WILLIAM COBBETT: ENGLISHMAN

WILLIAM COBBETT: ENGLISHMAN
A Biography

ANTHONY BURTON

AURUM PRESS

First published 1997 by Aurum Press Limited,
25 Bedford Avenue, London WC1B 3AT

Copyright © 1997 Anthony Burton

A catalogue record for this book is available from the British Library.

ISBN 1 85410 516 7

Typeset by Action Typesetting Ltd, Northgate Street, Gloucester
Printed and bound in Great Britain by Hartnolls Ltd, Bodmin

CONTENTS

For Pip

ACKNOWLEDGEMENTS

I should like to thank the following for help in the production of this book:

Mrs Eleanor Vallis of Nuffield College Library for help in research; the Warden and Fellows of Nuffield College, Oxford for permission to reproduce material from the Cobbett archives; Southampton City Heritage Services for providing copies of Cobbett letters and illustrations; Anne Jones, Curator of Farnham Museum; David Chun of the Cobbett Society; Molly Townsend and Surrey Local Studies Library for information and comments.

I should also like to thank the following for help with illustrations:

The two 'chopsticks', the reaper by Pyne (17016 s 69, p. 11) and the ploughman (8d 434 B5, opp. p. 176) are reproduced by permission of the Bodleian Library, Oxford; prints from *The Selections of Wonders* (012274 bb 7[3]) are reproduced by permission of the British Library; the portrait of Nancy Cobbett is reproduced by kind permission of Lady Lathbury; the sketch of Cobbett from his *English Grammar* is reproduced by kind permission of Janice M. Cobbett Robinson, photographed from an original sketch by Geremy Butler Photography; The Trustees of the British Museum; Guildhall Art Library; the Corporation of London; The Museum of London; Museum of Farnham; New Lanark Conservation Trust; Norfolk Studies Library; The Historical Society of Pennsylvania and the Victoria and Albert Museum Picture Library.

A.B.

PREFACE

There is only one good reason for writing a biography: the subject holds you so firmly in his grip that you simply cannot help yourself. I first encountered William Cobbett some twenty or so years ago, when researching factory conditions in the Industrial Revolution. I read his speech about the mill children and almost committed the indecorum of rising from my chair in Oxford's Bodleian Library and cheering. I can now cheer in print instead. From there, I moved on to *Rural Rides* and the dog-eared condition of the book is witness to how often it has been referred to and read. It was 1986 before I got round to writing about him, when I followed the track of one of his rides in *Britain Revisited*. After that, it was only a matter of time. I knew that one day I would have to write this book.

The formal acknowledgements can be found on another page, but I would like to indulge in a personal note. This is my fiftieth book, and in all that I have written, I have had the help of my wife in all aspects of the work. I hope that she has not found the experience of living with a writer to be too similar to that of Nancy Cobbett. The dedication at the front is a thank you not just for this book, but for the other forty-nine as well.

Anthony Burton
Bristol, 1997

1
THIS OTHER EDEN

This royal throne of kings, this sceptr'd isle,
This earth of majesty, this seat of Mars,
This other Eden, demi-paradise,
This fortress built by Nature for herself,
Against infection and the hand of war,
This happy breed of men, this little world,
This precious stone set in a silver sea,
Which serves it in the office of a wall,
Or as a moat defensive to a house,
Against the envy of less happier lands,
This blessed plot, this earth, this realm, this England.

William Cobbett did not approve of Shakespeare – he disapproved, indeed, of the theatre as a whole – yet John of Gaunt's famous speech perfectly expressed one of the central beliefs of his life. If there was an Eden on earth, then it was to be found in England, more particularly in the South East, in the rich, lush counties of Surrey, Kent and Hampshire, and most especially in the country around the town of Farnham where he was born. Yet here, at once, we find the first of many contradictions that make Cobbett's life so rich and at the same time so puzzling. He wrote about his early years as an uninterrupted idyll, but there are many reasons for believing that reality must have been a little different. There is no reason to think that he set out deliberately to mislead his readers, but there are good grounds for thinking he deluded himself. He knew what he wanted his early life to be – what he needed it to be for the sake of the arguments with which he bombarded his public for many years – so that was how it had to be. His past had to be pressed into service for the demands of the present. This has always to be borne in mind, because Cobbett's own words are the only source we have for his early life. It is necessary to test what he says against other accounts of life in the countryside at this time, in order to get, if not a true, then a truer picture of these years.

His date of birth is a little uncertain, since he frequently gave

conflicting versions of his age, but it is generally agreed to have
been at some time in 1763, and not, as he claimed in his autobiography, 1766. Cobbett described Farnham as a town set in a timeless
pattern of modest prosperity, thriving on the produce of a rich land,
content with a pattern of comfortable social stability. It is true that
Farnham had not yet felt the convulsions of the Industrial
Revolution, which was already gathering strength in other parts of
Britain, but it was not immune to change. When Daniel Defoe
visited the town earlier in the century he duly noted its prosperity.[1]

> It is a large populous market-town, the farthest that way in the
> county of Surrey, and without exception the greatest corn-
> market in England, London excepted; that is to say, particu-
> larly for wheat, of which so vast a quantity is brought every
> market-day to this market, that a gentleman told me, he once
> counted on a market-day eleven hundred teams of horses, all
> drawing waggons, or carts, loaden with wheat at this market.

He also, however, noted changes.

> but this also was, I suppose, before the people of Chichester
> and Emsworth on one side, and Southampton, Tichfield, and
> Redbridge on the other, took to the trade of sending their
> wheat in meal to London by sea.

In reality, Farnham was not so much enjoying a timeless idyll as
sinking into a stupor. In the seventeenth century it had been clam-
ouring for borough status, but soon there were few left to take any
interest in local affairs. Things became so bad that by the end of the
century the Vestry could only muster one member.

This was the town into which Cobbett was born and if it was not
high on civic pride, it was a comfortable spot whose way of life
went on as it had for years if not centuries, perhaps a little slower
than before but that if anything made it seem all the more pleasant.
It was a still point in a world that was beginning to bustle. The
surrounding country had a special kind of English beauty, but was
wild enough for a small boy to enjoy many adventures. In later
years Cobbett often looked back on those days in that place, and saw
them in a golden haze of nostalgia. At the very end of his life he
visited Scotland and found it a good deal more pleasant than he
expected – but it could not compare with the valley of the Wey
between Farnham and Alton.[2]

> It is a narrow valley, down the middle of which beautiful
> meadows are watered by the occasional overflowings of the
> little river WEY ... At *Farnham* this river is a very small

affair, which, if in America, would not be entitled to be called even a *creek*, but must be content to be called a *run*. Contemptible as it is, however, in point of magnitude, it was, about threescore years ago, quite broad enough, and deep enough, to have spared the borough-mongers and tax-eaters a monstrous deal of trouble, I, from one of the bathing places in it, having, about that time ago, been pulled out by the foot, which happened to stick up above the water, and to enable a brother-swimmer a great deal older than myself to preserve this everlasting torment to the *'higher orders'*.

He had by then travelled enough in the world to know that there were grander scenes to admire elsewhere, but he was not one of the new Romantics who longed for the picturesque – the ruined castle, the blasted oak. His taste was with those of a slightly earlier age who took their greatest pleasure in viewing a neat garden or a field of ripening corn. His language was often extravagant, but in writing on the countryside he adopted a quieter tone. He was a master of words who knew precisely what he was doing. His description of his home county was intended to convey tranquillity and order.[3]

This little river, which I used to think beyond all comparison the greatest in the world, does, however, cause there to be some of the prettiest meadows under the sun; and these continue along from a mile and a half on the east end of FARNHAM to the town of ALTON in Hampshire. On the south side of the river the ground rises very steeply from very near the edge of the meadows, and is generally clothed with very pretty woods, intermixed with hop-gardens: on the other side it rises more slowly, now and then spreading off into a level; and on this side, for the whole of the ten miles, there are the finest hop-gardens in the world, intercepted by very fine cornfields, bounded, generally, by beautiful hedges.

Beyond the rich valley were the wastes, heaths and commons, but even those had their very particular attractions.

Where the commons are greenish, and studded round with cottages and little gardens and fields, most assuredly the sight is the prettiest, and the life the happiest, in the world; because the soil is warm, the spring and the singing birds come early, the ground is dry; the air excellent, and the sand-hills, so convenient for boys to roll down, the finest places in the world for the breeding and rearing of Members of Parliament, and Prime Ministers.[4]

This was the background against which Cobbett played out the earliest years of life, and to which he returned time and again, but never perhaps finding the sweetness and freshness that he described in his boyhood. It was an Eden he had lost, and which was lost to others: he was to devote much of his life to trying to regain it.

He set his own life in the same rural mode, but it is here that one first begins to sense that all was not perhaps quite as straightforward as it seemed from his own robust statements.[5]

> All that I can boast of in my birth is that I was born in old England. With respect to my ancestors, I shall go no further back than my grandfather, and for this very plain reason, that I never heard talk of any prior to him. He was a day-labourer, and I have heard my father say, that he worked for one farmer from the day of his marriage to that of his death, upwards of forty years. He died before I was born, but I have often slept beneath the same roof that had sheltered him, and where his widow dwelt for seven years after his death. It was a little thatched cottage with a garden before the door. It had but two windows: a damson tree shaded one, and a clump of filberts the other. Here I and my brothers went every Christmas and Whitsuntide, to spend a week or two, and torment the poor old woman with our noise and dilapidations. She used to give us milk and bread for breakfast, an apple pudding for our dinner, and a piece of bread and cheese for supper. Her fire was made of turf cut from the neighbouring heath and her evening light was a rush dipped in grease.

And again at another time he wrote[6]

> I was bred at the plough-tail, and in the Hop-Gardens of Farnham in Surrey, my native place, and which spot, as it so happened, is the neatest in England, and, I believe, in the whole world. All there is a garden.
>
> I was brought up under a father, whose talk was chiefly about his gardens and his fields, with regard to which he was famed for his skill and his exemplary neatness. From my very infancy, from the age of six years, when I climbed up the side of a steep sand rock, and there scooped me out a plot four feet square to make me a garden, and the soil for which I carried up in the bosom of my little blue smock-frock ... I have never, for any eight months together, during my whole life, been without a garden.

What is interesting here is what is not mentioned, that his father was landlord of The Jolly Farmer pub, and it was here that he was born. Even when he returned to Farnham with his own son in 1825,[7] he pointed out 'The little old house' where he lived 'with my grand-mother Cobbett', and not the family home. The only other notable omission is any mention of his mother. The only reference he made to her in his autobiography was that he remembered her telling him that there was just four years between the youngest and eldest of the children – he was equally unwilling to discuss his brothers, who appear later as vague, shadowy figures in the Cobbett story. His mother, however, was clearly alive well into his infancy, and from a later reference (p.74) it seems she was still alive when Cobbett left the family home for good. But when, in later life, he sought an example of a good wife and mother, it was to his own wife he looked and not his mother. One can only speculate as to why so little is known about her – though it is worth bearing in mind that Cobbett was very selective in what he chose to tell the world about his early life. Facts that failed to fit the image he was trying to create were ignored. Similarly when he came to describe the education of himself and his father, he was keen to emphasize the degree to which they were self-taught. His father earned twopence a day as a little boy driving a plough and spent all his pay on school in the evening, learning 'what a village schoolmaster could be expected to teach'. But having received a basic training in the three R's, he went on to improve his arithmetical skills to the point where he could take on basic land surveying. This skill earned him a special place of respect in the community. He proceeded to pass on these same skills to his children. Cobbett says that he had some 'faint recollection' of going to an old woman who 'did not succeed in teaching me my letters'. It became a matter of great pride that what he learned came from his family or by his own efforts. What he does not mention is the apathy of Farnham, where the local school was kept in such poor repair it collapsed in ruins in 1758, and no one sought to replace it. Even if it had existed, however, he would have been forced to do as his father had done, for he was soon set to work in the fields.[8]

> I do not remember the time when I did not earn my living. My first occupation was driving the small birds from the turnip seed and the rooks from the peas. When I trudged afield, with my wooden bottle and my satchel over my shoulders, I was hardly able to climb the gates and stiles, and, at the close of day, to reach home was a task of infinite labour. My next employment was weeding wheat, and leading a single horse at harrowing barley. Hoeing peas followed, and hence I arrived at the honour of joining the reapers in harvest, driving the team and holding the plough. We were all of us strong and laborious, and my father used to boast, that he had

four boys, the eldest of whom was but fifteen years old, who did as much work as any three men in the parish of Farnham. Honest pride and happy days!

Once again one has to question this memory of a rural idyll. Even making allowance for the passage of years – and to those who live at the end of the twentieth century, almost any portrait of rural life is inclined to seem idyllic – there is surely something lacking here. And what is missing is any sense of the drudgery that was part of the life of any farm labourer, and which bore down especially hard on the very young. Richard Hillyer, writing some time after Cobbett, when life was certainly no harder, painted a very different portrait.[9]

> Every night I dropped asleep over my supper, and then woke up just enough to crawl upstairs, and fall into bed ... Sunday was the only break, and then the racked body cried out to be let alone for an hour or two, so that the muscles could loosen ... A black depression spread over me. 'This is what it is going to be from now on,' I thought ... 'Lifting, hauling, shoving, trudging about from day to day, nothing else through all the years.'

This must have been the reality of life for many. Equally, it must have been true that there were many compensations that made the drudgery bearable. Cobbett remembered with great affection the fairs and holidays, the cricket matches and 'single-stick' games. They remained bright in memory, later to be brought out, dusted down and polished and set against the garish symbols of a later age. In his day, men appeared at the fairs in white smocks with red handkerchiefs and the girls were neat and clean. He was to set this life as a standard against which he measured change – and seldom for the better. Returning to the fairs in 1822, he found men 'ragged and dirty' and the girls decked out in 'tawdry cottons, looking more like town prostitutes than country girls.'[10] The pleasures of life were simple but Cobbett describes them with a fresh enthusiasm that rings true, and certain elements recur in memories throughout his life, while other pastimes seem never to have palled.

One pleasure in particular seems to have a very special place in his memory. There was a sand hill near his home, which he used to visit with his brothers. He would clamber to the top, take his arms out of the sleeves of his smock and roll down like a little barrel. This was just the sort of robust game that delighted him: this set a boy up to grow into a man fit to take on the whole world.[11]

I am perfectly satisfied that if I had not received such an

education, or something very much like it; that, if I had been brought up a milksop, with a nursery-maid everlastingly at my heels, I should have been as great a fool, as inefficient a mortal, as any of those frivolous idiots that are turned out from Winchester or Westminster School or from one of those dens of dunces called Colleges and Universities.

Traditional country sports always enthused him. They were an essential part of the country scene.

When I was a little boy, I was, in the barley-sowing season, going along by the side of a field, near Waverley Abbey; the primroses and bluebells new spangling the banks on both sides of me; a thousand linnets singing in a spreading oak over my head; while the jingle of the traces and the whistling of the plough-boys saluted my ears from over the hedge; and, as it were to snatch me from the enchantment, the hounds, at that instant, having started a hare in the hanger on the other side of the field, came scampering over it in full cry, taking me after them many a mile.[12]

By the time he was eight, he had only to hear the bay of the hounds to set off in pursuit, 'leaving the hoe to do as best it could to destroy the weeds.' His eagerness went far beyond that. At about the same age he dashed in among the hounds at a kill to grab a hare's scut for a trophy, and got a slash from a hunter's whip for his pains. He soon had his revenge, by laying a false trail for the hounds at the next meet, which ended with the hunt floundering about in a bog.

No! damn her, where can she be? And thus, amidst conjectures, disputations, mutual blamings, and swearings a plenty they concluded, some of them half-leg deep in dirt, and going soaking home.[13]

Even if the story was only half true, here was no meek, subservient country lad, and there is some evidence that his rebelliousness and refusal to buckle under to mindless authority had its roots in a radical home life, in which politics and the discussion of politics played an important part. In later life, Cobbett preferred to present an intellectual history of himself, in which he reached his own conclusions by his own unaided abilities. It seems that he owed more to his family, and in particular to his father, than he was ready to admit. His daughter Anne began collecting notes on Cobbett after his death, and the picture that emerges is of a boy fascinated by this other world from a very early age.[14] She was able to draw on the memories of Cobbett's brothers – members of the family that Cobbett was assiduous in caring for in later life, but who he preferred not to present to the gaze of his public.

> My uncle Tom told me in 1835, talking about Papa ... that he was, when quite a young boy, fond of hearing their father read the newspapers. Their father used to read aloud of an evening, and it was tiresome to the other 3 boys to have to keep quiet the while –, but Bill used oftentimes to listen and pay attention to the reading ... and he would sometimes make remarks which showed he was taken up with the subject, and particularly he was (Uncle Tom said) interested with speeches in parliament, and would recollect for long times things in them, and remind his father by 'that's he, you know that said so-&-so.'

And when he was no more than seven years old, he would go out on the common at night 'throwing his arms about and making speeches to the furze bushes.'

The one subject which was known to have been discussed was the American War of Independence, on which his father held very firm views.

> My father was a partisan of the Americans: he used frequently to dispute on the subject with the gardener of a nobleman who lived near us. This was generally done with good humour, over a pot of our best ale; yet the disputants sometimes grew warm, and gave way to language that could not fail to attract our attention. My father was worsted without a doubt, as he had for antagonist, a shrewd and sensible old Scotchman, far his superior in political knowledge; but he pleaded before a partial audience: we thought there was but one wise man in the world, and that one was our father. He who pleaded the cause of the Americans, had an advantage, too, with young minds: he had only to represent the king's troops as sent to cut the throats of a people, our friends and relations, merely because they would not submit to oppression; and his cause was gained.[15]

There is a good deal here to suggest a strong streak of individuality inherited from an equally independently-minded father. It is unlikely that there were many vehement supporters of the American Revolution against British rule in the little market town of Farnham. The town was no breeding ground of rebellion and individuality, but here we have a portrait of a small boy prepared to take on the powerful adults of the local hunt, listening avidly to tales of rebellion in distant colonies and not so keen on what seemed set as his way of life that he was not prepared to abandon it when pleasure called. And all this before he was ten years old! It is small wonder that rebellion would soon take a more dramatic form.

2

BREAKING AWAY

As a boy growing up in the 1770s, young William could not necessarily expect to stay with the family at Farnham. It was quite common for children as young as ten to be hired out to farmers outside the home village. At any one time over half of those in their teens would probably be living twenty or more miles away, and that, given the long working day, meant that they would be totally cut off from their families. The hiring and firing of farm labourers was a wholly seasonal affair.

> How amazing is the contrast to the poor labourer between a severe and frosty winter and a mild and open one? During the former the earth is fast bound in chains which defy the plough, the spade and the mattock, and trifling is the compensation he receives from voluntary bounty or parochial allowance; in the latter, he goes forth to his work with almost as little interruption as in the warmth of summer, or the mildness of Autumn. [1]

Even the youngest labourers had to take such work as there was as it became available. So at the age of ten or eleven – though given Cobbett's muddle over his birthday he could have been older – he was entrusted with the task of taking a horse over to Steeple Landford in the Wylye Valley, west of Salisbury. He stayed there from June until autumn, when he returned to take a job weeding the gardens and clipping the hedges of the Bishop of Winchester's home, Farnham Castle. His enthusiasm for gardens came to him young, and remained with him throughout his life, so that when a visiting gardener from Kew told him about the wonderful gardens in which he had worked, he found an avid listener in young Bill Cobbett. The Royal Gardens were then quite new, established by Augusta, the Dowager Princess of Wales in 1759 and planned by Lord Bute, a keen amateur botanist, and his head gardener, William Aston. They had not yet become home to exotic plants from around the world, but they did have a reputation for great beauty and richness. The boy immediately decided that he had to see them for himself and that he should apply for a job there.

He set off next morning, on a hot June day, to walk to Richmond, about thirty miles away. He was not sure where he was going and took nothing with him but the clothes he wore and 'thirteen half pence in my pocket'. He kept stopping to ask the way, spent twopence on bread and cheese and a penny on small beer and contrived to lose one of the precious halfpennies. He arrived, after what was a decidedly brisk and energetic walk, in the afternoon, and it was now that he made one of the key decisions of his life.[2]

> I was trudging through Richmond in my blue smock-frock and my red garters tied under my knees, when, staring about me, my eye fell upon a little book in a bookseller's window: *Tale of a Tub*; price 3d. The title was so odd that my curiosity was excited. I had the 3d., but, then, I could have no supper. In I went and got the little book, which I was so impatient to read that I got over into a field, at the upper corner of Kew Gardens, where there stood a haystack. On the shady side of this I sat down to read. The book was so different from anything that I had ever read before: it was something so new to my mind, that, though I could not at all understand some of it, it delighted me beyond description; and it produced what I have always considered a sort of birth of intellect. I read on till it was dark, without any thought about supper or bed. When I could see no longer, I put my little book in my pocket, and tumbled down by the side of the stack, where I slept till the birds in Kew Gardens awaked me in the morning.

It is difficult to see just what it was in Swift's satire that appealed to the young boy. The notion from which the title is taken is that seamen when faced with an attack by a whale throw out an empty tub as a diversion. Swift's tub is a diversion from Hobbes's materialistic whale of a book, *Leviathan*. The story deals with a farmer's legacy to three sons, who symbolize the Catholic church, the Anglicans and the Dissenters. The Anglican is largely spared Swift's cruel wit but the other two are mercilessly attacked. As with the better known *Gulliver's Travels*, the *Tale* can be read as a story, but there is no denying the fact that this is sophisticated writing. Here, for example, Swift derides the ecstatic behaviour of many of the dissenting sects by comparing them with tipsy Irishmen.

> Now it is usual for a Knot of *Irish* Men and Women to abstract themselves from Matter, bind up all their Senses, grow visionary and spiritual, by Influence of a short Pipe of Tobacco, handed round the Company; each preserving the

Smoak in his Mouth, till it comes again to his Turn to take it
in fresh: At the same Time, there is a Consort of a continued
gentle Hum, repeated and renewed by Instinct, as Occasion
requires, and they move their Bodies up and down, to a
Degree, that sometimes their Heads and Points lie Parallel to
the Horizon. Mean while, you may observe their Eyes turn'd
up in the Posture of one, who endeavours to keep himself
awake; by which, and many other Symptoms among them, it
manifestly appears, that the Reasoning Faculties are all
suspended and superseded, that Imagination hath usurped the
Seat, scattering a thousand Deliriums over the Brain.[3]

What can an eleven-year old have made of this? One thing he
certainly did get was an instant infatuation with language. Swift's
influence on Cobbett the polemicist was considerable. The great
satirist could be whimsical or direct, flowery or pugnacious: he
could, in short, adapt his style to the needs of his subject. But what
principally characterizes his writing is its savagery towards those
with whom he disagreed, a savagery denounced by his opponents as
crudity. Much the same could (and would) be said about Cobbett.
That, however, lay in the future and one can now only dimly see
what it was in Swift that infatuated the child. There is a hint in the
phrase, the 'birth of intellect', suggesting that it was now that he
first realized the power of words themselves to move thoughts and
ideas as well as arouse emotions.

After the intellectual excitement, there were more mundane
matters to be dealt with. He was hungry and penniless, but he made
his way to Kew Gardens, where in all probability he did have the
rather cocky self-confidence that he described looking back over the
years.[4]

The singularity of my dress, the simplicity of my manner, my
confident and lively air, induced the gardener, who was a
Scotchman, I remember, to give me victuals, find me lodging,
and set me to work.

But it was not the gardens at Kew, however grand, that lingered in
his memory, but the little book he had bought with his last threepence.

The gardener, seeing me fond of books, lent me some gardening books to read but these I could not relish after my Tale of
a Tub, which I carried about with me wherever I went, and
when I, at about twenty years old, lost it in a box that fell
overboard in the Bay of Funday in North America, the loss
gave me greater pain than I have ever felt at losing thousands
of pounds.[5]

Cobbett wrote little about his life over the next few years, though there are occasional notes that pop up and can be pieced together to give a rough picture. He made several moves, and although this was by no means uncommon in boys of his age, it suggests that there was no great urge to rush back to Farnham. After Kew he spent some time in the Guildford area, where his employers included the Revd James Barclay who allowed Cobbett the use of his library. It is clear that already he was seen as something very different from the usual run of clod-hopping farm boys. At some time in 1781 he was in London and heard John Wesley preach – or 'Jack' as he called him, taking his cue from Swift's *Tale*. What impressed the boy was the ability of Wesley to grasp his audience, and the famil-iar 'slang' he used. At much the same time, he seems to have been staying at Ham Common, on the Thames, where he regularly read to his landlady, a widow, and her daughters from the newspapers of the day, after which he would go and practise impromptu speech-making. 'He said he had a feeling within him then, that he should one day be in Parliament.'[6] Everything at this period points to a restlessness, a desire to make his way in the world. Regardless of what he may have said about the virtue of honest toil on the land in later years, his own ambitions were set elsewhere. Whatever long term plans he may have had, he must have known that none of them could be achieved if he stayed as a farm labourer. How change would come he could not perhaps say, but he was ready for any move that might open up new opportunities. Such a chance seemed to have come in 1782. He had been staying with an uncle near Portsmouth, when he saw the sea for the very first time.

But it was not the sea alone that I saw: the grand fleet was riding at anchor at Spithead. I had heard of the wooden walls of Old England: I had formed my idea of a ship and of a fleet; but what I now beheld so far surpassed what I had been able to form a conception of that I stood lost between astonishment and admiration. I had heard talk of the glorious deeds of our admirals and sailors, of the defeat of the Spanish Armada, and of those memorable combats that good and true Englishmen never fail to relate to their children about a hundred times a year. The brave Rodney's victories over our natural enemies, the French and the Spaniards, had long been the theme of our praise and the burden of our songs. The sight of the fleet brought all these into my mind; in confused order, it is true, but with irresistible force. My heart was inflated with national pride. The sailors were my countrymen, the fleet belonged to my country, and surely I had my part in it, and in all its honours; yet these honours I had not earned; I took to myself a sort of reproach for possessing what I had no right to, and resolved to have a just claim by sharing in the hardships and dangers.[7]

The next morning he walked to Spithead, and took a boat out to the *Pegasus* to volunteer for service.

The Captain had more compassion than is generally met with in a man of his profession: he represented to me the toils I must undergo, and the punishment that the least disobedience or neglect would subject me to. He persuaded me to return home, and I remember he concluded his advice with telling me that it was better to be led to church in a halter to be tied to a girl that I did not like, than to be tied to the gang-way, or, as the sailors call it, married to Miss Roper. From the conclusion of this wholesome counsel I perceived that the Captain thought I had eloped on account of a bastard. I blushed and that confirmed him in his opinion.[8]

Humiliated and rejected, there was nothing to do but return home. But the experience only confirmed him in his drive to find a life that would show him a world wider than the fields around some farmer's door. He was still very much a young man with a zest for life, and it would seem had already developed a taste for young ladies, something which he relished for many years. So, in May 1783, he set out to collect 'two or three lasses' to take to Guildford Fair. He had on his holiday clothes, and cash in his pockets. His path took him across the London turnpike and there, by coincidence, was the stage coach for London. It was a spur of the moment decision, he declared, to forget the fair and the young ladies and hop on the coach for London and a new life.

It sounds a little too good to be true. He had on him, in fact, all his savings – 'which I had been years in amassing' and 'which I certainly did not intend to spend'. So why was he carrying it to a fair of all places, where he was most likely to lose it? It is difficult not to think that he was by now eager, almost desperate, to shrug off his rural life and turn to something new. In any case, off to London he went, spending virtually all his savings in the process. As a boy, he had cheerfully walked to Kew, as a strapping youth, he was riding in style and playing the young gentleman. It looks very much as if he was making sure that this was a journey with no return ticket. In a sense, it was Kew all over again.

By a commencement of that good luck, which has attended me in all the situations in which fortune has placed me, I was preserved from ruin. A gentleman, who was one of the passengers in the stage, fell into conversation with me at

dinner, and he soon learnt that I was going I knew not whither
nor for what. This gentleman was a hop-merchant in the
borough of Southwark, and, upon closer inquiry, it appeared
that he had often dealt with my father at Weyhill. He knew
the danger I was in; he was himself a parent, and he felt for
my parents. His house became my home, he wrote to my
father, and endeavoured to prevail upon me to obey his
orders, which were to return immediately home. I am
ashamed to say that I was disobedient. Willingly would I have
returned, but pride would not suffer me to do it. I feared the
scoffs of my acquaintances more than the real evils that
threatened me.[9]

Hurt pride may have had a part to play in his decision to refuse
to obey his father, but the story scarcely rings true. He was, after
all, a young man by now, not a child, and well able to make a rational decision about his future. The idea of William Cobbett, who
throughout his life would pugnaciously face down all opponents and
scoffers, being terrified at the possibility of encountering the banter
of his friends is not very plausible. He was desperate to stay in
London and prepared to take on almost anything rather than return
to the dead end of life in Farnham. The enthusiastic gardener, the
great lover of rural pleasure, was even prepared to become a lowly
pen-pusher.

My generous preserver, finding my obstinacy not to be overcome, began to look out for an employment for me, when an
acquaintance of his, an attorney, called in to see him. He
related my adventure to this gentleman, whose name was
Holland, and how, happening to want an understrapping quill
driver, did me the honour to take me into his service, and the
next day saw me perched upon a great high stool in an
obscure chamber in Gray's Inn, endeavouring to decipher the
crabbed thoughts of my employer.

It was an arrangement in which neither seemed to find much
pleasure. Cobbett may have been a sophisticated reader, but he was
not adept with his pen. The generous Holland went to great pains to
help his new employee.

He was a month in learning me to copy without almost contin-
ual assistance, and even then I was of but little use to him;
for, besides that I wrote at a snail's pace, my want of knowledge in orthography gave him infinite trouble.[10]

If it was hard work for Holland, it was drudgery for Cobbett.

The office – or dungeon as he preferred to call it – was so gloomy that he was often forced to work by candlelight, while the hours were deplorably long, from five in the morning to eight or nine at night. Everything about the place was abhorrent to him:

> Mr Holland was but little in the chambers himself. He always went out to dinner, while I was left to be provided for by the *laundress* as he called her. Those gentlemen of the law, who have resided in the Inns of court in London, know very well what a *laundress* means. Ours was, I believe, the oldest and ugliest of the sisterhood. She had age and experience enough to be Lady abbess of all the ruins in all convents of Irish-Town. It would be wronging the witch of Endor to compare her to this hag, who was the only creature who deigned to enter into conversation with me.[11]

On Sundays he walked in St James's Park 'to feast my eyes with the sight of the trees, the grass, and the water'. Whatever illusions he may have had about the glamour and excitement of life in the capital were broken: they would never return. The big city had failed, so he began to dream an old dream again. He saw a recruiting advert for the Royal Marines, and he decided that if the Royal Navy would not have him, he would settle for the next best thing. If he had any kind thoughts or felt any obligation to Holland, who had taken him in when he was destitute, he did nothing to show them. Without saying a word to anyone, he marched off to Chatham and took the King's shilling. It was only then that he discovered that instead of joining the Marines, he was now enlisted as a soldier in a marching [infantry] regiment.

> When I told the Captain that I thought myself engaged in the marines 'By Jasas, my lad,' said he, 'and you have had a narrow escape.' He told me that the regiment into which I had been so happy as to enlist was one of the oldest and boldest in the whole army, and that it was at that time serving in that fine, flourishing and plentiful country, Nova Scotia. He dwelt long on the beauties and riches of this territorial paradise, and dismissed me, perfectly enchanted with the prospect of a voyage thither.[12]

So it was that on 4 February 1784 young William Cobbett found himself in His Majesty's 54th Regiment of Foot, the West Norfolks, ready to embark for Canada. The American War had ended the year before with the signing of the Peace Agreement at Versailles, so there was no great urgency about sending troops across the Atlantic and they were left to languish in barracks in Chatham. It was not exactly a life of glory and adventure, and the fresh-faced farm boys who made up the bulk of the recruits found that the worst enemy they had to face was hunger. It was in many ways a thoroughly miserable time, living off their wretchedly low pay of sixpence a day – and Cobbett recalled seeing his fellow soldiers cry from hunger and some succumbed and died.

> Of my sixpence, nothing like fivepence was left to purchase food for the day. Indeed, not fourpence. For there was washing, mending, soap, flour for hair-powder, shoes, stockings, shirts, stocks and garters, pipe-clay and several other things to come out of the miserable sixpence! Judge then of the quantity of food to sustain life in a lad of sixteen, and to enable him to exercise with a musket (weighing fourteen pounds) six or eight hours every day.[13]

And there were times too when he was reduced to total despair.

> I remember, and well I may! that upon one occasion I, after all absolutely necessary expenses, had, on a Friday, made shift to have a halfpenny in reserve, which I had destined for the purchase of a red herring in the morning; but when I pulled off my clothes at night, so hungry then as to be hardly able to endure life, I found that I had lost my half-penny! I buried my head under the miserable sheet and rug, and cried like a child![14]

But Cobbett, whatever faults he may have had, was never a man to let any spare time be wasted in mere idleness. If it had done nothing else, his stay at Holland's had shown him that there were situations in life where a lack of education was a genuine barrier to advancement, and he had the wit to realize that what was true of a clerk might well be true of a soldier. So he began to read voraciously, if indiscriminately. He joined a circulating library and read everything from novels and poetry to history and philosophy. Holland had taught him one useful skill, and he was able to write a fair hand, which brought him the job of copyist to Colonel Debieg. It was Debieg who persuaded him that copying was one thing, but if he was ever to put his own words on paper, he would need also to master the rules of grammar. Cobbett seized on this advice, and began a period of intense self-education.

> The edge of my berth, or that of the guard-bed, was my seat to study in; my knapsack was my book-case; a bit of board lying in my lap, was my writing-table; and the task did not demand anything like a year of my life. I had no money to

purchase candle or oil; in winter-time it was rarely that I
could get any evening-light but that of the fire, and only my
turn even of that. And if I, under such circumstances, and
without parent or friend to advise or encourage me, accom-
plished this undertaking, what excuse can there be for any
youth, however poor, however pressed with business, or
however circumstanced as to room or other conveniences? To
buy a pen or a sheet of paper I was compelled to forego some
portion of food, though in a state of half-starvation; I had no
moment of time that I could call my own; and I had to read
and to write amidst the talking, laughing, singing, whistling
and brawling of at least half a score of the most thoughtless
of men, and that, too, in the hours of their freedom from all
control.[15]

He copied out Lowth's *Grammar*, and repeated it over and over
to himself on guard duty until he had learned it by heart. His knowledge of grammar was hard won, and he was both inordinately proud
of it and seldom missed a chance to show up the lack of such skills
in others. He often seemed more delighted, in later years, to find an
ungrammatical phrase in an opponent's words than he was to find an
easily refutable argument. He was equally haughty over bad hand-
writing, and declared that any badly written letter was not worth a
second's consideration, and should simply be thrown out. It was a
reflection of the intensely hard work he had put in to create William
Cobbett, master of prose out of William Cobbett, farm hand. He
was never a great one for seeing the other man's point of view, and
could not comprehend that those who had been fed reading, writing,
and the rules of grammar since childhood were not likely to regard
their mastery with any sense of awe.

His efforts were not unrewarded and by the time the regiment left
for Nova Scotia in March 1785, he had been promoted to corporal
and clerk to the regiment – not the least important aspect of which
was an increase in pay of twopence a day. His time with Colonel
Debieg had other far-reaching effects on his career, for the Colonel
was no great respecter of rank or persons when it came to asserting
his own opinions. He was twice court-martialled for insubordina-
tion, having taken on no less an adversary than the Duke of
Richmond. If a colonel could oppose a duke, should not a corporal
be able to take on a colonel in a reasonable cause? The cause had
not yet arrived, but Corporal Cobbett was already showing a distinct
lack of respect for the 'epaulet gentry'.
He set off for Nova Scotia with high expectations that were shattered with the first glimpse of land.

When I first beheld the barren, not to say hideous, rocks at the entrance of the harbour, I began to fear that the master of the vessel had mistaken his way; for I could perceive nothing of that fertility that my good recruiting captain had dwelt on with so much delight. Nova Scotia had no other charm for me than that of novelty. Everything I saw was new: bogs, rocks, and mosquitoes and bull-frogs.[16]

After a brief stay in Halifax, they moved westward to St John, New Brunswick. He was no more enamoured with that, and was quite unprepared for the harshness of the winter: the icy winds that blew down from the Arctic, and the snow that stayed on the ground for months on end.

The men going on guard were wrapped up in great cloth coats lined with flannel, their heads covered with caps of the same sort, leaving only an opening for the eyes and nose. I have seen half a dozen men at a time with their noses frost-bitten, which you perceive the moment you see them, by their having become white.[17]

There were novelties and compensations. He skated on the frozen river and saw the fish swimming under the ice beneath his feet. The snow falls were fierce, but were followed by crisp days, 'with a bright sun over our heads and with snow, dry as hair powder, screeching under our feet.' Then came the release of spring when ice floes as high as houses crashed down the river and 'the sun began to bless our eyes with the sight of grass, to make us cast off our furs, and to resume our dresses as men, instead of bears'. After that the summer sun brought fine grain harvests and luscious, exotic fruits such as melons. None of it, however, could really reconcile him to the region, and when he came to give advice to would-be emigrants to North America, he described Canada as 'the offal' and the United States as 'the sir-loins, the well-covered and well-lined ribs, and the suet.'[18]

Modesty was never a part of Cobbett's nature, but in his account of army days in Canada, his vanity is downright distasteful. He was admittedly using his life to make a general point: that if a young man was sober, serious and hard working he could achieve success, but even so the main point seems to be the glorification of William Cobbett.

In early life I contracted the blessed habit of husbanding well my time. To this, more than to any other thing, I owed my very extraordinary promotion in the army. I was always

ready: if I had to mount guard at ten, I was ready at nine:
never did any man, or any thing, wait one moment for me.
Being, at an age under twenty years, raised from Corporal to
Sergeant Major at once, over the heads of thirty sergeants, I
naturally should have been an object of envy and hatred, but
this habit of early rising and rigid adherence to the precepts I
have given you really subdued these passions; because every
one felt that what I did he had never done, and never could
do.[19]

He set himself up as a better man than his fellow soldiers, and
soon began to think of himself as a very much better man than the
officers set over him. One example of his own superiority as he saw
it came with the introduction of the 'new discipline' in 1788, based
on Sir David Dundas's 'Principles of Military Movements'. These
were, he wrote, 'excessively foolish from end to end' but had to be
put into practice. Cobbett studied them carefully, mastered their
intricacies and then proceeded to explain them to the officers,
including the colonel. He drew diagrams, wrote out the new words
of command, and then the teacher had to go and take his place with
the men.

Those who were commanding me to move my hands or my
feet, thus or thus, were, in fact, uttering words which I had
taught them; and were, in everything except mere authority,
my inferiors; and ought to have been commanded by me.[20]

He claims to have made no secret of his contempt for his officers
and they would have had him flogged 'had they not been kept in awe
by my inflexible sobriety, impartiality, and integrity, by the
consciousness of their inferiority to me, and by the real and almost
indispensable necessity of the use of my talents'. There is another
interpretation. One has to consider the circumstances. Here was a
regiment sent overseas to a country recently engulfed by war. But
now the war was over, the local population was friendly and there
was nothing whatsoever for an army to do. The main occupation
was the tedious repetition of drill. That was bad enough, but then
some fool back in England made things far worse by throwing out
the old drill book and bringing in a new. Up popped the over-eager
young sergeant-major, ready to take on the whole job of mastering
the new, oh so tedious, rules on their behalf. With what a sigh of
relief the officers must have handed over the odious task, and if he
had to be allowed to strut a bit as a reward then it was cheap at the
price. The services rarely admire the over enthusiastic volunteer,
but are all too ready to make use of him. This was something
Cobbett could never see. He was being used, and he foolishly

expected those who used him to acknowledge the fact. It happened time and again.

Cobbett had a particularly prickly relationship with the adjutant. One of the officer's tasks was to prepare the orders of the day, but he was no grammarian, and eventually a happy arrangement was reached in which he simply told his sergeant-major what the day's orders were and left it to Cobbett to put them into correct English. But on one occasion, in Cobbett's eyes, he went too far. He had volunteered to write a report for a Commission set up to enquire into conditions in Nova Scotia and New Brunswick. The actual writing was, as usual, left to Cobbett. When the report was handed in and duly praised, the officer handed it back saying: 'Here, Sergeant Major, go and make a fair copy.' Cobbett was outraged: 'This was the most shameless thing I ever witnessed.' Yet what did he expect? His superior officer, who had volunteered for the job, to say 'Actually, I didn't do it. This is all the sergeant-major's work'? If he did, he showed remarkably naïvety, and there is evidence that he was indeed something of an innocent abroad. He was still a very young man, who had come a long way in a very short time, and was quite unaware of the unspoken rules of this new society in which he existed. But there seems also to be a hint of a very strong character trait that would assert itself ever more firmly as the years went by. He would not adapt himself to a way of life that seemed to him fundamentally wrong. For now he followed his own precepts, working hard and honestly. Later he would go further and try to bring society closer to his own views of what was right and proper.

That Cobbett was hard-working is beyond question, but he did find time to think of matters other than soldiering. He met Anne (Nancy) Reid, the daughter of an artillery sergeant. She was a tiny creature, just four feet two inches tall and only thirteen years old, but he decided at once that she would be his wife. She was beautiful, which to Cobbett was an 'indispensable qualification', but he seems to have been even more taken with her 'sobriety of conduct'. His own account of how he reached a decision is scarcely the stuff of high romance and passionate love.[21]

It was now dead of winter, and of course the snow several feet deep on the ground, and the weather piercing cold. It was my habit, when I had done my morning's writing, to go out at break of day to take a walk on a hill at the foot of which our barracks lay. In about three mornings after I had first seen her, I had, by an invitation to breakfast with me, got up two young men to join me in my walk; and our road lay by the house of her father and mother. It was hardly light, but she was out on the snow, scrubbing out a washing-tub. 'That's the girl for me,' said I, when we had got out of her hearing.

He was determined to make her his wife – 'I never had a thought of her ever being the wife of another man, more than I had a thought of her being transformed into a chest of drawers.' He was now determined to leave the Army as soon as he could, and settle down to married life. Before that could happen, Cobbett was moved with his regiment to Fredericton, a hundred miles away from St John in the interior of New Brunswick, while at the same time arrangements were being made for the artillery regiment to return to England. Cobbett was alarmed: Anne might yet turn into a chest of drawers after all.

> I was aware that, when she got to that gay place Woolwich, the house of her father and mother, necessarily visited by numerous persons not the most select, might become unpleasant to her, and I did not like, besides, that she should continue to work hard. I had saved a hundred and fifty guineas, the earnings of my early hours, in writing for the paymaster, the quartermaster, and others, in addition to the savings of my own pay. I sent her all my money, before she sailed; and wrote to her to beg of her, if she found her home uncomfortable, to hire a lodging with respectable people; and, at any rate, not to spare the money, by any means, but to buy herself good clothes, and to live without hard work, until I arrived in England; and I, in order to induce her to layout the money, told her that I should get plenty more before I came home.[22]

Cobbett's chances of an early return were fatally harmed by international politics. In 1790 Pitt announced the rights of the British to trade in Nootka Sound, off the west coast of Vancouver Island. A dubious and now very dog-eared treaty had given all trading rights in the Pacific coast to the Spanish, and a diplomatic row brewed up. The chances of it ever involving British troops stationed in New Brunswick were slim to non-existent, but the regiment was kept in Canada to the young lover's huge annoyance: 'Oh, how I cursed Nootka Sound, and poor bawling Pitt, too, I am afraid.' So the regiment languished, and Cobbett found time for long walks of exploration in the surrounding forest. It was in this period that, as he later admitted, 'he did a wrong'. On one of his expeditions he got lost in the woods, and with night approaching he began to fear the cold and the bears. Happily, he stumbled on a creek that delighted him.[23]

> Here was about two hundred acres of natural meadow, interspersed with patches of maple trees in various forms and of

various extent; the creek ran down the middle of the spot, which formed a sort of dish, the high and rocky hills rising all round it, except at the outlet of the creek, and these hills crowned with lofty pines; in the hills were the source of the creek, the waters of which came down in cascades, for any one of which a nobleman in England would, if he could transfer it, give a good slice of his fertile estate; and in the creek at the foot of the cascades, there were, in season, salmon, the finest in the world, and so abundant, and so easily taken, as to be used for manuring the land.

There was also a log cabin, a well-tended farm with maize, buckwheat, a few cows – and the farmer's daughter. He may have sworn undying love to Anne Reid, but when he wrote about her, he seemed more impressed with her industry than anything else. The nineteen-year-old girl he met here produced a very different response. She had 'a complexion indicative of glowing health and farming, figure, movements, and all taken together, an assemblage of beauties, far surpassing any that I had ever seen but once in my life.' The 'but once' looks suspiciously like an afterthought.

The farmer was a 'Yankee loyalist' who had come north with his family after the War of Independence. They welcomed the young soldier, and had very little doubt as to what brought him back to the farm whenever he had time off. He had not seen his fiancée for two years, and now, whenever he had a day free, he would paddle his canoe right through the night to spend time with this girl and then paddle the whole of the next night to get back to barracks. As he admitted: 'If this was not love, it was first cousin to it.' He knew he was in the wrong, but he could not stay away and had he heard even the faintest rumour about Anne he never doubted that he would have declared his love. But the rumours never came and nothing was said. At last the regiment was called back to England, and to Cobbett's mortification, the father travelled forty miles to see him off. 'His looks and words I have never forgotten.' Was it merely loyalty to the teenage girl back in England that made him keep silence? Not entirely. He knew what he was turning away from.

I longed, exchanging my fine laced coat for the Yankee farmer's homespun, to be where I should never behold the supple crouch of servility: and never behold the hectoring voice of authority again; and, on the lonely banks of this broad-covered creek, which contained (she out of the question) everything congenial to my taste and dear to my heart, I, unapplauded, unfeared, unenvied and uncalumniated, should have lived and died.[24]

He surely knew, however, that this was not to be the pattern of his life, and he was already deeply involved in plans that were to set him moving in a wholly new direction.

THE SOLDIER'S FRIEND

Cobbett was back in Portsmouth on 3 November 1791 and immediately announced his decision to leave the army. He was
commended for his service in the warmest terms, and it was even
suggested that were he to stay on, he would be considered for
promotion to ensign, but he would have none of it. By 19 December
he was a civilian again, but retained the highest regard for the ordinary British soldier. In the army he had found friendship and
loyalty, and would fondly tell the story of Sergeant Smaller. The
two men were on one of their forest expeditions, when Cobbett
collapsed from exhaustion – this story is all the more remarkable for
this rare admission of physical weakness. Smaller put Cobbett on
his back, and carried him for five miles through deep snow. By the
time they reached safety, Smaller's feet and legs were covered in
blood. Cobbett went on to fame; Smaller died in Holland in the
Duke of York's army. Of his former comrades he was to write:
'Amongst soldiers, less than amongst any other description of men,
have I observed the vices of lying and hypocrisy.' He did not have
the same feelings for the officers.

Although he liked to see himself as a lone figure standing up to
his incompetent superiors, he was, in fact, part of the 'us' and
'them' of Army life. And the 'us' faction often showed remarkably
radical tendencies. In the 1780s, New Brunswick society was split
between a democratic egalitarian party, known as the Lower
Covers, and an élitist group, the Upper Covers, who wanted to
establish land ownership on a European pattern, with a few grandees
served by a low-wage majority. At election time, in 1785, it seemed
likely that the Lower Covers might win, and their opponents hit on
the bright idea of giving the soldiers a vote on the grounds that they
would vote as their officers demanded. It did not work quite like
that.

> Our *officers* were, of course, of the Upper Cove party; but it
> was far different with us ... It was odd enough, that we
> should have had this unanimous feeling in favour of the

popular party in the Province; but we had it, and all the cat o' nine tails at the command of the Holy Alliance would not have rooted it out of our hearts.[1]

Faced with these views, the idea of enfranchizing the army was quickly dropped. The episode is instructive in showing that Cobbett was then influenced by the men around him into taking a very radical position. But in his next disagreement with the officers, he took a more lonely, if no less principled stance. He was to come into direct conflict with them, in England, but first there were other matters to attend to.

He found Nancy working as a servant in the house of a Captain Brisac, slaving away for a miserable five pounds a year. In spite of her circumstances, she had left Cobbett's one hundred and fifty guineas untouched.

> Need I tell the reader what my feelings were? Need I tell kind-hearted English parents what effect this anecdote must have produced on the minds of our children? Need I attempt to describe what effect this example ought to have on every young woman who shall do me the honour to read this book? Admiration of her conduct, and self-gratulation on this indubitable proof of the soundness of my own judgement, were now added to my love of her beautiful person.[2]

One never hears the note of passion when he writes of Nancy: he seems more to be congratulating himself on having completed a successful deal. And so he had, for she was to stand by him loyally through many swings of fortune. They were married on 5 February 1792. She was not yet eighteen, and signed the register with her mark. The wife of one of the most distinctive masters of English prose was illiterate.

Cobbett had already set in motion a plan that had its origins in events back in Canada in 1787. He had discovered that the quartermaster had been taking his title somewhat too literally, keeping a quarter of the men's supplies for his own use. Everyone knew such things went on, but Cobbett was horrified. Ignoring the advice of his fellow sergeants, he decided to put in an official complaint, but was told very firmly to mind his own business. Minding his own business was never Cobbett's strong point, and he set about a systematic study of the regimental books to find evidence of the wholesale theft practised by the quartermaster with the active connivance of many of the officers. He was faced with a tricky problem. The evidence was there in the books, but how could he be sure that if official charges were laid the books would not simply disappear? He could copy extracts, but what would his unsupported word be against so many others? If he was discovered the best he could hope for was demotion and 'a pair of bloody shoulders'. He finally recruited another soldier, Corporal William Bestland, to join the plot. They beavered away, making copies of all kinds of records, which they both signed and stamped with the regimental seal. Now that Cobbett was clear of the army and there was no longer a threat of being court-martialled and judged by the very men he was accusing, he was ready to move.

Cobbett's great mistake was to assume that he had discovered an isolated example of fraud in an otherwise wholly honest Army. In fact, corruption was rife, known to be so, and largely ignored. However, with supreme self-confidence, he sent his accusations to the Secretary of State at the War Office, Sir George Yonge. The charges levelled against four officers were of falsifying musters, so that pay was sent to non-existent soldiers, and – his original discovery – of taking goods intended for the men and selling them off privately. He asked that the regimental records be secured so that the charges could be proved. Cobbett was summoned to Yonge's office, assured that charges would be brought, though only against three of the officers as one had since died. He was patted on the back, and sent off with assurances that all was well. Then silence fell, and by now there were ominous signs that his small scandal was only a part of a much larger affair.

Cobbett's naïvety contrasts with the general cynicism that pervaded the popular view of the management of the armed forces. Too many commissions had been purchased by officers who had no aptitude for the military life and even less interest in becoming competent at their job. As early as 1795, the Duke of York had found it necessary to call for a return of army captains under the age of twelve. Too many younger sons, sent to the service, expected profit from their appointments, and did not expect to offer much, if anything, in return. It was bad enough that there was widespread corruption, but what made the whole system infinitely worse was that the victims were too often the hapless ordinary soldiers. Cobbett was putting his faith in Yonge, but the latter was already showing the politician's tendency to favour the strong, rather than redress the wrongs endured by the weak. Ordinary soliders were entitled to three shillings a week, but often failed to receive even that paltry sum as dishonest officers used the regimental funds as if they were their personal banks. A just administration would have stamped out such blatant dishonesty; but Sir George Yonge was putting forward a bill in Parliament that failed to attack corruption, but only sought to allay its effects. He proposed that where the men's pay fell short of what was due, the difference should be made up out of taxation. In other words, the officers could continue to milk the funds, while the tax-payer footed the bill. And it was Sir George Yonge to whom Cobbett was looking for support in his personal campaign against what was, in the scale of things, a comparatively minor case of corruption. Cobbett was, however, not slow to learn the lesson.

An anonymous pamphlet was published, *The Soldier's Friend*, exposing Yonge's hypocrisy and feebleness in the face of entrenched corruption. Cobbett at first denied being the author, though he later admitted it. But no one reading it can deny the authorship: the style that was to serve him for many years was already in place. A favourite trick was to pick an unfortunate phrase by an opponent and turn it against him. Yonge had commented that it had 'so happened' that soldiers had received half pay. Cobbett pounced.

> Astonishing! It has 'so happened' that an act of Parliament has been most notoriously and shamefully disobeyed for years, to the extreme misery of thousands of deluded wretches (our countrymen), and to the great detriment of the nation at large; it has 'so happened' that not one of the officers have been brought to justice for this disobedience, even now it is fully discovered; and it has 'so happened' that the hand of power has made another slice into the national purse in order – not to add to what the soldier ought to have received; not to satisfy *his* hunger and thirst, but to gratify the whim or the avarice of his capricious and plundering superiors.[3]

This is pure Cobbett in its plain speaking. He would polish this rather rough language later, but never lose the ability to go to the heart of a matter and set out his main argument in words that all could understand.

It must have seemed ominous, however, that such a major scandal could be publicly aired and equally publicly ignored. What hope could he have with his comparatively minor fraud? He was soon to find out as officialdom began to close ranks. Events now become somewhat muddled, for Cobbett's own version does not tally with the official one. However, certain facts are clear. The first disturbing sign appeared when it was announced that the court martial was to be held in Portsmouth at Hilsea Barracks, where the regiment was quartered. This meant that the accused would be surrounded by friends, and would easily be able to exert an influence on the witnesses, most of whom were NCOs. Cobbett appealed over Yonge's head to the prime minister, William Pitt, and the trial was moved to London. That was one success for Cobbett, but there was more alarming news. In spite of Yonge's assurances, the regimental books had not been secured and the officers had had ample time to change the records. Then he found that the charges had been diluted, and rumours were rife that Cobbett was conducting a personal and malicious vendetta. He now faced a real dilemma. He had the support of just one officer, Lord Edward Fitzgerald, and he would have to rely very heavily on the corroborative evidence of Corporal Bestland. But Bestland was still in the army, and was all too likely to suffer the most dire consequences for opposing his own officers. This would be especially true if the case was lost, and there were increasingly good grounds for believing it would fail. Cobbett later made even more of this factor, and a promise he had made to Bestland not to involve him in the case until he was out of the army. The case against the officers was falling apart.

Cobbett had not really appreciated that, to many in authority, the need to present that authority as above reproach and criticism was a good deal more compelling than the need to explore what many saw as minor offences. Where he saw ordinary soldiers deprived of pay and the bare necessities of life, they saw a system of perks, reprehensible, perhaps, but established in a long tradition. If anything was to be done about them, it would be done quietly in the approved manner, not in public, and certainly not at the behest of one of the lower ranks. Cobbett may have been slow to appreciate the realities of the situation, but he was not so stupid as to ignore them once they became clear.

The court martial was called for 24 March, and duly convened with an impressive array of judges – seventeen officers, with three major generals at their head. Everyone was present, except for the man who had laid the charges. A messenger was sent round to Cobbett's London lodgings, but came back to report the Cobbetts gone, nobody knew where. There was no accuser, no one to argue the case and the officers were duly acquitted. The judge advocate general declared there was no case to answer and that, in all probability, this was an example of a malicious prosecution. When questioned as to whether Cobbett himself could be charged he replied in the negative, but indicated that a civil case might be brought. But in order to bring a civil case, Cobbett himself had to be produced, and it soon became known that he and his wife had fled the country.

The intricacies of this case can never be completely unravelled. Cobbett had worked for years to amass his evidence at, it has to be said, considerable risk to himself. Now, when the whole process reached its climax, he had abandoned the enterprise. His enemies, and there was never any shortage of those, attributed it to base cowardice. He claimed mere prudence. He had ample evidence that the action would fail, and if it did he would be transformed from accuser to accused. He also heard that there was to be a trumped up charge of sedition, a suspicion confirmed when he met several sergeants who had been sent from Portsmouth to London, ordered to swear that they had heard Cobbett propose the toast to 'the destruction of the House of Brunswick'.[4]

What is one to make of this curious episode? The only logical answer supports Cobbett's version of events. He was a doughty fighter but a canny one. While he had a chance of success he would battle on, but once that chance was gone he preferred to quit the field to fight another day. The odds against his accusations being upheld were growing, while at the same time the chances of himself becoming a victim were also increasing, and if he had fallen he would have brought others down with him. The sensible response was to drop the case and take himself and his young bride out of harm's way. Yet there is more to it than that. One of the problems with writing about Cobbett is his tendency to write of his own past in a way that suits his opinions at the time of writing. When he described this period of his life, his politics were Tory and he preferred to describe it in terms of an individual attempting to redress a particular and quite specific wrong, rather than as a radical fighting a social system. In a sense, this was fair: he had been stirred into action by the discovery of a quite specific crime, but he was not quite the political innocent he later claimed to be. He had, like many of his countrymen, come under the influence of the greatest radical thinker of the age, Tom Paine. He later tried to shrug off this influence by claiming that he was affected emotionally and had not yet developed intellectually.

> The fault, therefore, if there was any, was in the head, and not in the heart; and, I do not think, that even the head will be much blamed by those who duly reflect, that I was when I took up PAINE's book, a novice in politics, that I was boiling with indignations at the abuses I had witnessed.[5]

There was a great deal in Paine that must have struck a chord, not least the Radical's sympathetic attitude to the British soldier. They suffered, according to Paine, a double oppression – 'shunned by the citizen on an apprehension of being enemies to liberty, and too often insulted by those who commanded them'. And striking even nearer home, Paine united support for the soldier with that for the farmworker, and, incidentally supported Cobbett's father's views of the American war. It was waged, he declared, at the expense of 'the labouring farmer, the working tradesman, and the necessitous poor in England' who kept 'in prodigality and sloth, the army that is robbing both them and us'. How could Cobbett not be swept along by such arguments, and how could a susceptible young man, beginning to really stretch his intellectual abilities for the first time not be influenced by the most exciting thinker of the day?

Paine's words appealed to many aspects of Cobbett's personality. Because one thinks of Paine primarily as the great enthusiast for the democratic revolutions of France and America, one forgets how

often he played the patriotic card. He contrasted the American presidency, where the office holder had to be a native of the country,
and was answerable to the people at elections, with the state of
affairs at home.

> In England the person who exercises prerogative is often a
> foreigner; always half a foreigner, and always married to a
> foreigner ... Though such a person cannot dispose of the
> government, in the manner of a testator, he dictates the
> marriage connexions, which, in effect, accomplishes a great
> part of the same end. He cannot directly bequeath half the
> government to Prussia, but he can form a marriage partner-
> ship that will produce almost the same thing.[6]

Cobbett was profoundly influenced by these views. He felt
himself unable to get justice at home and, worse, faced persecution
for trying to obtain it. Paine spoke of new, free societies in France
and America, and he decided to sample both. As the authorities
searched for him, he had already left England and was taking a
belated honeymoon in France. The couple settled in the village of
Tilques to the south-east of Calais. The ostensible object of the visit
was to enable Cobbett to learn French, to help him begin a new
career as a schoolmaster, but he was undoubtedly influenced by
Paine's enthusiasms. It was, after all, not the most obvious place for
a young family to dash off to in search of peace and quiet. True, in
September 1791, Louis XVI had, however reluctantly, accepted the
new constitution, but his position was widely seen as hopeless, and
when the Cobbetts arrived in March 1792, the country was already
on the brink of war with Austria. The whole of France was ringing
with revolutionary rhetoric led by the orator Pierre Vergniaud.

> So, led by the most sublime passions beneath the tricolor flag
> that you have gloriously planted on the ruins of the Bastille,
> what enemy would dare to attack you ... *Union et courage*!
> Glory awaits you. Hitherto kings have aspired to the title of
> Roman citizens; it now depends on you to make them envy
> that of Citizens of France![7]

These were stirring times, and no one could have chosen to go to
France who was not also stirred by the idea of seeing the country at
that crucial time in its history. Even writing about the country in
1796[8] when he had gone through the first of his political *voltes face*,
he was able to describe the time he spent there as 'the six happiest
months of my life'. He wrote:

I went to that country full of all those prejudices that

Englishmen suck in with their mother's milk, against the French and against their religion: a few weeks convinced me that I had been deceived with respect to both, I met everywhere with civility, and even hospitality, in a degree that I had never been accustomed to.

This is interesting as the first indication that he had begun to think of Catholicism as something other than at best misguided and at worst evil – a theme he was to return to and develop later. He wrote little about those days, but a few remarks suggest that old habits had not quite fallen away with marriage. His American girl had been deserted, but there were free and easy French girls to dally with.

When I was in France, just after I was married, there happened to be among our acquaintance a gay, sprightly girl of about seventeen. I was remonstrating with her, one day, on the facility with which she seemed to shift her smiles from object to object; and she, stretching one arm out in an upward direction, the other in a downward direction, raising herself upon one foot, leaning her body on one side, and then throwing herself into a flying attitude, answered my grave lecture by singing, in a very sweet voice (significantly bowing her head, and smiling at the same time), the following lines from the vaudeville, in the play of Figaro:

> *Si, l'amour a des ailes,*
> *N'est-ce pas pour voltiger?*

that is, if love has wings, is it not to flutter about with? The wit, argument, and manner, all together, silenced me.[9]

Cobbett was fond of describing his New Brunswick episode, as 'the only sin that I ever committed against the female sex.' But he enjoyed a little dalliance. There are few hints of love and passion in his own marriage, and judging from his advice to young husbands his ardour rapidly cooled. 'Nature has so ordered it, that men should become less ardent in their passion after the wedding-day, and that women should not.' Poor Nancy! Dragged off to a foreign land, where other women seemed to have a great deal of amusement that was denied to her. Cobbett loudly approved the old doctrine about the French: 'pigs in the parlour and peacocks on the promenade.' A Cobbett wife was expected to be beautiful, because it put the husband 'in good humour with himself' and made him 'pleased with his bargain'. Her foremost duties were to be up early, hard at work running the household frugally and efficiently. Her rewards were certainly not to be material – no 'outward and visible and vulgar signs of extravagance', which meant no jewellery – 'the hardware which women put upon their persons'. He was scathing about all amusements and pitied the woman, 'who had been brought up to play music, to what is called draw, to sing, to waste paper, pen, and ink, in writing long and half-romantic letters, and to see shows and plays and read novels.' Peacock promenades were definitely out.

> I never dangled about at the heels of my wife; seldom very seldom, even walked out, as it is called, with her; I never 'went-a-walking' in the whole course of my life; never went to walk without having some object in view other than the walk; and as I could never walk at a slow pace, it would have been hard work for her to keep up with me; so that in the near forty years of our married life, we have not walked out together perhaps twenty times.[10]

Nancy's role was to be homemaker and wife, and there must have been times when she felt that a servant's life in England was not a great deal worse than a wife's existence in France. And having fled England, it now seemed they would be forced to flee France as well. The Revolution was clearly entering a new and more dangerous stage. France was at war with Austria by April, and Prussia joined the conflict in July. Cobbett saw the clouds gathering and, although he had intended to stay longer in France, he decided to leave almost at once for America. He planned one last trip to see Paris, but heard *en route* that the king had been dethroned. The Swiss Guard who defended him were not merely beaten, but hunted down one by one, massacred and mutilated. The gruesome events of 10 August 1792 could not be ignored. The Cobbetts turned round and headed straight for the port of Le Havre.

It was a terrifying journey. Nancy Cobbett remembered the events clearly, and told her children the story. They were frequently stopped, their papers inspected and their baggage searched, and the officials became convinced that she was a French aristocrat trying to escape. Their suspicions were confirmed by her refusal to speak English: she was, in fact, too frightened to speak at all. At the port things became even worse.

> The people in the streets came running to the carriage and climbed up to look in at the windows, the coachman being much frightened thereat: he begged them to put the windows down.[11]

When he had left the army, his father had begged him to settle down near Farnham, and Cobbett had said that once he had mastered French he would return as a schoolmaster, but the truth was that he had no more wish for the dull life of a provincial teacher than he had for the life of a farm labourer. He had fled the latter for London as a young man, and now he and his young wife were to make an even more decisive break. By the end of August they were on board a small American sloop, the *Mary,* bound for New York. Some seven weeks of rough seas gave Cobbett time to brood over his experiences and to conclude that the French Revolution had not, after all, created a paradise on earth.

4

A NEW BEGINNING

If revolutionary France was a bitter disappointment, what would Cobbett make of America? Paine, who had praised the first, had also been one of the keenest advocates of American independence, not as a theoretical possibility, but as an imminent course of action. 'We ought not now to be debating whether we shall be independent or not, but anxious to accomplish it on a firm secure, and honourable basis.'[1] Cobbett had, of course, been brought up to believe in the justice of the American cause, so one might have expected him to be well disposed to Paine's arguments. But Paine had written in equally enthusiastic terms about the glories of French republicanism, and Cobbett was now a good deal less inclined to take him at his word. He approached America with a scepticism born in France. He had left England with a taste for 'liberty, equality, fraternity' which was beginning to turn bitter.

Cobbett's first concern, however, was not with political theory so much as with the more prosaic matter of earning a living. After landing in New York, he made his way to Philadelphia, the then capital of the country. He had a letter of introduction to Thomas Jefferson from William Short, American Minister at The Hague. It was a standard, polite form of words, for Short did not know Cobbett personally, and it is not at all clear who persuaded him to write it. Cobbett himself did not expect much from it, but his own letter to Jefferson[2] is interesting in shedding some light on his views on America and how he saw his own career developing. He wrote: 'Ambitious to become the citizen of a fine State, I have left my native country, England, for America: I bring with me youth, a small family, a few useful literary talents and that is all.'

If he had any doubts about democratic republics he was wise enough not to air them, but given his outspokenness one can fairly conclude that he was genuinely hopeful about the future of his new country. And he was already dwelling on his 'literary talents' which, so far as we know, had then only been expressed in *The Soldier's Friend*. He went on, however, to say that although he promised to repay any favours Jefferson might award him, he would 'feel but little disappointment' if nothing happened and was confident that 'my own industry and care will make me a happy and useful member in my adopted country'. He did not even bother to deliver the letter while he was still in Philadelphia, but sent it after he had moved some thirty miles down the Delaware River to Wilmington. Jefferson took the hint and failed to offer the young immigrant a job.

The Cobbetts, for all William's easy optimism, were not in the happiest of positions. Their money was almost gone, Nancy was heavily pregnant, and he had no job, but Cobbett had already laid his plans. The region was full of French émigrés, some were escaping from the Revolution, others alarmed by slave uprisings had come north from the West Indies. There was ample opportunity for the now bilingual young man to make money as a teacher. He soon found pupils, one of whom was so enthusiastic that he moved in as a boarder. Cobbett enjoyed the company and there was a good deal of horseplay, 'stealing each others bread at supper, and so on',[3] but Nancy was less amused. She was eighteen years old, expecting a child and running a household in a new land – but she never, it seems, complained at the time. And her husband was gracious enough to give her the credit for seeing them through the first difficult period: 'it was perhaps owing to her care, industry, and sweetness of temper.'

At first he was kept far too busy earning a living and getting the family settled in to worry about politics. Although he generalized about family life in America more than he described his personal circumstances, there is little doubt that he drew on his own experiences in later writings. Nancy was not happy in Wilmington, and he put his own interpretation on her unhappiness.

> Women, and especially English women, transplant very badly, which is indeed a fact greatly in their praise. It is amiable in all persons to *love their homes*, their parents, their brethren, their friends and their neighbours; and, in proportion as they have this love in their hearts, they will be reluctant to quit their home, and especially to quit their country. English women have an extraordinary portion of this affection and, therefore, they are to be treated with all possible indulgence in the case here contemplated, provided that indulgence do not extend so far as to produce injury to their families and themselves.[4]

And he had little patience for comparisons between the old life and the new. The woman who complained that 'the flies settle upon the *preserved peaches*, and that they do *not do this in Old England*'[5] needed to be reminded that in Old England the family had no peaches for them to settle on.

On 3 January 1793 Nancy gave birth to a son, Anthony. As one would expect, her husband had firm views on everything from the delivery to bringing up the child. He objected most strongly to having anyone but a female midwife present: to allow a doctor at the birth was the height of immodesty. And once the child arrived, it was the clear duty of the mother to breast-feed him.

> No woman ever suffered more than my wife did from suckling her children. How many times have I seen her, when the child was beginning to draw, bite her lips while the tears ran down her cheeks. Yet having endured this, the smiles came and dried up the tears; and the little thing that had caused the pain received abundant kisses as its punishment.
>
> Why, now, did I not love her the more for this? Did not this tend to rivet her to my heart?[6]

He was, however, equally adamant that the father also should take his full share of child-rearing. 'There is nothing more amiable, nothing more delightful to behold, than a young man especially taking part in the work of nursing the children.'[7] He described his own routine at the start of the working day – and with Cobbett every day was a working day. He was an obsessive believer in early rising and, once up he began to help his wife look after the baby:

> get up, light her fire, boil her teakettle; carry her up warm water in cold weather, take the child while she dressed herself and got the breakfast ready, then breakfast, get her in water and wood for the day, then dress myself neatly, and sally forth to my business. The moment that was over I used to hasten back to her again.[8]

Thunderstorms frightened Nancy, and he would always leave his pupils to dash home to comfort her. This greatly amused the French, who when making an appointment would add '*Sauve la tonnerre toujours*, Monsieur Cobbett' – unless it thunders.

His concern for his wife did not include any consideration that she might in any sense have an equal share in the running of the home. She had vowed to obey, and 'a woman when patiently reasoned with on the subject, must be a virago in her very nature not to submit with docility to the terms of her marriage vow'.

He had no great faith in women's ability to keep faithful to their husbands and declared that the best way of ensuring that was to keep them safe at home, with as few visitors as possible. There were, he declared, no such things as 'innocent freedoms'. And he applied some of the same strictures to men.

What must that man be made of who does not prefer sitting by
his own fire with his wife and children, reading to them, or
hearing them read, to hearing the gabble and balderdash of a
club or a pot-house company![9]

He, however, felt himself quite at liberty to enjoy 'innocent freedoms'. He might wish to keep his wife at home, and regard a visit
from a doctor as the height of immodesty, but he enjoyed female
company and flirting, or, as he put it, 'to romp most famously'.
There was, however, a distinction to be made between a pretty girl
and a wife.

> Your 'free and hearty' girls I liked very well to talk and laugh
> with; but never, for one moment, did it enter my mind that I
> could have endured a 'free and hearty' girl for a wife.
> Skipping, capering, romping, rattling girls are very amusing,
> where all costs and other consequences are out of the ques-
> tion.[10]

He also expressed the view that infidelity in a man was 'less
heinous' than in a woman. Nevertheless, he seemed genuinely
astonished when his wife objected to his behaviour – but he gave in
to her wishes.

> My wife said to me, in a very gentle manner. 'Don't do that:
> I do not like it.' That was quite enough: I had never thought
> on the subject before: one hair of her head was more dear to
> me than all the other women in the world, and this I knew that
> she knew; but I now saw that this was not all that she had a
> right to from me; I saw that she had the further claim upon
> me that I should abstain from everything that might induce
> others to believe that there were any other women for whom,
> even if I were not at liberty, I had any affection.[11]

He stayed at home, rocking the cradle, while he began work on a
textbook for his French students.[12]

His early enthusiasm for Wilmington and America began to
wane. It is difficult to say just when this happened, as he only set
down his views after disillusionment had already set in. He wrote of
his first American home town:

> The land was bad – rocky – houses wretched – roads impass-
> able after the least rain. Fruit in quantity, but good for
> nothing ... The seasons were detestable. All burning and
> freezing.
>   The people were worthy of the country – a cheating, sly,

roguish gang. Yet strangers made fortunes in spite of all this, particularly the English. The natives were by nature idle, and sought to live by cheating, while foreigners, being industrious, sought no other means than those dictated by integrity.[13]

At this time he still had very little concern with politics, though being surrounded by French *émigrés*, he could hardly avoid being aware of the tumults in Europe. He wrote to a friend:

Every time the newspapers arrive, the aristocrats and democrats have a decent quarrel to the admiration of all the little boys in town ... God preserve you from the political pest. Let them fright and tear one another's eyes out: take care of your business, and let the devil and them decide their disputes.[14]

But European politics could not be shrugged off. The Americans supported revolutionary France almost by instinct: they had cast off the imperial chains of Britain, as propagandists never tired of reminding them, and they were naturally well disposed to fellow republicans. There were, however, awkward matters to overcome. The French revolution was following a bloody path never trodden by the Americans – and among the potential victims was none other than one of the heroes of their own revolution, Lafayette. At home, he had a more ambiguous role: he supported the movement towards democracy, but as an aristocrat himself – his full name was Marie Joseph Yves Gilbert du Motier, Marquis de Lafayette – he still owed allegiance to the king. When war broke out with Austria, he was one of the French military leaders, but he found himself in a difficult position. He was leading his men against one enemy across the border, while another – the Jacobins – was, as he saw it, threatening the legitimate government at home. He went so far as to propose to the Austrian ambassador that the war should be suspended while he marched back to Paris to sort out the revolutionaries. At the fall of the monarchy, Lafayette found himself turned willy-nilly from revolutionary to counter-revolutionary, arraigned before the National Assembly. In the event, his position was hopeless and he fled France, only – with ultimate irony – to be imprisoned by the Austrians, and then the Prussians, as a dangerous revolutionary. Cobbett took on the task of translating the documents relating to the impeachment of Lafayette for the American public, and these were published in February 1793. He remained strictly neutral – producing virtually the only document in his literary career in which his personal views did not predominate. In any case, it was not controversial, in that the proceedings tended to show Lafayette in a favourable light, and the American hero's reputation remained untarnished. The interesting questions (as far as Cobbett is concerned) are why and how he came to be involved in the project. One obvious answer is that translators were not readily available: he was and he needed the money. But there was surely more to it than that, for Cobbett was not the man to go against his principles. Was he already trying to tell the American people that the French Revolution was not the great, spontaneous movement towards freedom that most believed it to be? And was he chosen as translator because of his known growing opposition to the events in France? Both seem likely: France and England were at war in 1793 and he was always a patriot first and foremost. The widespread support in America for fellow revolutionaries disgusted him, and this was his first attempt to show the Americans that the French were not quite the idealists that they were believed to be. Here, he declared, is one of your very own heroes threatened with the guillotine and forced to flee the country. Can this be right? At this stage, however, he was content to lay out the facts of the case without additional comments of his own.

By the end of 1793, spurred on by Nancy, who found Wilmington not at all to her taste, he began to plan for a move to Philadelphia. They set off early the next year, and they had scarcely settled in before they were devastated by a double tragedy: Nancy's second baby was stillborn and their first child, Anthony, died. They were both totally overwhelmed by the events. Cobbett wrote movingly of the tragedy in a letter to a friend in London.

> Oh, Miss Smither! I hope you will never experience a calamity like this – All I ever felt before was nothing at all to this – The dearest sweetest beautiful little fellow that ever was seen – We adored him – Everybody admired – When we lived at Wilmington people came on purpose to see him for his beauty – he was just beginning to prattle, and to chace the flies about the floor with a fan. I am sure I shall never perfectly recover his life.[15]

Nancy would not eat for days and there was, for a time, a real fear that she would not survive the double shock. She took to her bed, but sleep was denied her. Cobbett was so concerned that when howling dogs disturbed her rest, he sat up all night throwing stones to keep them at bay. It was one of the low points of his life, and it was at just this period that political events forced themselves upon him. Quite when he began to turn away from the American ideal is uncertain, but it seems likely that the motivation came from outside. Britain and France were at war, and the natural reaction of the Americans was to side with their fellow republicans against the nation which had so recently been their oppressor and opponent. The tricolour was hoisted everywhere, and this was more than ex-sergeant major Cobbett was able to tolerate. He had been told that France was the land of liberty, but his own experience had been less than happy, and every day his *émigré* pupils brought news of fresh atrocities. If American politics meant supporting France, then he was opposed to American politics as well. He recalled the words of his old mentor Paine:

> There, the poor are not oppressed, the rich are not privileged. Industry is not mortified by the splendid extravagance of a court rioting at its expense. Their taxes are few, because their government is just; and as there is nothing to render them wretched, there is nothing to engender riots and tumults.

And against that he set what he now considered his own experience.

> Instead of that perfect freedom, and that amiable simplicity, of which PAINE had given me so flattering a description, I found myself placed under a set of petty, mean, despots.[16]

In the midst of all this personal misery, America delivered what Cobbett considered the ultimate insult: they brought out the flags, beat the drums and blew the trumpets to welcome Joseph Priestley. The object of Cobbett's wrath was one of the great men of the age, chiefly remembered for his work as a chemist and the first man to isolate the element oxygen. He was at the forefront of the Industrial Revolution, counting among his friends such eminent figures as Josiah Wedgwood and Matthew Boulton. In politics he was radical, welcoming, as did many others, the onset of the French Revolution, and he was a dissenter in religion, a leader of the Unitarian church. In 1791, he had been present at a Bastille Day dinner, and that was quite enough for the mob. In what became known as the 'Church and King' riots, they had an obvious victim, pro-revolution and against the established church. They burned his Birmingham home, destroying all his scientific papers, and drove him into exile. It was clear that the outrages had a measure of official political support, as Wedgwood made clear when he wrote a letter of consolation.

> You will have occasion for all your philosophy, and for all your Christianity too to support your mind under the highly aggravated injuries you have received. If they had arisen merely from the ungovern'd madness of a mob, from the lowest order of our species, one would then lament all its effects like those of a storm or hurricane, but if there is reason to believe the rabble were acted upon and encouraged

to such proceedings by those who should be their superiors, one cannot but perceive the too evident spirit of the times or of the place at least by which you and so many of your worthy neighbours have suffered.[17]

Cobbett claimed still to be an apolitical animal, who heard about the affair almost by accident.

One of my scholars, who was that we call in England a Coffee-House Politician, chose, for once, to read his newspaper by way of lesson; and it happened to be the very paper which contained the addresses presented to Dr Priestley at New York, together with his replies. My scholar, who was a sort of republican, or at best but half a monarchist, appeared delighted with the invectives against England, to which he was very much disposed to add. Those Englishmen who have been abroad, particularly if they have had time to make a comparison between the country they are in and that which they have left, well know how difficult it is, upon occasions such as I have been describing, to refrain from expressing their indignation and resentment; and there is not, I trust, much reason to suppose, that I should, in this respect, experience less difficulty than another. The dispute was as warm as might reasonably be expected between a Frenchman, uncommonly violent even for a Frenchman, and an Englishman not remarkable for *sang-froid*; and the result was a declared resolution on my part to write and publish a pamphlet in defence of my country, which pamphlet he pledged himself to answer: his pledge was forfeited: it is known that mine was not.[18]

Cobbett had every reason to dislike Priestley. He was a scientist – and science for Cobbett was meaningless mumbo-jumbo. He was a dissenter, and Cobbett held such men in low esteem, a position he seems to have first adopted on reading *A Tale of a Tub* as a boy. In that work the character of foolish Jack was a lampoon on John Wesley. At a time when England was at war, an Englishman was siding with the enemy. And all this at a most difficult period, when American popular opinion was moving strongly in the direction of joining in the war on the French side. He set out to put his own ideas into print, though his first reception when he approached the bookseller Matthew Carey was not encouraging.

Mr Carey received me as booksellers generally receive authors (I mean authors whom they hope to get but little by): he looked at the title from top to bottom, and then at me from head to foot. 'No, my lad,' says he, 'I don't think it will suit.'

My lad; God in heaven forgive me; I believe that, at that
moment, I wished for another yellow fever to strike the city.[19]

The pamphlet was published eventually by Thomas Bradford,
who shared Carey's anti-British sentiments, but recognized a good
profit when he saw it. Like *The Soldier's Friend,* it appeared anonymously, but it had such an immense impact that the pamphlet[20]
launched Cobbett on his career as a political journalist. It displays
many of the traits that were to remain constant through the years,
starting with Cobbett's distaste for Priestley's religion.

> Those who know anything of the English Dissenters, know
> that they always introduce their political claims and projects
> under the mask of religion. The Doctor was one of those who
> entertained hopes of bringing about a revolution in England
> upon the French plan; and for this purpose he found it would
> be very convenient for him to be at the head of a religious
> sect.

It continues even more scathingly to personalize the attack on his
Unitarianism. 'He preached up a kind of deism, which nobody
understood, and which it was thought the Doctor understood full as
well as his neighbours.' Cobbett could use the rapier as well as the
cudgel. Soon he was deploying another weapon which was to
become a standard part of his armoury. He was always looking for
the opportunity to detect a weakness in the form of hypocrisy, and
he found just such a chink. Priestley, he claimed had argued first for
the abolition of tithes, and when that notion failed had demanded
that dissenting churches should get their share in proportion to their
numbers. 'A very modest and disinterested request truly.' Having
established a minor hypocrisy in one area of life, he could then turn
to a far greater one in a much more important cause. The mob who
attacked Priestley had been punished: of four ringleaders found
guilty, two had been hanged. He had demanded and received cash
compensation for over £2500 from the town of Birmingham. Yet
this was the man who had the temerity to stand up and praise mob
rule in Paris. It was when it came to discussing Priestley's support
for the French Revolution that Cobbett's passion was truly aroused
– and his prose starts to erupt with the exclamation marks and italics
that were to become a notable feature of all his polemical writings.

> What! The rights of man yet? I thought that *liberty and equal-
> ity, the rights of man* and all that kind of political cant had
> long been proved to be the grossest imposition.

He continues to berate the French, and also to cast doubt on the hallowed institutions of American democracy as well.

> In speaking of monarchies, it has often been lamented, that
> the sovereign seldom or never heard the truth; and much
> afraid I am, that this is equally applicable to democracies.
> What court sycophants are to a prince, demagogues are to a
> people.

He ends with another theme that was to become a *leit-motif*
throughout his writings.

> Perhaps a cobler [*sic*], with his hammer and awls, is a more
> valuable acquisition than a dozen philosophi- theologi- politi-
> cal empires, with all their boasted apparatus.

Cobbett was firmly set on a new career as an author, and he had
found the subject matter that was to occupy him for the next six
years. He would defend Britain and Britain's interests in the New
World, and if democracy and the republic were determined to take
the side of the bloodthirsty godless French, why then, he would
stand by King and Country.

> From that time (the summer of 1794) to the year 1800 my
> labours were without intermission. During that space there
> were published from my pen about twenty different
> pamphlets, the whole number of which amounted to more
> than half a million copies. During the three last years a daily
> paper, surpassing in extent of numbers any ever known in
> America, was the vehicle of my efforts; and by the year 1800
> I might safely have asserted that there was not, in the whole
> country, one single family in which some part or other of my
> writings had not been read; and in which, generally speaking,
> they had not produced some degree of effect favourable to the
> interests of my country.[21]

5

PETER PORCUPINE

Cobbett entered the American political scene at a particularly difficult time. The republic had, after all, only been in existence for a decade and although a constitution was safely in place, a great many questions still remained to be resolved. By far the most important concerned the fundamentals of power: should authority ultimately reside with a strong central government or with individual states? This in turn reflected the differing interests of a new mercantile state and another, agricultural community. The question was finally to be decided more than half a century later, by civil war, but in the 1790s the divisions affected all affairs both at home and abroad. The President, George Washington, dreamed of a unified nation working towards a common goal, and did his best to mediate between the factions. He could not, however, prevent distinct parties emerging each with its own leader. The Republicans under Jefferson largely represented the agrarian interest; the Federalists under Alexander Hamilton spoke for the new men of town and city. Such internal divisions were inevitably reflected in views on foreign affairs. Jefferson labelled the Federalists 'Monocrats', supporters of the regime of king and aristocracy. To support France was to stand firm for the republic; to fail to do so was, in his eyes, to come out in favour of Britain and turn back to the old, discredited order. Washington did not wish to support either side; he wanted time for America to develop in peace, and he saw international trade as the key to prosperity. When Cobbett attacked Priestley, he was in effect, if not in intention, taking sides in American politics.

When war broke out between Britain and France in 1793, there was an intense outburst of anti-British feeling and anti-British actions, much of it fomented by the French diplomat, Edmond Genêt, who was as passionate a supporter of the French interest as Cobbett was of the British. Genêt went much further, moving from words to deeds, including an attempt to fit out a privateer with an American crew to attack British shipping. That was one step too far, and the plan was abandoned in the face of Washington's implacable opposition. The President was not about to be forced to abandon his neutrality by the actions of a foreigner. Genêt retaliated by plotting against Washington with the help of the Democratic Clubs that were springing up everywhere, and which represented the views of the more extreme supporters of the French Revolution. John Adams, recalling those days in old age, wrote of 'the terrorisms excited by Genêt in 1793, when ten thousand people in the streets of Philadelphia, day after day threatened to drag Washington from his house'.[1] This was a gross exaggeration, but it says something about the fever of the times.

This was the situation in America when Cobbett's pamphlet appeared. His attack on mob rule, by any faction, struck a chord with moderate opinion. His anti-French views were equally well received by the Federalists, who were desperately trying to keep out of the war but were fighting against the background of an almost entirely pro-French press. The pamphlet quickly went into five editions in Philadelphia. It was all the spur Cobbett needed, for there were great issues to be decided and a fight to be fought – and, as he was rapidly discovering, he had an ability to move opinion with his prose. Just as importantly, he revelled in a good scrap. He was self-appointed Champion of the British cause, and the Democratic Clubs and Societies of America were the enemy.

The issues were never as simple and straightforward as either Cobbett or the Democrats declared. In 1794 everything centred around the issues of trade and the freedom of the seas. Having dealt with one threat from France, a more real one now appeared from Britain. The British issued a Provision Order in 1794, which allowed them to take any ship trading with any French port, no matter how innocent the cargo. Whether they were legally entitled to do so or not was beside the point: their ships ruled the seas and they had the power to act. Not content with seizing ships they were impressing American sailors into the British Navy. Opinion in America was, not surprisingly, outraged. It certainly did nothing to help Washington retain his carefully balanced position of neutrality: the general view among the Federalists was that the British had gone mad. They were making the position of their American friends insupportable. Someone had to go and sort out the mess and bring about a new understanding. The job went to Chief Justice Jay. As he set off on his talks, pro-French propaganda became ever more clamorous – and against it was raised the increasingly powerful voice of William Cobbett.

What is most striking in Cobbett's early works is the way in which he could take on an opponent's argument and use it against him, holding the original up to ridicule. A common cry at the time was that Britain was the home of tyranny, France the land of liberty, a view given extra weight by the United Irishmen, bringing stories of impris-

onment and transportation for Irish patriots. Cobbett was quick to
agree: wrongful imprisonment was a terrible thing. But, on the other
hand, they had wanted to overthrow the government, depose the king
and set up a French-style republic. Still, perhaps – just perhaps – the
courts were wrong and the sentences a little hard. So, let us look at
how such things were dealt with in freedom-loving France. The citizens of Lyon had, in 1793, stood by the earlier 1791 constitution: had
not attempted to oppose approved laws, but supported them. They
had, it was true, rejected the more violent Jacobin measures, which
included using the cathedral for a fête de Raison, in which anti-
Christian hymns were sung. But, demanded Cobbett, would any God-
fearing American approve such blasphemy? As punishment for this
opposition, a decree was issued in which aristocrats and their supporters were to be killed. No one knows exactly how many died, but the
guillotine was kept so busy that people complained of blood overflowing the gutters. To help speed up the process, prisoners were
lined up in front of cannon and blown to pieces. Well, said Cobbett,
after recounting this grisly tale, perhaps the English have been at fault
– but what can you say about the French? How can leaders of religion
praise a country which allows an ass to be dressed as a clergyman and
paraded through the streets, while Jacobins hold mock communions?
How could they possibly justify the massacre of thousands of inno-
cents? Then he turned on the Democratic Clubs themselves, the
upholders of freedom, who were mainly drawn from the slave-holding
communities of the South.

> And these are the people, my God! who talk about the *natural*
> and *unalienable* rights of man – and who make such a boast
> of the purity of their principles. Never was there any thing in
> the world, that exhibited such a dishonourable, such a base,
> odious, and disgusting contrast as the profession and the
> conduct of this race of patriots.[2]

Cobbett himself was no abolitionist, then or later, but then he never
claimed to be the promoter of universal liberty either. It was not
slave-owning he objected to, but the hypocrisy.

At this time, the influence of his first inspiration can still be
seen. Swift used extravagant allegories to drive home his arguments, and Cobbett tried his hand at something similar. He invented
an anatomical feature which he called the 'crumena', which needed
to be filled before the body would work. This was a rather laboured
metaphor, intended to represent the purse of political hacks. He then
went on to belabour the image:

> When the crumena becomes empty, the sympathetic intestines
> are immediately contracted, and the whole internal state of the

patient is thrown into insurrection and uproar, which commu-
nicating itself to the brain, produces what a learned state
physician calls the *mania reformationis*; and if this malady is
not stopped at once, by the help of an hempen necklace, or
some other remedy equally efficacious, it never fails to break
out into Atheism, Robbery, Unitarianism, Swindling,
Jacobinism, Massacres, Civic Feasts and Insurrections.

This passage suffers from two faults: the imagery and its language
are crude, and at the same time the metaphor itself is unclear. One
can see the appeal for the young writer of indulging in the sort of
fanciful flights that make Swift one of the satirical geniuses of all
time. At the same time, it is equally obvious that Cobbett was not
Swift. It is to his credit that he was probably the first to realize this
fact. It was not the fanciful that appealed to his readers, but the
direct, the sense of one reasonable human being talking to another,
without humbug. He would always be at his best when he met an
argument head on, and whacked it into submission.

The pamphlet, *A Bone to Gnaw for the Democrats* was published
anonymously, and was a great success. It combined common sense
– it was in America's interests to make a treaty with Britain as a
solid and reliable trading partner if nothing else – with brilliant and
often sharply witty attacks on the opposition. One reviewer,
however, was not altogether favourable. Samuel Harrison Smith of
the *American Monthly Review* was not notably unkind to Cobbett's
arguments, but had the temerity to attack his grammar. This was
one area where Cobbett was decidedly prickly, and he replied under
a suitably prickly pseudonym, Peter Porcupine, a name that he was
to keep for the rest of his American writings. He did what he would
always do: he went on the attack, devoting nine whole pages to a
pamphlet on the unfortunate Smith's own departure from the rules
of grammar.[3]

Cobbett's writing career was well and truly launched, and was
already showing traits that were to characterize it for years to come.
He showed a brilliant ability to espouse a cause in language that all
could understand, a ruthless determination to ridicule his political
opponents, and an equally strong determination to do the same to
anyone else who earned his displeasure. He vigorously defended his
attacks on personalities as well as ideas.

I never could see how abuses were to be corrected, without
attacking those to whom they were to be attributed. If swindling and debauchery prevails, how are you to check it
without exposing the *swindler* and the *debauchee*?[4]

Inevitably, there was no shortage of opponents to return the fire, and the more there were the more he revelled in it.

When I had the honour to serve King George, I was elated enough at the putting on of my worsted shoulder-knot and, afterwards, my silver-laced coat; what must my feelings be then, upon seeing half a dozen authors, all *Doctors*, or the devil knows what, writing about me at one time, and ten times the number of printers, bookbinders, and booksellers, bustling, running, and flying about in all directions, to announce my fame to the impatient public? What must I feel upon seeing the newspapers filled from top to bottom and the windows and corners of the houses placarded with a *Blue Shop for Peter Porcupine, a Pill for Peter Porcupine, Peter Porcupine Detected*, a *Rooster for Peter Porcupine*, a *History of Peter Porcupine*, a *Picture of Peter Porcupine*? The public will certainly excuse me, if after all this I should begin to think myself a person of some importance.[5]

If Cobbett had discovered a skill as a writer, he had also found a zest for a fight.

The pamphlets flowed freely now, and as details of the Jay Treaty became known, there was a desperate need for someone to argue in its favour. Jay had won a few concessions for America – the border dispute over Canada was settled and American ships were given limited trading rights in the West Indies. But in return, he had virtually agreed to the main demand – that goods sent to France could be seized, and had also agreed an embargo on American vessels carrying to Europe any commodities – including cotton – that were also grown in the West Indies. It was not, by any standards, a good deal, but it secured the peace. Washington reluctantly gave his agreement. Now it had to be ratified by the Senate. Cobbett spearheaded the ratification movement, and one can sense his growing mastery of sophisticated argument.

One of his opponents was 'Franklin', a pseudonym for Alexander Dallas, the Secretary of State for Pennsylvania. Dallas argued against a communal treaty with Britain and for a treaty with France. He fulminated against England. 'She is famed for perfidy and double dealing, her polar star is interest, artifice with her is a substitute for nature.' All the more reason for a treaty, replied Cobbett: 'no individual would ever think of dealing to any amount with a person famed for perfidy and double-dealing, without binding him down by written articles.'[6] And then neatly reversed his argument: there is surely no need for written agreements with open, honest magnanimous France. As was often the case, Cobbett had swiftly pounced upon a weak point casually thrown in by his opponent.

Dallas chose to argue that if Americans imported British goods, they would be importing monarchial ideas along with them. This was too silly to be worth refuting. 'To suppose this man in earnest would be to believe him guided by something below even the imbecility of a frenchified republican.'[7] Dallas called the king 'a tyrant that invaded our territory.' Actually, Cobbett mildly points out, it was his territory at the time but he does so magnanimously: never mind that. Who says old enemies cannot make up their differences? Has not France just made a treaty with Prussia? And so he goes on, neatly demolishing the opponent and making a thorough fool of him.

One of Cobbett's most admirable qualities was his willingness to take on any opponent, regardless of whether it was in his personal interest or not. In 1795 he was happy to take on American majority opinion, and made personal enemies out of men of considerable power in the community. He often seemed not to know where boldness ended and foolishness began, and more than once suffered the consequences.

This was a most hectic time for Cobbett. A daughter, Anne, was born; she proved healthy and was to survive into old age. He still had his lessons, and his work. He had always been a busy man who despised idleness.

Till I had a second child, no servant ever entered my house, though well able to keep one; and never, in my whole life, did I live in, ate or drunk, or slept or dressed, in a manner so perfectly to my fancy, as I did then. I had a great deal of business to attend to, that took me a great part of the day from home; but whenever I could spare a minute from business, the child was in my arms. I rendered the mother's labour as light as I could; any bit of food satisfied me; when watching was necessary, we shared it between us.[8]

He even took on extra paid work, which must have been pure drudgery for him, all too reminiscent of the miserable days spent copying law documents. Now he was translating Martens's *Law of Nature* from the French at a quarter a page.

I made it a rule to earn a dollar while my wife was getting the breakfast in the morning, and another dollar after I came home at night.[9]

He was either a very rapid worker or his wife a very slow cook if he could translate four pages of legal French during breakfast preparations, but the message is clear. Cobbett was working flat out during every waking hour. As a result, he was steadily able to put money away for the day when he could become independent. He was already moving in that direction in early 1796 as he began to shrug off the persona of William Cobbett, language teacher, and assume the much more congenial role of Peter Porcupine, controversial pamphleteer.

Cobbett was well served for material in Philadelphia. The notion of the founding fathers that America would be a nation untouched by a party faction was visibly collapsing. Intrigue and rumour were the commonplaces of conversation in the capital, and one of those rumours proved a gift to Cobbett in his fight for the British interest. Accusations had been made against the Secretary of State, Edmund Randolph. He was well known as a French sympathizer; some called him a Jacobin, but what shook George Washington was an allegation that he had asked for French bribes. He was confronted with the charges, denied them, but at once resigned. He now turned his fury against Washington himself, and published his own version of the quarrel.[10] He also used it to attack the Jay Treaty, claiming that Washington had vacillated, frequently changed his mind and finally given in to anti-French factions. There was much bluster, but as Cobbett was quick to notice, there was no real attempt to explain or refute the allegation made against him.

> On the article of corruption, of which we before doubted, we now doubt no longer; and as to his accusations against the President, it only serves to show that one who, with unblushing front, can ask a bribe, will never be ashamed to publish his ingratitude and apostacy.[11]

It is a common accusation that Cobbett at this time was violently pro-British and anti-American. That he was the former is beyond argument, and when British and American interests collided he was never in any doubt over where he stood. But it was more than mere sophistry to argue that in the case of the Jay Treaty there was no such conflict. It was in America's interests to bolster trade with Britain and keep out of the European war. The Southern States were just beginning to send cotton to Lancashire and the trade was already showing signs of phenomenal growth. And Cobbett was not a lone voice: it was, after all, the President himself, one of the most revered men in American history, whose side he was taking. It was no more possible in early 1796 than it would be later to tie a meaningful party-political tag to William Cobbett's coat-tails. He would have been a modern party whip's worst nightmare.

Other pamphlets followed, one of which, *The Bloody Buoy*[12] was more a book than a tract, a sustained polemic listing the savageries of the French Revolution and drumming home the point that the victims included ordinary men and women, not just the wealthy and aristocratic. He made the point, and a good point it was too, that it is easier to start a revolution than to control its course.

His personal life was in as great a turmoil as the national life on which he was commentating. He had a furious row with his publisher, Samuel Bradford, and his son, and took two pamphlets away to another publisher. Those who quarrelled with Cobbett inevitably found themselves deposed from the ranks of the just and the good and set down among the demons. There were no half measures, and when Bradford made matters worse by declaring that he had 'made use of the British Corporal', his wrath overflowed. To be told he had been made use of was bad enough, but to be demoted was even worse. He had a fine turn of invective. Bradford was 'this hatter-turned-printer, this sooty-fisted son of ink and urine, whose heart is as black and as foul as the liquid in which he dabbles'.[13] Bradford said that Cobbett had described Americans as being 'aristocrats and royalists at heart' and was guilty of gross hypocrisy. No, replied Cobbett, not all Americans, just the Bradfords, who he had caught out poring over books of heraldry trying to find a family connection to Lord Bradford. The Bradfords should perhaps have remembered the title of that early pamphlet, A Kick for a Bite: they were fairly trampled underfoot.

By now, in any case, Cobbett felt sufficiently secure to set up in business on his own as publisher, bookseller and writer, and in the spring he began negotiating for a house in Second Street. He had good reason to be confident. Peter Porcupine was famous, and as more and more people began to discover his identity, there was no reason to be coy. He was attracting attention everywhere: even those he had flailed with words were curious to meet him. Talleyrand, one time Prince de Benevento and Bishop of Autun, later a leading member of the Revolution and resident in Philadelphia, was an obvious target. Cobbett called him 'an apostate, a hypocrite, and every other name of which he was deserving', though this can hardly have kept Talleyrand awake at night. He loved shocking the Quakers and devoutly Puritanical Philadelphians by promenading the streets, his black mistress on his arm. Still one does not expect a man to invite a vitriol-penned opponent round for a social call; nor perhaps, would one expect the opponent to accept. But what fascination they must have felt for each other. For Cobbett, here was one of those revolutionaries he was spending all his time denouncing in the flesh: for Talleyrand, it was an opportunity to brighten a dull existence by meeting the literary man of the moment. The Frenchman began by making flattering remarks about Cobbett's pamphlets, even though he still officially declined to formally acknowledge authorship. But when Talleyrand asked – and his tongue was surely stuck firmly into his cheek – whether Cobbett had been at Oxford or Cambridge, it all proved a bit too much.

I had kept my countenance pretty well; but this abominable stretch of hypocrisy, and the placid mien and silver accent with which it was pronounced, would have forced a laugh from a quaker in the midst of a meeting ... I gave him to understand that I was no trout, and consequently not to be caught by tickling.[14]

When Talleyrand asked Cobbett to give him English lessons, he refused, later claiming that it was a feeble attempt to subvert him to the French cause. It is interesting to note that he never lashed out at Talleyrand with half the vigour with which he attacked other opponents. They even continued to meet at the house of an *émigré* who had fled the Terror. Cobbett always reserved his hottest fire not for those who he most vigorously opposed, but for those for whom he had no respect. He was bright enough to see that Talleyrand was playing a game, but he was also bright enough to see that it was not intended to succeed.

The time was getting close for Cobbett to open up for business. There was no longer any point in pretending that William Cobbett bookseller-to-be and Peter Porcupine were not the same man, so the bookshop and publisher would be seen as an ardent advocate of the British cause. Very well then, if he was going to come out of concealment, he would do so with no hint of cowardice or hypocrisy. He had been told that the Democrats could muster a mob that would at the very least break his windows, might pull down the whole house and possibly murder him. Caution was urged, but Cobbett was surely right in thinking that if he gave in even to the threat of violence, his reputation as a robust, independent thinker would be shattered. He would not pretend to hold opinions other than those he had so vigorously promoted in print, so if pretence was out he might just as well opt for boldness.

I saw the danger; but also saw that I must at once set all danger at defiance, or live in everlasting subjection to the prejudices and caprices of the democratical mob. I resolved on the former; and, as my shop was to open on a Monday morning, I employed myself all day on Sunday in preparing an exhibition, that I thought would put the courage and powers of my enemies to the test. I put up in my windows, which were very large, all the portraits that I had in my possession of kings, queens, and nobles. I had all the English ministry; several of the Bishops and Judges; the most famous Admirals; and, in short, every picture that I thought likely to excite rage in the enemies of Great Britain. In order to make the test as worthy as possible I had put up some of the worthies of the Revolution ... Early on Monday morning I took down my shutters. Such a sight had not been seen in Philadelphia for twenty years. Never since the beginning of the rebellion had anyone dared to hoist at his windows the portrait of George III.[15]

Having braved the wrath of the pro-independence American, he set about offending the Francophile Democrats: he set up two prints of Lord Howe's naval victory over the French on the 'Glorious First of June, 1794'. Actually, this was not quite as brave as Cobbett made out: for Howe had opposed the British role in the War of Independence and actually resigned his command rather than fight the Americans. Still, all in all, it was a calculated act of defiance. It worked. There was one semi-literate anonymous letter, but no mob, no smashed windows. Peter Porcupine was open for business.

6

DISILLUSIONMENT

Cobbett was wont to claim that the Jay Treaty was forced through entirely as a result of his own Herculean efforts. The British government seems to have held much the same opinion and Sir Robert Liston of the British Embassy offered him a cash payment or, if that was unacceptable, promotion for any of his family who happened to be in the army and help, unspecified, for others. Cobbett, quite rightly and justifiably, prided himself on his independence, and regularly refused any offers that might endanger it. This altogether admirable trait was slightly marred by the pomposity with which he flourished his superior morality.

> As to my relations in the army, I can ask for no promotion for them, because I have not an opportunity of knowing whether such promotion would be consistent with the good of the service; and, with respect to my relations out of the army, a sudden elevation might, perhaps, be very far from contributing to their happiness.[1]

He then rather spoiled the effect by adding

> The Government did nothing wrong in making the offer; for my services to England were so great, so manifest that it would have been criminal not to.

Cobbett was certainly not a man to underestimate his own worth. His was an influential voice, but George Washington probably saved the treaty, not from anything that happened in France, England or even America, but as a result of actions by Spain. The Spanish saw an Anglo-American alliance as a threat to their own American interests, and promptly set out a treaty of their own, giving Americans access to the Mississippi. Treaties were, it seemed, no bad thing after all, and were a great deal better than trying to fight a war at sea – particularly when America had no navy whatsoever. The Jay Treaty was the last major act of Washington's presidency. It was a

course of action that was certainly sensible, could be described as
statesmanlike, but was deeply unpopular. America had, it seemed,
given in to threats from a country they had decisively trounced just
a few years before. The great George Washington was to bow out
of the political arena, not with cheers ringing round him, but to the
accompaniment of catcalls and jeers. His final response was almost
as comical as it was pathetic.

> As some of the gazettes of the United States have teemed with
> all the invective that disappointment, ignorance of facts, and
> malicious falsehoods could invent, to misrepresent my politics
> and affections – to wound my reputation and feelings – and to
> weaken, if not entirely destroy, the confidence you have been
> pleased to repose in me; it might be expected at the parting
> scene of my public life that I should take some notice of such
> virulent abuse. But, as heretofore, I shall pass them over in
> utter silence.[2]

With an election due, there was real concern that Washington's
fall in popularity would reflect on the chances of his chosen successor, John Adams. The hopes of Thomas Jefferson and the
Republicans ran high. Cobbett was inevitably involved on the side
of Adams, and he found the perfect subject matter for a pamphlet,
presented to him courtesy of the French Minister, Pierre Adet. He
threatened that the French would follow the English lead and attack
neutral ships trading with the enemy, but hinted that if only the
Americans would elect a Republican government the threat would
be removed. There were two basic defects: the French did not
control the seas, and could not make good their threat and they were
blatantly interfering in America's internal affairs. It was a perfect
opportunity for some good Porcupine ridicule.

> When we see an unprincipled, shameless bully, 'A dog in
> forehead, and in heart a deer', who endeavours, by means of
> a big look, a threatening aspect, and a thundering voice, to
> terrify peaceable men into compliance with what he has neither
> a right to demand, nor power nor courage to enforce, and
> who, at the same time, acts in such a bungling, stupid
> manner, as to excite ridicule and contempt in place of fear;
> when we see such a gasconading, impudent bluff as this (and
> we do every day), we call him a *Blunderbuss*'.[3]

Having set the tone for the debate, Cobbett simply withdrew and
reprinted Adet's own letters as perfect examples of a diplomatic
blunderbuss at work. It was a brilliant and witty pamphlet. Even
George Washington, who did not care for political rough and tumble

and deplored Cobbett's 'strong and coarse expressions', admitted 'it is not a bad thing'. It was generally agreed that the Adet affair had lost Jefferson votes, and when at the end the electoral college came out for Adams by a narrow 71–68 majority, it looked as if it had cost him the election as well.

It is difficult today, when the name of George Washington is so generally revered, to realize with what intense loathing he was regarded by the Republicans. Benjamin Bache, an old opponent of Cobbett's, published a set of anti-Washington articles of immense ferocity, to mark Adams' inauguration in 1797.

> If ever there was a period of rejoicing, it is this moment. Every heart, in unison with the freedom and happiness of the people, ought to beat high in exultation, that the name of Washington ceases from this day to give a currency to political iniquity and to legalize corruption.[4]

Cobbett, not surprisingly, took a very different view. He admired Washington and looked forward to Adams continuing the same policies. He had already begun a monthly publication, *The Political Censor*, the ostensible aim of which was to inform the public about major debates in the government, but was at least as important as a forum for Cobbett's own views and commentaries on events. With a new administration, and one which Cobbett at least believed he had been instrumental in putting there, the way seemed open to an even more ambitious project. On 4 March 1797 the world was presented with the first edition of a new daily paper, *Porcupine's Gazette*.

> I began my editorial career with the presidency of Mr Adams, and my principal object was to render his administration all the assistance in my power. I flattered myself with the hope of accompanying him through his voyage, and of partaking in a trifling degree of the glory of the enterprise.[5]

He had achieved a position that he was to cherish for the rest of his life. At last he was truly independent: he was publisher, editor and writer. Each and every day, the public would be kept informed of the great events, would keep up with the manoeuvres and debates of politicians and would be guided through the labyrinth by Peter Porcupine in person. There were no restraints to gag him, no one to impose on him. At the base of his quarrel with Bradford, was a chance remark made by the son, that the Bradfords would like a follow-up to the successful pamphlet of 1796, *A Prospect from the Congress-Gallery*. His father had promised one, and the customers would be disappointed if one failed to appear.

> What! a bookseller undertake to promise what I should write,
> and that I should write to please customers too! No; if all his
> *customers*, if all the Congress, with the President at their
> head, had come and solicited me; nay, had my life depended
> on a compliance, I would not have written another line.[6]

Now there would be no more Bradfords. He could put his own
views forward as forcibly as ever, and attack his opponents' arguments, and their personal character and morality as he chose. What
he did not perhaps appreciate at this time was that those he attacked
might have friends in high places who could make life extremely
difficult for him, to say the least. But then it was never Cobbett's
way to worry too much about what opponents might do: 'prudence'
was not a word that featured in his journalistic lexicon.

There is no doubt, however, that it was precisely this rough-and-
tumble approach that made Peter Porcupine so popular. His paper
was as informative as any, but its style was unique, and ensured it
a huge circulation for its time. Even those who disagreed with its
views – or, perhaps one should say, especially those who disagreed
with its views – were aware of the importance of Peter Porcupine.
This importance was especially noted by those whose job it was to
promote British interests in America, for they recognized that an
independent voice, and no one could ever say that Cobbett was not
his own man, was worth far more than the most carefully composed
official pronouncements when it came to swaying political opinion.
The only trouble as far as officialdom was concerned was that one
could never be absolutely sure in which direction such a very independent character might move.

Cobbett's position in the political spectrum could often be
gauged by his attitude toward Tom Paine. He had been an early
admirer, but had become disillusioned with revolutionary France
and was inclined to blame Paine for enthusing him in the first place.
America also had proved less appealing than he had been led to
expect, and then, at the end of 1796, Paine had popped up again,
opposing Washington.[7] Just as there is no sterner opponent of
tobacco than the ex-smoker, so the ex-Painite now became his most
vehement critic. A wholly scurrilous and mainly untrue biography
of Paine had been written by George Chalmers[8] and Cobbett
reprinted it in America adding his own embellishments. In this work
Paine was depicted as a cheat, a philanderer, a brutal husband and
much more. It was a view that fitted well with Cobbett's own view
of revolutionaries: it might sound very fine in theory, but was liable
to go horribly wrong in practice.

> Paine's humanity, like that of all the reforming philosophers
> of the present enlightened day, is of the speculative kind. It

never breaks out into action. Hear these people, and you would think them overflowing with the milk of human kindness. They stretch their benevolence to the extremities of the globe: it embraces every living creature – except those who have the misfortune to come into contact with them. They are citizens of the world: country and friends and relations are unworthy the attention of men who are occupied in rendering all mankind happy and free.[9]

It was, of course, a criticism that could be levelled against all great reformers who were prepared to sacrifice anyone for their principles. It was equally applicable to Cobbett himself, even if he would rather not have admitted it. Over the next few years, common prudence would have told him to tone down some of his attacks in order to protect his family and income, but he would have scorned such advice. It did not prevent Cobbett gloating over Paine's falling out with the French revolutionaries he had supported. 'There he lies!' Cobbett gleefully declared, 'manacled, besmeared with filth, crawling with vermin, loaded with years and infamy.'[10]

Cobbett should have recognized a fellow spirit. But Paine was a man he had once revered and now he turned against him, just as Paine in turn had turned against his old ally, Washington. He had made promises in his revolutionary writings and those promises had been broken: worse, he had turned against his own country, England. This, for Cobbett, was the unforgiveable sin. However many times he changed his own political opinion, in this at least he was constant: William Cobbett was first, foremost and always an Englishman. His vehemence rose in direct proportion to his disappointment.

Cobbett is usually depicted at this stage of his career as the archetypal Tory. In the sense that he was disillusioned with violent change, he was a conservative. Insofar as radical opinion was pro-French and anti-English, he was enthusiastically right-wing. His country was at war and led by a Tory government, so he supported king and country and the Tory party. But at this stage he was too far removed from domestic politics in Britain to have any view whatsoever on local policies. He was not even clear where his future lay, in the New World, or the Old, but whichever it was to be he was not going to throw over his old allegiances: 'whenever, and wherever, I meet with any *malicious aspersions* on Britain, her king, or her subjects, the bitterest drops of my pen shall be employed in retaliation'.[11] His was, at this stage, a simple ethic: Britain's friends are my friends, her enemies are my enemies. Arguments in favour of Tory or Radical, Federalist or Republican were all measured against this creed. His support for Washington and his successor Adams would last precisely as long as they were seen to support

British interests: the moment they wavered, Cobbett would turn on them. In this, at least, he was and remained wholly consistent.

There was still no shortage of campaigns to be waged and French atrocities to reveal. As part of the continuing battle over maritime trade, the French were issuing letters of marque, in effect licences for anyone and everyone to use the French West Indies as a base for privateering, and American ships were as likely to be victims as British. Each and every attack was duly reported, with a good deal of lurid detail in *Porcupine's Gazette*. There was considerable American support for the rising of the United Irishmen against London rule in 1798, with the active support of the French. Cobbett had been first to denounce the continuing enthusiasm for all things French.

> I have heard more than one young woman, under the age of twenty, declare that they would willingly have dipped their hands in the blood of the Queen of France. A third part of the children, at least, were decorated like their wise sires, in tri-coloured cockades. 'Danson la Carmagnole', pronounced in a broken accent, was echoed through every street and alley of Philadelphia, by both boys and girls. Some ingenious democrat poet had composed the following lines:
>
> > Englishman no bon for me
> > Frenchmen fight for liberty.
>
> Poor devils! thought I when I used to hear them, little do you know about liberty![12]

Then when the rebellion failed, he made much of French half-heartedness, if not downright perfidy. He published an account, said to have been written by a patriotic rebel, Martin McLaughlin,[13] describing the brutality of the French command. After a minor fracas with a drill sergeant, an officer intervened and shot McLaughlin's friend dead: 'I then began to think Billy was a little mistaken when he said 'that the French were our best friends'.' The Irish were given the menial tasks until it came to the fight when the French ran away and left them to it. The ordinary Irishmen were the misguided victims, the French out-and-out villains and the Irish leaders little better. Many fled to America, much to Cobbett's disgust: the country was meant as 'an asylum for the oppressed' not as a 'sanctuary for the infamous'.

The British did not always do a great deal to make their Philadelphian defenders' task an easy one. Liston of the British Embassy was involved in a hare-brained scheme to annexe Florida, using the British Navy and local Indians, which Cobbett did his best to put in a favourable light – no easy task, but if it won him no new friends in America, it was at least well received back in Britain.

Happily for Cobbett, the French were even more prone to dropping diplomatic bricks than the British. Just as Washington had sought to make peace with Britain by treaty, so Adams was anxious to prevent the attacks on American ships by the French. A diplomatic mission was sent over to Paris who instead of meeting high-ranking officials were fobbed off with nobodies, simply known as X, Y and Z. They were happy to agree to a peace. All they wanted in return was a cash payment of £50,000, a loan of 32 million Dutch florins and for Adams to retract every derogatory remark he had ever made against France. Publication of this farcical correspondence created an uproar. Not even the Republicans could find words to defend Messieurs X, Y and Z. This was a situation made for Cobbett. He produced yet another tirade on French atrocities, this time not against aristocrats but good Republicans in other European countries. Liberty must be defended, the vicious French repelled.

> Independence, with all its attendant blessings, is yet within your power; but as it was obtained by arms, so it must be maintained; and you have not a month, nay not a day left to you to consider, whether you shall assume those arms, or basely bend your necks to the galling yoke of the insolent, bloodthirsty tyrants of France.[14]

The pamphlet was a huge popular success and did a great deal to turn opinion against the French. What it did not do, to Cobbett's extreme disgust, was provoke Adams and the American government into declaring war. He fulminated against the House of Representatives who were shilly-shallying over what to do.

> no energetic measure is adopted, no *strong alien bill or sedition law is passed*, nor is any declaration of war made, by which *traitors* can, in the eyes of the law, be found guilty and punished. Dreadful, awful state. If ever people on earth were dancing on the edge of a precipice, we are at this moment.[15]

Then worse news came. Adams was actually planning to negotiate with France to resolve the issues. This was precisely what Washington had done, with very much the same motives, in securing the Jay Treaty. That was not how Cobbett saw it. He had been betrayed, and there was no longer a politician or a party in America which he felt he could trust or support.

Cobbett's position by the end of the 1790s was a sorry one. His political star was fading: it is difficult to hold a readership when you oppose everyone, and his personal and financial problems were increasing. He had been storing up troubles for the future ever since the first edition appeared. His no-holds-barred approach to his enemies often went beyond what many saw as acceptable. His hatred of the Democrats was extreme. On hearing that one of their supporters had lost an eye in a naval engagement, he wrote, 'So far so good' and added, 'but he should have lost two'.[16] He was, inevitably, himself the subject of threats, which worried him not a jot. When a correspondent threatened to horse-whip him, Cobbett simply replied: 'I know he is a base scoundrel, and that he no more dares attack me, than he dares to go to any country where there is a gallows.'[17] This was his best rough-and-tumble style, and did no harm whatsoever to the *Gazette*'s circulation, but carried dangers.

Cobbett was a brave and determined adversary, but not a prudent one. It was all very well making enemies, but he chose one who was well placed to do him real harm. Judge Thomas McKean was a man of high prestige, a convinced Democrat and one of the signatories to the Declaration of Independence. In 1777 he was appointed Chief Justice of Pennsylvania, and it was one of his decisions that incurred the wrath of Peter Porcupine. Two Quakers were brought before him and charged with treason for serving under the British forces. The jury found them guilty, but strongly recommended mercy. McKean ignored the plea and they were executed. Inevitably, Cobbett was enraged and, equally inevitably he made his rage public, denouncing McKean as a murderer. It is doubtful if he thought for a moment about the personal consequences should he ever become involved with the law in Pennsylvania, and if he did consider them he would probably have written his denunciation all the same. He was soon to pay the price.

In 1797, Cobbett found a new target in Don Carlos Martinez de Yrugo, Spanish minister in America. His sin was the familiar one of supporting the French cause, and Cobbett followed the equally familiar routine of combining a denunciation of policy with a denigration of person. Yrugo became 'Don Sans-Culotte de Carmagnola Minor', and even the king of Spain was referred to as a 'degenerate prince' – all rather mild stuff by Porcupine standards, but enough to infuriate the Spanish grandee. Yrugo tried to persuade the Secretary of State to do something to quieten his tormentor, but when there was no sign of immediate action, a better idea appeared. Yrugo had a son who was busily courting the daughter of Judge McKean. Why not issue a libel writ to be heard in Pennsylvania? He did, and was saved the expense and bother of actually going to court by the Judge's enthusiasm. McKean chose to ignore his personal interest – a known hatred of one party and an approaching family connection with the other might have suggested the possibility of prejudice to some, but not it seems to the Judge. Cobbett was commanded to McKean's presence. He arrived without legal representation, unaware that the matter was to be decided then and there. He was ordered to pay a surety of $2000 and give a guarantee to end his attacks or go to gaol. He paid up. There was worse to come.

That year, there was an epidemic of yellow fever, which Cobbett seems to have regarded as being sent deliberately to make life difficult for him. He wrote to a friend, Edward Thornton apologizing for sending in an account with somewhat unseemly haste, 'but I am absolutely blocked up – I am fast, like the poor frigate at Boston. The yellow fever has taken away all those who should have paid me, and sent in all those to whom I owe.'[18] There were compensations in the popularity of the pamphlets such as *The Cannibal's Progress* being read by families of all types, from poor to rich. But already, he was speaking of a yearning to be home. He wrote to Thornton:

> You make me very happy Sir, in telling me that I am highly esteemed in England; that is the place where I wish to be esteemed ... a few years will most certainly see me once more in dear old England.

His view of his new homeland was not improved when the Governor responded to the fever epidemic by issuing a proclamation that the authorities should be informed of all cases and the patients removed from the city. This infuriated Cobbett, who exclaimed, 'What? Forcibly enter my house, and drag from thence my wife or my child, for no other offence than that of being sick!' His main invective, however, was reserved for the fashionable physician of the day, Dr Benjamin Rush. He believed that all disease came from a single cause, over exertion of the body, and could be cured by bleeding and violent purgatives, such as mercury. How many victims might have survived had they been spared the doctor's 'cure' cannot be known, but Cobbett had at least a notion. He wrote to a friend.

> Dr Rush, in that emphatic style which is peculiar to himself, calls *mercury* the '*Samson* of medicine.' In his hands, and those of his partisans, it may, indeed, be justly compared to *Samson*: for I verily declare they have slain more Americans with it than ever Samson slew of the Philistines.[19]

Rush sued for libel.

Cobbett argued that, as a British subject, he was entitled to a hearing in the Federal Court rather than in McKean's Pennsylvanian Court: the ruling on that was given by McKean himself. Cobbett could scarcely have been surprised at the result. Everything was going wrong in America. In August 1798, he wrote to Thornton describing not only his public worries, but also his private woes. Nancy was expecting another child – William was to be born in December of that year – and was increasingly unhappy and home-sick, but resolute.

> Whether I shall escape the scourge that continually hangs over us here, I know not; but, if I do, a few years will most certainly see me once more in dear Old England, far distant from Yellow Fevers and universal suffrage. If Mrs Cobbett's health continues to decline, which I am afraid will be the case, it is impossible for me much longer to resist her solici-tations, which grow more and more ernest [*sic*] every day.[20]

He continued:

> It is the misfortune of most wives, to be *cunning* on these occasions. 'Ah, did I not tell you so!' – Never did I hear a reproach of this kind from my wife. When times are *smooth* she will contradict and blame me often enough in all conscience; but, when difficulties come on me, when danger approaches us, then all I say and do, and all I have said and done, is *right*.[21]

The case was slow to reach the courts and Cobbett did nothing to help his own cause by continuing his attacks on McKean. Cobbett well knew the likeliest outcome, and in November 1799, a month before the trial, he had packed up his furniture and the stock of his bookshop and sent them to New York. The trial itself was a farce, not helped by the hopeless incompetence of Cobbett's attorney, who spent half his speech saying what a good doctor Rush really was. Rush was heard to remark in a surprised voice that he had not 'feed' the attorney, while Cobbett commented that he should have paid to keep his own lawyer out of court. The jury found for Rush and imposed damages of what was then a colossal sum, $5000. In a moment of supreme irony, not lost on Cobbett, the verdict was announced on the day George Washington died – having been treated by excessive bleedings and purgatives in the approved Rush manner.

Cobbett was advised to leave America, but he retained a stalwart front, for a brief time at least.

> No, Sir, the miscreants may, probably, rob me of all but my honour, but that, in these degenerate times, I cannot spare. To flee from a *writ* (however basely and illegally obtained) is what I will never do ... such a step might, for aught I know, be very proper if taken by a *sovereign citizen*; but, to an

Englishman, a subject of George the Third, it would be an insupportable disgrace.[22]

Meanwhile, his remaining goods in Philadelphia had been confiscated, and a whole edition of *Porcupine's Works* was destroyed. His disillusionment with America was complete. There were exceptions to be made for individuals, but 'with the exception of the Quakers of Pennsylvania, many other individuals in that State, and the people of New England, I hate the United States and all their hypocritical system of rule'. And his greatest condemnation was reserved for officialdom.

I never saw and heard so much place-hunting, profit-hunting, political intrigue, bargaining about jobs and bills, in short, no such low, filthy, odious, political corruption, as I had before my eyes, and in my ears, in one single fortnight while I was at Harrisburgh, the seat of the government of Pennsylvania.[23]

By now *Porcupine's Gazette* was no more, but he still wanted a voice, and began a new journal *The American Rush Light*, sub-titled 'by the help of which, wayward and disaffected Britons may see a complete specimen of the Baseness, Dishonesty, Ingratitude and Perfidy, of Republicans, and the Profligacy, Injustice and Tyranny of Republican Governments'. With its brief existence of just five issues the last shots of the war with Rush were fired. But already there were fresh lawsuits threatening, and Cobbett was in no mood for another hopeless action that could only end in his ruin. On 31 May 1800, Cobbett had an announcement printed in the leading newspapers. It is worth quoting in full as a measure of his disillusionment with America and the Americans.

When people care not two straws for each other, ceremony at parting is mere grimace; and, as I have long felt the most perfect indifference with regard to a vast majority of those whom I now address, I shall spare myself the trouble of a ceremonious farewell. Let me, however, not part from you in indiscriminating contempt. If no man ever had so many and such malignant foes, no one ever had more friends, and those more kind, more sincere, and more faithful. If I have been unjustly vilified by some, others have extolled me far beyond my merits; if the savages of the city have scared the children in my cradle, those children have, for their father's sake, been soothed and caressed by the affectionate, the gentle, the generous inhabitants of the country, under whose hospitable roofs I have spent some of the happiest hours of my life.

Thus and *thus*, Americans, will I ever speak of you. In a very little time I shall be beyond the reach of your friendship and your malice; beyond the hearing of your commendations and your curses, but being out of your power will alter neither my sentiments nor my words. As I have never spoken anything but truth *to* you, so I will never speak anything but truth *of* you; the heart of a Briton revolts at an emulation in baseness, and although you have as a nation treated me most ungratefully and unjustly, I scorn to repay you with ingratitude and injustice.

To my friends, who are also the real friends of America, I wish that peace and happiness which virtue ought to ensure, but which I greatly fear they will not find; and as to my enemies, I can wish them no greater scourge, than that which they are preparing for themselves and their country. With this I depart for my native land, where neither the moth of *Democracy* nor the rust of *Federalism* doth corrupt and where thieves do not, with impunity, break through and steal five thousand dollars at a time.[24]

To his friends, he made no bones about his motives for attacking his old neighbours and former friends in Philadelphia.

In all my publications about them, revenge is predominant over every other passion ... Damnation seize them, body and soul! If I can give them a foretaste of the torments of hell I will do it.[25]

On 1 June the whole family, William, Nancy, Anne and young William, were on board a ship bound for Nova Scotia and England.

7

RETURNING HOME

Whatever Cobbett might say, however he might bluster, there was no denying the fact that the family was escaping their enemies, avoiding a fight there was no chance of winning. He was, by nature, an optimistic man, supremely confident of his own abilities, yet even so it was a nervous time, a move towards a very uncertain future. There were, however, encouraging signs. The ship called in at Halifax, Nova Scotia, where the Cobbetts were personally welcomed by the governor, Sir John Wentworth, and the commander of British forces in North America, the Duke of Kent. They were fussed over and introduced to everyone of importance, which was all very gratifying – doubly gratifying when contrasted with the last time they were there. Sergeant Major Cobbett had stood in the ranks obeying the orders of the 'epaulets', now he reviewed the troops in the company of a royal duke. The ladies sent their carriages for Nancy Cobbett, who as Anne Reid had scrubbed soldiers' shirts. Cobbett would have needed far more modesty than he ever possessed not to feel immense pride in the changed circumstances, and in the knowledge that his reputation rested entirely on his own gifts and efforts.

The voyage to England on the *Lady Arabella* was less successful. The fellow passengers either felt that the Cobbetts had been fêted long enough or simply had no idea why such a fuss was being made. Even the Captain proved a great disappointment.

> Porteus, of whom I had such a good opinion, proved the greatest blackguard I ever met with, and he was nobly backed by a brace of lieutenants of the 26th Regiment, who accompanied us from Halifax. Mrs Robertson had a maid (I mean a female servant), with whom these fellows made free, almost in the presence of our wives; they smoked Mrs Cobbett almost to death; they talked in the most vulgar strain, and even sung morsels of bawdry in her presence.[1]

There were unwelcome excitements along the way, including an

encounter with a French privateer. By the time the ship reached
Falmouth, relations between the Cobbetts and the officers had
reached such a bad state that the latter tried to get them detained, on
the grounds that Cobbett's secretary, Edward Demonaison, was a
foreigner and probably a spy. To Cobbett's immense delight, the
little plot failed. The Customs Officer not only refused to act, but
turned out to be an enthusiastic reader of Peter Porcupine and gave
the family the full VIP treatment. So the Cobbetts eventually made
their way to London in high spirits.

Anne, although she was a small child at the time, remembered
the return to London as a high point in her young life.

> We entered Hyde Park Gate, and I recollect it quite well, so
> sunny and all in a glare ... Papa has told us that he said to
> Mama that though she might feel ashamed at their appearance,
> the humble post chaise and pair, and all inside as well as the
> outside, covered with dust, that she should see that by that
> day ten years he would have made himself so celebrated in
> this country that all those lords and ladies riding in their fine
> carriages should have heard of him.[2]

The prophecy was to be fulfilled, though not quite in the way
Cobbett intended. Ten years to the day, he was sent to prison: but
he was undeniably famous.

William Cobbett has come down to posterity as 'a great
Englishman', yet here he was, thirty-seven years old, having spent
nearly half his life living abroad. He had left the country as a
clumsy, semi-literate, but undeniably intelligent country lad and had
returned as one of the most famous political journalists of the age,
with a reputation that had spread throughout Europe and America.
But he had not yet arrived at the persona that he was to make his
own throughout the second part of his life. He liked to portray
himself as a gruff, honest son of the soil and made a point of acting
and dressing the part. The great essayist William Hazlitt gave a
thumb-nail portrait of him a few years later – a portrait of which the
subject would surely have approved.

> The only time I ever saw him he seemed to me a very pleas-
> ant man – easy of access, affable, clear-headed, simple and
> mild in his manner, deliberate and unruffled in his speech,
> though some of his expressions were not very qualified. His
> figure is tall and portly. He has a good sensible face – rather
> full, with little grey eyes, a hard, square forehead, a ruddy
> complexion, with hair grey or powdered; and had on a scarlet
> broad-cloth waistcoat with the flaps of the pockets hanging

down, as was the custom for gentlemen-farmers in the last century, or as we see it in the pictures of Members of Parliament in the reign of George I. I certainly did not think less favourably of him for seeing him.[3]

But how does this Cobbett compare with the man who arrived in London in 1800? A quarter of a century had gone by since he had last worked the land, handled a scythe or walked behind the plough. For the last few years he had lived a city life, surrounded not by fields and trees and friendly country folk, but by brick and stone and squabbling politicians. This was the atmosphere in which he thrived, and this was the atmosphere to which he wished to return, exchanging one political capital for another. He now knew far more about the machinations of diplomats than he did about the changes that had revolutionized the agriculture of England during his absence. He was a man with a gaze set on nothing less than influencing the policies of nations.

He had some hopes of continuing to exert the influence in England that he had enjoyed in America. His work was widely known, largely thanks to the efforts of leading anti-Jacobean writers, William Gifford and John Richards Green, who had propagated and praised his writings and in their letters to America had given him a view of the British political scene, albeit a somewhat lopsided one. Thanks to his work in America, Cobbett also had letters of introduction from Liston to important men in the Pitt administration, notably George Hammond, Under Secretary for Foreign Affairs. This suited Cobbett very well. His preoccupation was still the defeat of France and the evils of revolutionary republicanism. In America he had tacitly assumed that because he was in whole-hearted agreement with the government's foreign policy, he was likely to agree with them on other matters as well. If the Tories were anti-Jacobin, then William Cobbett would support the Tories; and now the Tories seemed flatteringly eager to welcome Cobbett into their ranks. He was wined, dined and generally fêted and was soon making important friends and influential connections. At a dinner party given by Hammond, he met William Windham, a somewhat pedantic politician much given to worrying over moral niceties, and at the time Secretary of War in Pitt's cabinet. The two men became good friends, perhaps because of rather than in spite of their differing temperaments. It is a measure of how far the opinions of the Cobbett who had left England had swung by the time he returned. He had left as an admirer of Paine's polemic written against Edmund Burke's *Reflections on the Revolution in France*, now he was finding an ally in a man who had been a close friend and admirer of Burke.

There was every encouragement for him to take up his career as publisher, editor and main contributor to a political journal. But he

faced serious problems when it came to trying to re-create Peter
Porcupine in an English setting. He had been away for a very long
time, and the world had changed dramatically. He was well
informed on foreign affairs and the war with France, but was almost
wholly ignorant of the domestic scene. When he left England, the
Industrial Revolution was just getting into gear. Now spinning and
weaving had left the cottage for the factory, powered first by water
but increasingly by steam. A network of canals and turnpike roads
had spread across the country. A new industrial proletariat had been
created, which looked back with nostalgia at the old rural life, a
view expressed in a popular ballad of the day, 'The Factory Bell'.[4]

> Oh happy man, oh happy thou,
> While toiling at thy spade and plough,
> While thou admist thy pleasures roll,
> All at thy labours uncontrolled:
> Here at the mills, in pressing crowds
> The high-built chimneys puff black clouds,
> And all around the slaves do dwell
> Who're called to labour by a bell

The misery endured by many factory workers was real enough, but
the idyllic picture of rural life was a fantasy. The agrarian revolution was less dramatic than the industrial, but its effects were as far-
reaching. Enclosure had been steadily advancing throughout the
eighteenth century, and the old open field was already an anachro-
nism when Cobbett was a boy. The most striking change in land use
at the end of the century was the transformation of the old commons
and wastes into arable land. Changes cost money, so there was a
tendency for farms to get larger, while at the same time moving
away from the old system of farmer and labourer living under the
same roof. Smallholders and the poorer tenant farmers were swept
up under the new system and reduced to paid labourers. And all the
time prices were steadily rising and agricultural prices fastest of all.
Where manufacturing prices had risen by fifty per cent since the
middle of the century, by 1800 farm prices had more than doubled
and wages were nowhere near keeping pace.

It was in the interest of the new generation of farmers to have a
large pool of cheap labour available on demand. There was a strong
incentive to keep the labourer wholly dependent on the farmer.

> When a labourer becomes possessed of more land than he and
> his family can cultivate in the evenings ... the farmer can no
> longer depend on him for constant work, and the hay-making
> and harvest ... must suffer to a degree which ... would
> sometimes prove a national inconvenience.[5]

As for the parish poor, they were 'designing rogues, who, under various pretences attempt to cheat the parish'. Not everyone took such a harsh view of the poor. In May 1795, there was a meeting of Berkshire magistrates at Speenhamland, near Newbury, to fix a minimum wage for the county. This they did, but instead of insisting that farmers paid this wage, they set in place a system where ever 'poor and industrious person' received funds from the parish to make up the difference between what the farmers wished to pay and what was deemed the minimum needed to keep a family alive. What was begun in Berkshire soon spread rapidly to other counties. That this was a direct incentive for large employers to pay low wages and have the differences made up by their neighbours was not immediately obvious to the men who dreamed up what they thought was a way of helping the labouring poor. Such, however, it turned out to be. Cobbett returned to an England of poor harvests, high prices and low wages, which was only saved from widespread revolt by the patriotism evoked by war. Nothing is more conducive to getting unpopular policies accepted than a popular war.

Cobbett was, not surprisingly, largely unaware of the nature of the changes in society, and, in particular, their impact on the rural poor. Nor were such subjects likely to feature strongly in the conversations at the salons and round the dining tables of his new political friends. It would have been easy for him to be swayed by the adulation he received in London, but one advantage of his egotism was that he did not see it as being anything other than his due as saviour of the British interest in America. He remained his own man. It was not just that he was supremely confident of his own abilities, but his American experience had taught him, if nothing else, that it was unwise to rely on the constancy of politicians. He had begun as one of Adams's most ardent supporters and defenders and had ended as one of his most bitter opponents. The change had little to do with personalities: Cobbett was, and always remained, a cause man, not a party man. If A supported his cause and B opposed, when then he was all for A, but if A dropped the cause and B took it up, then Cobbett would as enthusiastically praise B as he had once condemned him. So when Hammond offered him the control of one of the two government supported papers, *The True Briton* and *The Sun*, he turned the offer down. This was a brave decision. He was short of funds and still something of a stranger in his own land. He was being offered financial security and there was something undeniably right as well as attractive in the title 'William Cobbett, *The True Briton*'. He explained his decision to Hammond by quoting the fable of the wolf and the mastiff. The fat, sleek dog persuades the wolf to give up the hard life of hunting in the cold, wild woods and come back with him to a warm house and regular meals. On the way, the wolf notices a mark round the dog's neck

and asks him what it is. The dog replies that it is just the mark of
the collar his master puts on to tie him up.

> 'Tie you up!' exclaimed the wolf, stopping short at the same
> time; 'give me my ragged hair, my gaunt belly, and my
> freedom!' and so saying he trotted back to the wood.[6]

It was not just a brave decision: it was a wise one. Cobbett was
not just more wolf than dog, he was a notably lone wolf. He
followed his own paths. Even so, at this stage, he still saw his role
as it had been in America, as a supporter of government policy. He
disagreed with Hammond only on the question of how this could
best be achieved: 'for me to be able to do government any service,
I must be able to say, that I am *totally independent* of it, in my
capacity as proprietor of a newspaper.'[7] The views that his paper
would express would be, and would be seen to be, his own. But
Cobbett's views did not arrive fully developed from his own brain,
however much he might wish to think they did. He was, in fact, as
susceptible as anyone to rational argument and current opinion. He
had been won over by Paine's logic and passion and it was only his
first-hand experience of revolutionary France that caused him to
change his mind. He was a great pragmatist: the eloquence of the
lesson was of less importance than the value of the results.
Nevertheless, he was influenced by the important writers of the age,
and if he says frustratingly little about those writers, perhaps this
was because it was not a Cobbett trait to admit to being influenced
by others at all. We know that he regularly read philosophy, and we
can get some idea, even this early in his writing career, of the
impact on his thinking of what he read.

He scorned 'feelosofers', but there is considerable evidence that
he thought about their writings, and adapted their ideas for his own
use. In 1800 he was writing about 'the vile Rousseau',[8] not surpris-
ing as Rousseau was a cult figure for the Revolutionaries and particularly admired by Robespierre. Cobbett was somewhat coy about
his reading of Rousseau – 'I happened, by accident, to look into his
'Emile',' he wrote later in life, describing a time in the early 1800s
when the children were small. It is difficult to see his reading a
book which he himself had brought into the house as accidental.
And Cobbett found in Rousseau's views on education much that
echoed his own developing ideas. When Rousseau wrote in *Emile*
that moral rules can be found 'in the depths of my heart, written by
Nature in ineffaceable characters' and that 'we can be men without
being learned' he found a willing reader. It was not perhaps so
much philosophical ideas or attitudes of mind that struck a chord
with Cobbett. Rousseau could write as directly as Cobbett when he
chose to. In a letter to a doubter in Dijon, it is the correlation

between town and useless luxury on one side and the rural world of simpler needs, thwarted by the former, that is to be a major theme in Cobbett's own writings.

> Luxury feeds one hundred poor people in our towns and causes one hundred thousand to perish in our rural areas. The money pouring from the hands of the rich to those of the artists, in order to supply their unnecessary things, is lost to the subsistence of the husbandman; and the latter has no coat precisely because others must have braid; our kitchens need gravy, that's why so many sick people lack bouillon; our tables need vegetables, that's why the countryside drinks only water; our wigs need powder: that's why so many poor people have no bread.[9]

But when it comes to the best known of Rousseau's works *The Social Contract*, the influence seems to be a good deal less than that of the English writer John Locke and his eighteenth century followers. At this period in his life, Cobbett was still developing his own fundamental ideas, but some notions were already plainly formed – and the notion that some form of contract existed between government and governed was certainly a part of the framework. It is interesting to compare the two. Here is Locke:

> The great and chief aim of men uniting into commonwealths and putting themselves under government, is the preservation of their properties.[10]

And here by way of comparison is the mature Cobbett.

> Men made themselves a compact, or an agreement, to divide the land and its products in such a manner that each should have a share to his own exclusive use, and that each man should be protected in the exclusive enjoyment of his share by the united powers of the rest.[11]

He had built a platform out of various planks on which he would stand and view the political scene. It would be a time before he could take in the whole panorama, and begin the process of reassessment. He quickly came to realize that it was not just England that had changed, but his own perceptions of it. The first shock came when he returned to his old home at Farnham.

> Everything was so pitifully small! I had to cross, in my post-chaise, the long and dreary heath of Bagshot. Then, at the end of it, to mount a hill, called Hungry Hill; and from that hill I

knew that I should look down into the beautiful and fertile vale of Farnham. My heart fluttered with impatience mixed with a sort of fear, to see all the scenes of my childhood; for I had learnt before, the death of my father and mother. There is a hill, not far from the town, called Crooksbury Hill, which rises up out of a flat, in the form of a cone, and is planted with Scotch fir trees. Here I used to take the eggs and young ones of crows and magpies. This hill was a famous object in the neighbourhood. It served as a superlative degree of height. 'As high as Crooksbury Hill' meant, with us, the utmost degree of height. Therefore, the first object that my eyes sought was this hill. I could not believe my eyes! Literally speaking, I for a moment thought the famous hill removed, and a little heap put in its stead; for I had seen in New Brunswick a single rock, or hill of solid rock, ten times as big, and four or five times as high! The post-boy, going downhill, and not a bad road, whisked me, in a few minutes to the Bush Inn, from the garden of which I could see the prodigious sand hill where I had begun my gardening works. What a nothing! But now came rushing into my mind, all at once, my pretty little garden, my little blue smock-frock, my little nailed shoes, my pretty pigeons that used to feed out of my hands, the last kind words and tears of my gentle and tenderhearted and affectionate mother! I hastened back into the room. If I had looked a moment longer I should have dropped. When I came to reflect, what a change! I looked down at my dress. What a change! What scenes I had gone through! How altered my state! I had dined the day before at a Secretary of State's with Mr Pitt, and had been waited upon by men in gaudy liveries! I had had nobody to assist me in the world. No teachers of any sort. Nobody to shelter me from the consequence of bad, and no one to counsel me to good behaviour. I felt proud. The distinctions of rank, birth, and wealth, all became nothing in my eyes; and from that moment (less than a month after my arrival in England) I resolved never to bend before them.[12]

There were other differences in his personal life. His parents were dead, and his brothers, settled with large families, were unmistakeably poor. This was perhaps the first time he had become directly aware of the poverty that had engulfed so much of once prosperous and rural England. For the moment this was not a national cause in which he was to become embroiled, but a personal one he could do something about in a very positive way. It was, he declared, the first time in his life he had really understood the value of money. He was able to relieve the distress of his family, but soon discovered that the changes that had overtaken their lives were part of another, bigger social movement. He was dismayed to find that the old social categories were equally changed. When he left, a 'Squire' was a well understood term, he was the gentleman at the manor, the leader of the rural community. He had seen pamphlets, sent out from England, and had assumed that because there was an 'Esquire' after the author's name he was receiving the views of independent-minded gentlemen. Instead they were written by professional authors, 'all, in one way or another dependents on the government; and, out of the public purse, profiting from their pamphlets'. Cobbett was no 'Esquire' and he would never pretend to be one, but he would show these government hacks what a truly independent writer could achieve. Peter Porcupine had gone his own way in America, and won great prestige. He was now determined to introduce the character to the British public, and set out to repeat his success. In 1800 he opened a bookshop in Pall Mall and began a publishing business from an office in the Strand. There was a need for urgency for there was his own growing family to support – a son, John, was born that year. He was not that unaware of the value of money. There was also a real need to cash in on his reputation as quickly as possible, while the memory of his American deeds was still fresh in the public mind. So he launched a new journal, with a familiar name, on the British public. *The Porcupine* was born.

8

A TIME OF CONFUSION

Everything that had seemed so clear-cut in America looked a good deal more confusing in Britain. The war against France which in Cobbett's mind had all the character of a holy crusade, in which the might of virtuous England was set against the ungodly hordes of France, was an altogether more muddled affair of shifting alliances and political expedients. Cobbett's preoccupation with the Jay Treaty had inevitably led him to concentrate on the war at sea, where the British fleet was supreme. Napoleon had been assembling a fleet of small vessels for the invasion of England, but declared that nothing could be done until he was convinced that the British did not command the seas. Devastating proof to the contrary was provided by Nelson in the first action he commanded in 1798, the Battle of the Nile, and was confirmed by his even more daring victory at Copenhagen in which he famously applied his telescope to his blind eye when ordered to retreat. On land, matters were very different. Here Britain's role was rather more that of paymaster to the allied armies than of an active belligerent. There was disunity not just among the allies, but even inside the government as to what the aims of the war should be: the defeat of France and the overthrow of the republican government, or a policy of containment within existing frontiers.

Their allies were a cause for concern to the British Government. Austria had been given loans on the understanding that she would join the alliance, but had spent the money and declined to sign up. Some regarded the Prussians as being altogether more dependable, but Frederick William II shared the disinclination to fight. The Russians would join in provided others footed the bill. In the event, it was the 'unreliable' Austrians who proved the most effective force while the 'reliable' Prussians were soon to prove the least trustworthy. But the greatest humiliations were reserved for the British in Europe. The first fiasco involved an invasion of Holland. Prussia promised to deliver over 200,000 troops for the battle, in return for £3 million credit from the British government, but before the invasion had begun the Prussians had started peace negotiations with

France. The Russians agreed to take part on payment of £88,000 at the start of the campaign and £44,000 a month until it ended. The British contribution was made up of battalions of footguards and twice as many ill-trained, ill-equipped volunteers. At first, things went well, but Abercrombie, the commander, halted to await reinforcements under the Duke of York. The French had by now had time to gather their forces, and the result was huge losses among the Russian and British troops and total withdrawal back to Britain. In 1800, frantic for a victory, the British army embarked on an even more desperate adventure – the capture of strongly fortified Cadiz. In the event, storms kept the ships at sea and eventually the seasick soldiers returned home without having set foot on European soil. Lord Cornwallis wrote bitterly of 'Twenty-two thousand men floating round the greater part of Europe, the scorn and laughing stock of friends and foes'.[1] While all this was going on, Napoleon had crushed the Austrians at Marengo, and reached agreement with Russia. Napoleon was successfully isolating Britain and was prepared to talk peace, from a position of strength.

France had one great advantage: once Napoleon had been made First Consul in 1799, he spoke for the whole country. He had no need to talk to, let alone appease, anyone else. At the end of the year, he wrote to George III offering peace which the king contemptuously rejected in a reply which offered agreement only on the absurd condition, in the circumstances, that the French reinstate the monarchy forthwith. Pitt received the full support of Parliament in agreeing to fight on, but when it came to deciding how it was to be done, given the somewhat abject record of the Army, all was confusion. For all the bellicose talk, there was an air of disillusionment spreading throughout the government.

Cobbett arrived full of patriotic fervour, seeing the whole situation in the simplest terms. There was a just war to be fought and it needed to be fought to a conclusion. If he knew the problems that faced the government, he ignored them; and if he had ideas on how victory could be achieved with a demoralized Army and a crumbling alliance he was uncharacteristically silent. He had arrived in Britain at a most confusing time, and he was neither well enough informed nor yet sufficiently in touch with public opinion to make a meaningful contribution. It was not a situation that could, or would, last and it was not long before he found his voice again. In the meantime, the government had just as many problems to solve at home as they had abroad.

The first was the growing militancy of the work-force. There were two sets of very different attitudes to what was happening in the new manufacturing towns. There were a few dispassionate observers. John Ferriar was a doctor in Manchester who described conditions in the slums, where many people were crammed into crumbling houses or dank cellars. Writing in 1792, he described the horrors of disease that haunted the poor.

> The lodging houses, near the extremities of the town, produce many fevers ... The most fatal consequences have resulted from a nest of lodging houses in Brooks's entry ... In those houses, a very dangerous fever constantly subsists, and has subsisted for a considerable number of years. I have known nine patients confined in fevers at the same time, in one of those houses, and crammed into three small, dirty rooms ... Four of these creatures died, absolutely from want of the common offices of humanity ... The horror of those houses cannot easily be described; a lodger fresh from the country often lies down in a bed, filled with infection by its last tenant, or from which the corpse of a victim to fever has only been removed a few hours before.[2]

He saw people forced to live and die in atrocious conditions.

Others viewed the same conditions in a different light. Andrew Ure was the Pangloss of the manufacturing world, a writer who saw industry as creating a Utopia, which would arrive all the sooner if only the work-force would obey the always reasonable demands of their employers. Sadly, in Ure's eyes, they seemed not to know what was good for them.

> Manufacturers naturally condense a vast population within a narrow circuit; they afford every facility of secret cabal and co-operative union among the work people; they communicate intelligence and energy to the vulgar mind; they supply in their liberal wages the pecuniary sinews of contention, should a spirit of revolt become general, and the ample means of inflaming their passions and depraving their appetites by sensual indulgences of the lowest kind. Persons not trained up in moral and religious nurture, necessarily become from the evil bent of human nature, the slaves of prejudice and vice; they can see objects only on one side, that which a sinister selfishness presents to their view; they are readily moved to outrage by crafty demagogues, and they are apt to regard their best benefactor, the enterprising and frugal capitalist who employs them, with a jealous eye.[3]

Ferriar's urgent pleas were ignored: there was a serious outbreak of cholera in 1796, but nothing was done to improve the underlying conditions and it was to break out again in 1832. The most famous account of all, that by Engels in the 1840s, paints a picture almost identical to that of Ferriar. Ure, too, was right in a sense.

Conditions in the manufacturing towns did breed discontent, though whether this was due to 'prejudice and vice' or a natural response to living in conditions of degrading squalor is a different matter. Groups such as the framework knitters of Nottingham were notoriously militant, and when the Oxford Blues were sent in to break up a protest in 1791, they were not attacked by bricks and stones, but suffered the humiliation of being deluged by 'night soil' from the privies as they marched beneath the castle rock. To the poor, legitimate protest often had little meaning. The knitters attempted to use the law to prevent work which had been granted by charter to adults being handed over to children – and the law turned them away. There were, as they saw it, two options: to organize themselves into Unions or to let loose the mob. To the government, the Unions were spearheading the movement of revolutionaries and Jacobins and Pitt banned them under the Combination Laws of 1799. It is a trait of paranoid governments and regimes under stress to see all opponents as part of a wider conspiracy, much as Western governments were inclined to see communist organizations behind all protest movements in modern times. Government then acts as if the myth were a reality, and as a result disparate groups are drawn together and united by shared grievances; politicized by the very measures designed to prevent this. So the protesters who were badly paid and hungry, and sought nothing more complicated than a little extra cash and more food on their plates, began to organize into a formidable radical force. Government policy did, however, have an advantage for those in power: it is easier, and a good deal cheaper, to fight a fictitious foreign-inspired conspiracy than it is to right a genuine grievance.

If the industrial workers had not been politicized before, they were now. There were sporadic outbursts of rioting, which the government dismissed as unjustified malice. Cobbett at this stage was still prepared to accept the government view without much question.

> We have had some mobs, and we have to thank for it nobody but the silly writers against monopolizing. The mobs in London (and I presume the rest even like them) seem to have assembled more from a love of fun than from want of bread. First they got drunk, and then they wanted something to eat.[4]

He went on to outline his own very conservative position: that trouble had been fomented by the opposition press, and that if only people would keep to the old, tried and trusted way of doing things, all would be well. He was quite unaware of how far the poor had tried all the ways and as a consequence how little they trusted them.

The other great question of the day was Ireland, and in particular the contentious issue of Catholic emancipation. Pitt was concerned that Ireland offered Napoleon a back-door invasion route to England and two failed attempts did not lessen his worries. The second, in 1798, found some local Irish support and lasted for two weeks. He was aware of the widespread disaffection among the Catholics, who were kept firmly under control by the Protestant landlords. Even Protestant tenants who had the vote were expected to do the bidding of the grandees. Castlereagh, who was to win for himself a prominent place in the Cobbett book of demons, was first elected to the Irish Parliament in 1790 at the age of twenty-one, and thanked Lord Moira for getting his tenants out to vote – if not quite all of them.

> Perhaps it may be necessary to make those who from interested motives opposed your wishes feel your resentment. Such conduct when overlooked serves to increase that inattention to the landlord's recommendation.[5]

There was no question of power and privilege voluntarily slackening its grasp, and attempts by the Catholics to put their claims for equality of treatment were firmly put down by the Orange lodges. Pitt still hoped to have Irish interests more closely allied with those of England, and the Act of Union of 1801 was to bring them into the United Kingdom. The great question still remained. How were the Catholic majority to be given a voice? The most vehement opponent of emancipation was George III, who declared it to be the most Jacobinical thing he had ever heard of and announced that any man who proposed such a thing was his personal enemy. This was, to say the least, unfortunate, since the main proponent was Pitt, the King's Prime Minister. Pitt was in personal financial difficulties. He still had the official backing of Parliament, but was well aware that his foreign policy was geared to little more than buying time. He was brokering a peace with France which he, of all people, must have known could not hold, but he was happy to find an issue that gave him the opportunity to stand down. His successor would be left with an inevitable mess, and a possible catastrophe. Pitt was confident that when disaster came, his country would look to him again. In February 1801, his resignation was made public and a new administration installed under Henry Addington.

This was a crucial time for Cobbett. He was increasingly allied to William Windham who had been a fervent supporter of Pitt, particularly over the emancipation issue, but who was a good deal less enamoured with Addington. From being surrounded by out and out government supporters, Cobbett found himself in a group increasingly questioning and criticizing policy. It was a situation which suited Cobbett's temperament: he was always happiest when he had something to fight against. But for the moment he was side-lined, reduced to taking up minor issues – minor, at least, in terms of most of the great themes of the day.

One matter that came to his attention was the case of Jekyll: a writer who had dared to voice criticism of the army. As a result, although he had not himself been charged with any crime, he had the unhappy experience of hearing himself ridiculed and his reputation blackened in the course of a court martial. Cobbett had personal experience of the treatment likely to be meted out in such circumstances, and had very little faith in the impartiality of courts martial, so he was quick to step in on Jekyll's side. The whole affair he said gave the military the status of 'the only privileged slanderers in the realm'.[6] Even Members of Parliament were free from litigation only when they spoke in the House. If the matter was allowed to rest, it would be an open invitation to traduce anyone who dared question Army decisions. Jekyll should sue and claim damages. There is a delightful irony in Cobbett of all people proposing that anyone should sue for slander or libel. In the same letter he touches on another theme which was soon to preoccupy him – the large numbers directly employed by the government: '50,000 persons in the taxing offices, not to mention the battalions of clerks at Whitehall.'

Another theme appeared that was very much to his taste, when a gentleman called Williams tried to bring a number of parsons to account for failing in their parish duties, by holding plural livings, drawing pay from more parishes than they could possible serve with diligence.

> Whoever has seen a shot fired into a rookery in the month of June, when the young rooks are just beginning to flutter from the nest; whoever has heard the cawing, the sort of half-squalling, and seen the fluttering and dashing about of the old ones among the boughs; whoever has witnessed this uproar amongst these feathered incumbents of the tops of the trees, may form some faint idea of the bustle among the black-coats and bush-wigs.[7]

There was one major theme that remained dear to his heart, the war against France. He had made his reputation in America as a doughty defender of the British position, and on his return home he had been fêted for his efforts. In October 1800, he brought out the first edition of his new daily paper, *The Porcupine*, and in case the name did not make it quite clear that it was to continue the trends he had set in motion on the far side of the Atlantic, he later extended the title to *The Porcupine*, and *Antigallicum Monitor*. He declared the paper wholly independent of any party, and made his own rules.

With memories of Dr Rush all too painfully alive, he refused to take adverts for patent medicines – 'death-dealing nostrums'. Having rejected a government-supported paper, he was now faced with a demand of the exorbitant fee of five guineas per copy per annum for sending the new paper to his old readers in America. He refused to pay, complained at length and publicly, and lost both overseas sales and post office advertising. It was not a good financial omen. There was, however, a far greater obstacle in his way before he could repeat his earlier success.

Cobbett in America had gone against the current of much popular opinion, and must have felt that back in England he had rejoined the mainstream. Enthusiasm for the war was on the wane. There were few victories to cheer and the costs were escalating. The introduction of income tax in 1798 to pay for the war was hugely resented. Rises in customs and excise duties were scarcely better received. The alternative, which the government increasingly favoured, was to borrow money by inviting the public to purchase the government securities collectively known as 'the funds'. The trouble with this system was that while it provided the government with capital, it did so at the cost of continuing obligation to pay high interest rates to the lenders. This was good news for wealthy investors, but did nothing to help a weakening economy. Cobbett argued fiercely against the system with his usual mixture of sound argument and personal invective which could be notably ugly. Concessions over policy in the West Indies were being pushed by 'the hypocritical sect of negro-loving philanthropists'.[8] If Napoleon was giving up the war of guns and sabres, it was in order to concentrate on a trade war, which would include cutting off Britain's vital cotton supplies from South America.[9] To Cobbett's chargin, his bullish patriotism was making him even fewer friends at home than it had abroad. He found, in fact, things were a good deal worse. He refused to support the peace proposals. The citizens of London proved less tolerant than those of Philadelphia.

I naturally opposed the Preliminaries of the Peace of Amiens in 1801. From the scenes of violence and outrage, which had taken place in some parts of the town, not far from my shop in Pall Mall, I had reason to expect that, on the arrival of the Ratification of the Preliminaries, my dwelling house there, as well as my printing-office in Southampton Street, would be attacked, because my sentiments respecting these Preliminaries were publicly known. It happened precisely as I had expected: about eight o'clock in the evening my dwelling-house was attacked by an innumerable mob, all my windows were broken, and when this was done the villains were preparing to break into my shop. The attack continued at

intervals, till past one o'clock. During the whole of this time
not a constable nor peace officer of any description made his
appearance; nor was the smallest interruption given to the
proceedings of this ignorant and brutal mob, who were thus
celebrating the Peace. The 'Porcupine' office experienced a
similar fate.[10]

When it came to the actual signing of the Peace in 1801, he was
equally defiant. His only concern was the safety of his wife and
children, but Nancy announced that she would go away for a time
rather than force him to compromise his principles. All over
London, businesses and private houses were illuminated to celebrate
the peace. It would have been the act of a hypocrite and coward if
Cobbett had joined in. He was neither.

> My wife's removal had not taken place many hours before I
> had reason to congratulate myself upon it. A numerous and
> boisterous rabble, coming from Cockspur Street, began to
> assault the house, at about half-past nine o'clock. The Bow
> Street Magistrate with his men used their utmost exertions to
> prevent violence, but in vain. The attack continued, with
> more or less fury, for about an hour and half, during which
> time a party of horse-guards were called in to the aid of the
> civil power. Great part of the windows were broken; the sash
> frames of the ground floor almost entirely demolished; the
> panels of the window shutters were dashed in; the door nearly
> forced open; and much other damage done to several parts of
> the house.[11]

It was one thing to protect Cobbett's house, but quite another to
look after the *Porcupine* office. His clerk and wife managed to get
away, and tried to summon help.

> He went to the public office at Bow Street and there related
> the danger to the officers who, so far from being disposed to
> render him any protection, literally pushed him from the
> door.[12]

It was not just an unpleasant, and potentially very dangerous
episode, it was a costly one. The *Porcupine* was steadily losing
money, and Cobbett lacked the funds to support it. Yet although he
was out of step with much public opinion and increasingly disen-
chanted with the Addington government, he was strengthening his
ties with Windham and his faction, who shared many of Cobbett's
attitudes. They needed a public voice, and Cobbett seemed the very
man to supply it. Windham knew better than to try to tie Cobbett to

any political strings and can hardly have expected their two views would always coincide – or even coincide very often. What was important was that there was a vigorous voice of opposition, and that was an area in which Cobbett was wholly reliable. The *Porcupine* was sold off and Windham put up the money to found a new weekly paper, the *Political Register*. It was to offer an independent news service, informing the public about government and the proceedings of Parliament. It also provided a forum for Cobbett to speak directly to his readers on whatever subject he chose. The very first issue appeared in January 1802 and it was to continue week in, week out, right through to Cobbett's death in 1835. It was in the pages of the *Register* that Cobbett came into his glory, not merely as one of the great commentators of his own age, but as one of the greatest political journalists of all time.

Gillray's version of life at the Jolly Farmer, with young William encouraging his pet dog to attack a cat. It was one of a series brought out to coincide with Cobbett's publication of his memoirs in 1809. (British Museum)

Fashionable Kew Gardens in the eighteenth century, which not surprisingly impressed the young William Cobbett. (Museum of London)

Two more Gillrays, showing (left) Cobbett leaving the plough to join the army and (below) Cobbett trying to kick sense into the officers in Canada. (British Museum)

Tom Paine in a portrait by George Romney of 1792. (Norfolk Local Studies Library)

The junction of Second and High Streets, Philadelphia in 1801. (The Historical Society of Pennsylvania)

The very imposing house at Botley in an engraving of May 1817.
(Southampton City Heritage Services)

A Rowlandson
cartoon, showing
Burdett sent to the
Tower, but still
keeping a strangle-
hold on the borough-
mongers.
(British Museum)

Crowds gather at the
hustings in a
Parliamentary
election at
Westminster. This
scene was depicted in
1796, but little had
changed a decade
later. (Museum of
London)

Hunt shortly after he had addressed the crowds at Spa Fields.
(British Museum)

A caricature showing the reformers as revolutionaries. A banner held aloft on a pitchfork refers to Cobbett as 'The Hampshire Hog Reformer' and as ancient rights are burned Parliament is sacked and set on fire.
(British Museum)

Cobbett on board ship, heading back to America. (The Warden and Fellows of Nuffield College, Oxford)

The three Cobbett sisters painted by Nancy, but not identified. (Southampton City Heritage Services)

9
THE VOICE OF OPPOSITION

Without a periodical work in my own hand I can do nothing
... with it I can do almost anything.[1]

When it first appeared, the *Political Register* seemed little more
than Peter Porcupine with a change of clothes. It was as viru-
lently anti-Jacobin and just as enthusiastically in favour of traditional values – or, to put it another way, whole-heartedly
reactionary. Some of the views expressed would have even seemed
reactionary a century or more before. It is hard to imagine anyone
who had actually lived in Britain during any part of his adult life,
writing words such as these about the Hanoverian monarchy.

> The King gives the weakest and poorest of us some degree of
> consequence ... in his justice, his magnanimity, his piety, in
> the wisdom of his councils, in the splendour of his throne, in
> the glory of his arms, in all his virtues, and in all his honours,
> we share, not according to rank or to riches, but in proportion
> to the attachment that we bear to the land which gave us birth,
> and to the sovereign, whom God has commanded us to honour
> and obey.[2]

Yet even Cobbett, still groping his way through the often dimly lit
alleys of the British political scene was aware that, in Parliament,
there was a government of inconsequential nincompoops. His
instincts, on his return, had led him to support the Parliament he
had defended so resolutely in America. A lesser man would have
done so still: who knows, perhaps even Cobbett would have done so
had he been brought up inside the system. It seems unlikely; but he
was not, in any case, an insider. He was the new boy in the class,
who had come from a school where they did things very differently.
Even a casual reading of any copy of *Porcupine* shows the sheer joy
he felt in fighting as an underdog, reveals him revelling in ridicule
and thoroughly enjoying a literary rough-house. He was born and
bred for opposition, not sycophancy. Even so, he could well have

remained a government supporter had not government itself changed direction. What he did not see, or did not want to see, was that a weak government was following, rather than leading, political opinion. Even the violent response to the Peace of Amiens was seen as an aberration, a response by an illogical, wayward, bloodthirsty mob that had been led astray by demagogues. As such, it fitted everything he had ever heard about and condemned in France. As he wrote when he complained to Lord Pelham about the lack of help when his house and business were attacked, what was he supposed to do – repay force with force, or yield to the mob? The question was purely rhetorical.

Cobbett underestimated the war-weariness of Britain, and the misery that held so much of the country in thrall. The country's finances were in a desperate position. Gold reserves were shrinking, and the Bank of England was forced in 1797 to depart, at least temporarily, from the position where the words on their notes promising to 'pay the bearer' an equivalent amount in gold could, or would, be honoured. This may have done well enough for the Bank of England, but when small country banks issued notes with little to support them but blind faith, the seeds of rapid inflationary growth were sown. Prices rose and with them taxes to provide funds to pursue the war. Things were made worse by wretched harvests in both 1799 and 1800, and food prices climbed steeply. The high prices made landlords rich, and gave them spare capital to feed the boom: it did nothing but harm to those lower down the scale. They saw a simple equation: the war costs money, taxes provide the money – we provide the taxes out of an income that is certainly not increasing and, in terms of essential costs, is actually in retreat. Small wonder that they welcomed the peace with enthusiasm – and treated those who refused to join them with disgust.

This period is so crucial to the whole of Cobbett's future that it really is necessary to stand back and try to view the situation from many viewpoints. To many people, and especially to the poor, the war had brought misery. They cared little or nothing about how continental Europe was rearranged in terms of new power blocs, so long as they could get on with their own lives. They were far less interested in the negotiations over boundaries between diplomats from France or Prussia than they were in the decisions taken by the magistrates of Speenhamland and their attempts to determine subsistence levels and set the wages of rural labourers. Cobbett was not well informed about such things; arguably not, even at this stage, particularly interested. He had spent the whole of his working life as a political writer concentrating on just one issue. He had returned from America as a hero, applauded by the most powerful men in the land for the stand he had taken. He had not altered his position in any way whatsoever – but the government had. He remained as convinced of the rightness of his own position as he had been when that position was under constant and vigorous attack by the Democrats in America. Something had gone wrong, and if it was not William Cobbett, then it must be the government.

If his had been a lone voice raised in opposition, he would, no doubt, have gone on campaigning in exactly the way that he had always done, fighting the battle against Napoleon and Jacobinism. But his was not a solitary opposition. There were a great many men of influence and perspicacity who were also opposed to the notion that the Peace of Amiens was likely to bring in any lasting value and who felt that, on the contrary, it was likely to produce real harm. What followed now seems inevitable. Cobbett's loyalties began to drift away from those he had first supported. They saw this, as others of his former supporters were to see it, as a betrayal by Cobbett, a wilful change of allegiances. To Cobbett this was quite the opposite of the true situation. He had remained steadfast, and they had moved away from him. The radicalization of William Cobbett was never really a conversion to new ideals. He was, and remained, an issues man, not a party-political man. If the opponents of Amiens had been arch-reactionaries, then he would have travelled that road – at least as far as the next crossroads, when a new issue commanded his allegiance.

The most common accusation levelled against Cobbett was wilful inconsistency, and he could never see it. He was the immovable rock around which the tides of party opinion flowed. A dispassionate observer might observe that the tides rolled him along the party political beach, so that he started at one end and ended up at another: but that did not make him any less rock-like. The image should not be extended too far. What did remain true was that there were issues throughout his life on which he formed an opinion on which he never wavered: they were the fundamentals against which everything else was measured. The Peace of Amiens was the first great test. Had the peace held, had Europe settled down to a long period of calm and prosperity, then Cobbett would have been quickly marginalized, a ranter, a fighter of old battles. But his judgement of the situation was sound: he saw the peace as an opportunity for Bonaparte to rest and gather his resources for a fresh onslaught. In a way, he admired Napoleon for his unbending resolution as he began to lambast the weaklings who ran Britain. More and more, the pages of the *Register* read like the pages of an opposition paper. Cobbett was invariably driven to make friends with those who supported his views on this one issue – no matter where they stood on other matters. He was equally invariably convinced of the need to stand by his own views, and he did so with increasing self-confidence. He saw himself as 'a sort of self-dependent politician. My opinions were my own – I dashed at all prejudices. I scorned to follow anybody in matter of opinion.'[3]

He was not quite as independent as those words suggest, for he was strongly influenced by Windham and his faction. But his opposition to the Addington administration was fierce and wholly Cobbett in tone. In his criticism, however, he still looked backwards to what he saw as a better tradition. If he sometimes underestimated the abilities of the new men, quite difficult to do in the case of this government, he certainly overstated the talents of the old order.

> We believe Mr Addington to be a very *honest* man, but what is that? Honesty alone is not a recommendation for a footman, and shall it be for a first minister? He is not altogether destitute of talents as an orator, and even, perhaps, as a financier. In truth, he is what may be called a clever man. But he wants those great and commanding qualities which mark the statesman, and which are at this time, more than ever, necessary to the preservation of the country. There are several persons in the ministry possessed of very good talents, nor are they at all deficient in point of industry and zeal; but they want weight, they want consequence, they want birth. At no period of our history were the powers of Government ever shared by so few men of family. The ancient nobility and gentry of the kingdom have, with very few exceptions, been thrust out of all public employments: this part of the aristocracy has been, in some measure, banished from the councils of the State. A race of merchants, and manufacturers, and bankers, and loan-jobbers, and contractors, have usurped their place, and the Government is very fast becoming what it must be expected to become in such hands.[4]

The longer the peace lasted, the weaker the government seemed to become. It only needed Napoleon to complain about the harsh criticism he received in sections of the British press for the controlling hand of government to be applied, and the criticism faded away. France led and England followed, and the English markets rose and fell in response to events across the Channel. Even the French press were amused by the situation, *Mercure de France* commenting that such deference 'suits very well in a nation, where everything is bought and sold'. Cobbett saw a great country feebly capitulating to one that had recently been a foe. Legislation, such as the stipulation that English wool could only be sent to Spain via France, was made law with little opposition, other than in the pages of the *Register*. He saw France strengthening her armed forces as Britain's were steadily eroded, while all the talk was of winning the war of money and prosperity. Cobbett would have none of it. He attacked on two fronts. The first was an emotional argument: how could Britain allow herself to become so weak and impotent? He wrote satires which if they were less sophisticated than those of his first mentor, Swift, were still powerful. And what was important for the circulation of the *Register* was that they amused the readers. Here is part of a 'Receipt for affecting the Ruin of a Great and Independent Country.'[5]

Take 6 oz. 5 penny wt. 19 gr. of self-sufficiency. 8 oz. 10 penny wt. 23 gr. of ignorance or inexperience.

N.B. these two drugs, though of different appearance, and taste, produce so precisely the same effect, that they may always be used indiscriminately.

3 oz. 16 penny wt.9gr. of doubt.

N.B. This medicine made up of diffidence, integrity, and love of good fame on the one hand, of procrastination, fear of censure and overscrupulous prudence, on the other hand, is to be found in the greatest perfection at a certain apothecary's, not a hundred miles from Bedford-square.

Mix these three ingredients carefully together till they are completely amalgamated and incorporated with each other. Then pour them into a quart of a mixture, one part milk and three parts water, and let it boil well on a slow fire for eight hours. In the mean time you must carefully fling into the liquor, every half hour, one quarter of an ounce of a powder made up of the following ingredients all in equal quantity, viz. Pomp, flippancy, slovenliness, passion – After this mixture has boiled some time it will be reduced to a thin poor jelly of weak substance. – Let it be well sweetened by a proportionate quantity of places, pensions, and reversions of places, and ornamented *on the surface* with painted emblems of candour, flattery, and smiles – openness of conduct, and gentle manners.

This jelly, though thus sweetened and decorated, will suit but few palates; it must therefore be forced down the throats of unwilling patients by great and high-sounding professions and assurances. Even then it will not always be quietly taken. In that case it must be reduced to the shape of pills, and covered with a double coat of leaf gold.

As part of the general decline, he saw the spread of what he called 'Italian-like effeminacy' which had even reached the 'yeomanry'. They could be found 'turning up their silly-eyes in ecstasy at a music-meeting, while they should be cheering the hounds, or measuring their strength at the ring.'[6] This was a theme that was to stay with him for the rest of his life.

The other great theme that was to preoccupy him was the inex-

orable rise of government place-men and those who made fortunes
out of financial dealings: 'The stock-jobbing lovers of peace and
plenty; the omnium-eaters; all the innumerable swarm of locusts
who, without stirring ten miles from the capital, devour three-
fourths of the produce of the whole land.'[7]

He had a new enemy in his sights, and he saw that the enemy had
a new weapon – 'paper money.' Cobbett had become acquainted
with the implications of the system for the first time. He was offered
scrip for a government loan, which authorized him to participate in
that loan. To his horror, he found that he could trade in the scrip
and make a profit even before he had paid out a penny of his own
money. He saw men speculating in stocks and shares who would
once have put this money into building up estates that could have
provided employment for the rural poor. The 'paper aristocracy'
was taking over from the old aristocracy. Everything was turned
topsy-turvy, and it was no surprise to find that a system 'which
elevates bottle-corkers to country gentlemen, should reduce country-
gentlemen to bottle-corkers'. He began to read up on the subject,
and found enlightenment in the oddest place, in the works of the
once-derided, violently-opposed Tom Paine. In 1793 Paine wrote a
pamphlet[8] decrying the funding system of paying for work by
borrowing money. It could, he declared, only lead to a growing
national debt, increasing interest rates and a debased currency. The
work was gleefully seized on as propaganda by the French government, who had it translated into a number of languages and widely
distributed. The argument is soundly based if one assumes a country
has a static economy – and it would have seemed particularly sound
in 1793 when the whole country was gripped in a mania of speculation. The dire consequences would not follow in a country that was
enjoying real economic growth, firmly based on increased produc-
tivity. Cobbett, however, was never a great one for niceties. He
delighted in the argument – 'the stream was clear and strong' – and
made it his own. It is no wonder that those who had welcomed him
back to Britain now began to have second thoughts. Who would
have expected to hear William Cobbett, of all people, singing the
praises of Tom Paine?

Cobbett himself did not see things in that light. Yes, he had
attacked Paine with all the vigour he could muster for his support of
revolutionary France, because Paine was then wrong. He was
certainly not about to become a Jacobin himself. But, in this case,
Paine was clearly right, and he saw no reason why he should not
proclaim that fact with equal vigour. But once the door of a closed
room filled with noxious fumes opens, even a little way, the fumes
start to disperse. Cobbett had opened the door on the closed cell of
his hatred for Paine, and the respect that was starting to blow
through would eventually disperse all the ill feelings. However

much he might protest to the contrary, his opponents were right: Cobbett was starting to change.

Once his views on paper money were clear in his own mind, he began to share them with his readers in his usual vigorous way. What did the phrase 'promises to pay' mean in reality on a bank note at a time when the price of silver against which it could be exchanged was falling? It meant nothing: it might just as well be replaced by 'a stanza from Nancy Dawson or Chevy Chase'. The amount of paper money in circulation went up from £11 million in 1797 to £18 million in 1803. 'What a charming prospect', he noted with heavy sarcasm, to see national prosperity almost doubled in four years. But it was all a chimera – 'factitious wealth' – and he cheerily prophesied doom and gloom. All this paper money made it possible for fortunes to be made and for the government to spread its influence throughout society by patronage. He saw the system at work when he first began to look at the state of society in Ireland.

In 1803, there was a brief and wholly ineffective rebellion against British rule, led by Robert Emmett. It was quickly suppressed, but it was an excuse to pass draconian measures, imposing martial law and suspending habeas corpus. One of the more endearing features in Cobbett's character was his deep implanted suspicion of all attacks on personal liberty, no matter what the cause. He was prepared to concede that the measures might be necessary, 'but every man who retains in his bosom any attachment to real liberty, or any regard to justice' must attack such measures unless the case for them could be completely proved.[9] He was certainly not convinced that such a case had been made, and when a Dutch correspondent asked for permission to write about the venality of English rule in Ireland, Cobbett opened the pages of the *Register* to him. The articles appeared under the *nom de plume* 'Juvena' at the end of 1803. They attacked the government for depriving the army of funds while spending a fortune on 'ridiculous alterations and fantastic improvements at the country palaces of the Lord Lieutenant and his Secretaries.' It was a system that left the Irish subjected to the 'plunder of the clerks' while exposed to 'the pikes of the rebels'. The authorities responded by attempting to silence the criticisms rather than countering them. Cobbett and the Register were sued for libel in front of a special jury, each member of which was paid by the government for attending the court. No one was surprised by the verdict of guilty, nor by the fine of £500. This was followed by a second civil trial and a second £500 fine. The authorities did not know their man! Nothing could have been better devised to stir him into furious action. He began to write a whole series of stinging articles on the state of the poor, the unhappy labourers who were close to starvation, and the iniquity of their rulers who took so much and gave so little back.

Cobbett had turned against France and its revolution because he had seen for himself that whatever fine words philosophers and political theorists might pen about it, the reality was butchery and misery. In America he had been far enough removed from domestic policies to feel that those who opposed France deserved his support, not just over this issue but over other issues as well. Now, faced with a double disappointment at home – a government that weakly caved in to French pressure on one hand, while acting with wholly unreasonable harshness to its own citizens at home – he began to change his attitudes. Disillusionment was setting in fast.

When he had made arrangements to return to England, he had worked out that he would have around $10,000 which would give him 'a pretty tolerable start in London', and although he was aware he would 'feel very awkward for a time', he was confident for the future. 'It is in my power', he wrote, 'to do a great deal of good.'[10] For the time being, although there was a considerable faction in opposition to Addington in Parliament, and it was generally recognized that Pitt was only biding his time and waiting for a suitable opportunity to take control back into his own hands, yet the voice of that opposition was muted – with one notable exception. Cobbett continued to be heard, preaching the need to prepare for war in times of peace, speaking out for a set of values that were out of fashion and prophesying an end few thought would come. That is, until May 1803 when the prophecies were realized, and France and Britain were indeed once more at war. Now, with the country under threat of invasion, there was an urgent need to rally the spirit of the people. It is perhaps an exaggeration to compare Cobbett at this time with Churchill in 1939, for Cobbett was no statesman, but there are striking similarities. Churchill's speeches resounded in the nation's heart because they seemed to come so clearly from his own. Both men were capable of searing denunciations of the enemy, Hitler or Napoleon, and both were capable of invoking a simple and sentimental love of country. And just as the government turned to Churchill, so in 1803 they turned to Cobbett. He was asked to write a handbill that could be put on display in every parish in England and Wales.

In America he had given blood-curdling details of atrocities conducted in the name of Liberty Equality and Fraternity, and he had no hesitation in opening another cabinet of horrors now and putting the contents on display. But back in England, the love of his country, the vision of a rural idyll, had been strengthened. He was able to write, in a way that would have been embarrassing if it had not been so obviously deeply felt, to remind his countrymen just what they were fighting for.

The sun, in his whole course round the globe, shines not on a spot so blessed as this great, and now united Kingdom. Gay and productive fields and gardens, lofty and extensive woods, innumerable flocks and herds, rich and inexhaustible mines, a mild and wholesome climate, giving health, activity, and vigour to fourteen millions of people; and shall we, who are thus favoured and endowed; shall we, who are thus abundantly supplied with iron and steel, powder and lead; shall we, who have a fleet superior to the maritime force of all the world, and who are able to bring two millions of fighting men into the field; shall we yield up this dear and happy land, together with all the liberties and honours, to preserve which our fathers so often dyed the land and the sea with their blood; shall we thus at once dishonour their graves, and stamp disgrace and infamy on the brows of our children; and shall we, too, make this base and dastardly surrender to an enemy whom, within these twelve years, our countrymen have defeated in every quarter of the world? No; we are not so miserably fallen; we cannot, in so short a space of time, have become so detestably degenerate; we have the strength and the will to repel the hostility, to chastise the indolence of the foe. Mighty, indeed, must be our efforts, but mighty also is the need. Singly engaged against the tyrants of the earth, Britain now attracts the eyes and the hearts of mankind; groaning nations look to her for deliverance; justice, liberty and religion are inscribed on her banners; her success will be hailed with the shouts of the universe, while tears of admiration and gratitude will bedew the heads of her sons who fall in the glorious contest.[11]

Cobbett now had one less battle to fight: he no longer needed to persuade the country to prepare for war. The country had no choice. But if the government hoped that by asking him to act as a kind of patriot laureate they would still his criticism, they were to be disappointed. He had raged against the profiteers of peace, and he would now be doubly vehement in his denunciation of the profiteers of war.

10
FARMER BILLY

By the time the war restarted, Cobbett could feel well satisfied that he had indeed established both a considerable reputation and a not inconsiderable income. The latter was not something that ever gave him concern for long. He was supremely confident that no matter what financial calamities descended on him, he had only to pick up his pen to restore his fortunes. But, for the time being, prospects looked as bright as they ever had, and it was time to think of a permanent home for the family. In 1803, there were four surviving children: Anne, aged eight, William, five; John, three; and new-born James. He wanted them to be brought up, as he had been, in the country, and there was another good reason to look for a farm. When he wrote in the *Register* of the sound common sense of investing in land rather than speculating in the money markets, he was not just giving advice to his readers. He was expressing a firmly held conviction, and one that he would apply in his own life. So he set out to look for somewhere to live, and found just what he wanted in Botley on the River Hamble in Hampshire. Even today, when it has been almost joined by the spreading suburbs of Southampton and a busy main road takes traffic through the heart of the village, one can still admire the surroundings of wooded hills, fields and orchards. In Cobbett's day, it represented his ideal.[1]

> Botley is the most delightful village in the world. It has every-thing in a village, that I love; and none of the things I hate. It is in a valley. The soil is rich, thick set with woods; the farms are small, the cottages neat; it has neither workhouse, nor barber, nor attorney, nor justice of the peace ... Two doctors, one parson. No trade, except that carried on by two or three persons, who bring coals from the Southampton Water, and who send down timber. All the rest are farmers, farmers' men, millers, millers' men, millwrights, publicans who sell beer to the farmers' men and the farmers; copse-cutters, tree-strippers, bark-shavers, farmers' wheelwrights, farmers' blacksmiths, shopkeepers, a schoolmistress, and in

short, nothing but persons belonging to agriculture, to which indeed, the two doctors and the parson belong as much as the rest.

He bought Botley House and four acres of land in 1804, and over the next few years began to expand his holdings in the area. In 1805, he bought a farm for his brother and his family in Droxford, half a dozen miles away in the Meon valley – an arrangement which was not quite the success that William had hoped. Over the years he was to invest a good deal in Botley, extending and improving his holdings, using what he could spare from the *Register*'s profits and taking out a number of mortgages. At this stage, he was not farming the land: Botley was a retreat, the serious business of making money went on in the London office. He did, however, start planting trees with the idea that they would grow as the children grew and prove a lasting memorial and legacy. The locals thought him slightly mad to be 'planting such little bits of twigs'. Nancy was highly critical. She was not over impressed by her husband's business acumen, and would have preferred him to be planting profitable crops. He saw this as a sound long-term investment. She preferred a more immediate return. She took a generally dim view of any of Cobbett's activities that did not make the money she felt they should. One can sympathize with her, for married life so far had scarcely run on a steady track: whisked away to France and scarcely settled before she was off again to America, where the family fortunes had followed an equally erratic course. She had had first-hand experience of what Cobbett's controversial writings could lead to – litigation, fines and near ruin. Small wonder, then, that she looked for something a little more reliable. She was quite prepared to accept that land represented solid value, but why use it for ornament instead of profit? Insecurity dogged her life. The neighbours did not help, by constantly suggesting he should take some high-paid office as others did: 'why should not *you* Mrs C. ride in *your* carriage?'[2] She had quite enough sense not suggest *that*.

Cobbett's life seemed now to have fallen into two parts: in London, he was the increasingly famous, controversial, political journalist; in Botley, the jovial country landowner. In practice, the two were inseparable. Cobbett's shift along the political spectrum had left several people confused, his new friends scarcely less than his older political allies. He needed, if he was to be taken seriously, to shine with a more consistent light. Hampshire gave him the opportunity. Increasingly over the years, he would be able to speak directly to a broad readership as Billy Cobbett, the sensible farmer who could speak in a plain language to plain people. It is a sound policy to treat with the greatest distrust anyone who claims to be using ordinary common sense and speaking for the common man:

what usually follows is an ugly spew of prejudice and bigotry. Cobbett's case is different – though he certainly was capable of both prejudice and bigotry of the lowest kind. In a political age, where influence was traded like groceries, anyone who claimed to speak with an independent voice had to prove his credentials. He had certainly given evidence of independence, but now he needed to show that he could be trusted as well. The blunt-spoken farmer was a good deal more likely to win that trust than the professional journalist.

His new role gave him something more than a new persona. It gave him a new standard against which everything could be measured. He even invented a new name for a whole group of the population. They were the honest hard-working men and women who lived on the land, and made use of time-honoured benefits such as going out on the common for firewood: they were 'the chopsticks'. He was their self-appointed spokesman, a role which actually had a good deal of credibility. He was, after all, born a chopstick himself and now, back in the country, he was among them again. Now he could live, for a part of the year at least, the sort of life he was constantly praising in print.

There is no doubt at all that Cobbett really did love the traditional world of the British countryside. During the years of dubious peace, he had railed against what he saw as the growing effeminacy of social life, sometimes comically. He complained about 'the increase of those cuttings and stabbings, those assassin-like ways of taking vengeance, formerly heard of in England only as the vices of the most base and cowardly foreigners'.[3] He did not specify what a lethal, thoroughly English vengeance might be. He did, however, become incensed when a man who had killed another in a boxing-match was charged with murder. It was not boxing that was wrong, but the softness of the judiciary.

> In general they are sad dotards, and ten out of the twelve, are, perhaps, much more afraid of displeasing the well-dressed, lisping, soft-tongued rabble, than they are of breaking their oath. Their *palaverings* from the bench; their miserable exhibitions of dignity and *wit* at the county towns; their never-ceasing babbling efforts to obtain popularity; all these appearances make me fear their decision upon any point, in which the good of the country is concerned.[4]

It was not just a case of being a traditionalist in spirit, it reflected a wider concern with a tendency in the national life. He was soon taking up the matter in the pages of the *Register*.[5] Boxing involves bravery, which 'consists not in a readiness or capacity to kill or hurt, but in a readiness and a capacity to venture, and to bear the consequences.' From there it is only a short step, from sporting hero to military hero, and they, he declares, are the heroes everyone remembers and admires.

> Renowned soldiers are never forgotten. We all talk of Alexander the Great and of Julius Caesar; but very few of us ever heard, or ever thought of inquiring, who were the statesmen of those days. There is not, perhaps, a ploughman in England, who has not a hundred times repeated the names of Drake and of Marlborough; and of the hundreds and thousands of them, there is not one, perhaps, who ever heard, or ever will hear pronounced the name of Cecil or of Godolphin ... Where is the man, woman, or child, in this kingdom, who has not heard and talked of Nelson? And does not the reader believe that there are many parishes in either of which the knowledge of Pope or of Johnson's having existed is confined to two or three persons?

Those who opposed boxing were setting Britain on the road to ruin, a road marked out in six stages: 'Commerce, Opulence, Luxury, Effeminacy, Cowardice, Slavery.' The anti-boxing propagandists were leading the country through the fourth stage. Cobbett would not only put the opposite case, but at Botley he could see his own ideas put into practice.

In 1805, he organized the first of a series of single-stick contests, a sort of cross between quarter-staff fighting and fencing, in which the issue was generally decided by a bloody head. Blood running 'an inch' was considered wholly satisfactory. He not only set up the matches, but also provided the purses and prizes. His daughter Anne remembered them clearly. 'What pains he took, and what money he spent to get that thing up! Devoting his time to it, just as he did to everything he took up. He had it very much at heart to encourage country pastimes, all the things that produced courage and hardihood.'[6] The writer Mary Russell Mitford visited Botley during one of the contests and left a portrait of Cobbett at that time.[7] She remembered the 'well-filled purses' he provided but also recalled the immense good spirits of the man in his prime; tall, stout and invariably red waist-coated, he was the very picture of the country squire. And whatever lessons he might draw from his games to be spelled out for the readers of the *Register*, they were not elaborated for the guests at Botley. There, at such times, the subject of politics was never raised.

The Cobbett of those days was a man full of vigour, enjoying the traditional sports, such as coursing, and often to be found in the early morning alongside his gardener, scythe in hand, mowing the grass – and generally being first to finish his plot. Only the cynical

would suggest that it would be a very foolish gardener who took the
lead. Here at Botley he could have the life he recommended to
others, and revel in it. This was also the life he wanted for his
family and, having got the Cobbetts settled, he tried to do the same
for his wife's family. He had a particularly soft spot for her brother,
Frederick Reid, who, in spite of all Cobbett's efforts to woo him to
a life on the land, was determined on a career in the Army. He was
a thoroughly exasperating young man, in a very conventional way –
just the sort of young man, with a taste for frivolities that Cobbett
would have lampooned and ridiculed in his writings. Yet, even
when he was dressing him down, he indulged him.

> Your sister has heard, that you are going to Croydon to a ball.
> I know you cannot afford it: I see that it will be plunging you
> into new debts; I see in it ills of all sort; and I beseech you to
> have no hankering after any such things, which lead to
> expences and to mischief – You have enough to do, in all
> conscience, without going there and I do hope you will not go
> – I will get you a greyhound before spring of the year.[8]

From the family letters, he seems to have been a charmer, in the
way that so many far worthier relations are not. Anne loved him,
and wrote a series of lively letters.

> I did not like to write to my Uncle Thomas because he is such
> a sober old bachelor. I was affraid [sic] my letter would be to
> harum scharum for him and I can not write a dull letter it
> must be full of nonsense.[9]

To which she added with all the tact of a thirteen-year-old that she
had heard he had a bride: 'I long very much to see her. To see
whether she is pretty, but from all I can learn she is not.' The bride
did not appear. The jokey letters continued, even as she grew older.
Uncle Fred was not a great correspondent, and she told him that on
the whole she preferred writing to old maids than to old bachelors,
since at least they replied. Her father took, or tried to take, a firmer
line. He sent instructions for him to put his sister on a coach for a
visit, to write twice to confirm the arrangements and to buy her 'a
dove-coloured pelisse, trimmed with ribbon, and not fur, and *I* will
pay you.' He was to write twice to confirm the arrangements –
'Now, don't be a damned baby, but do all this like a man.'[10] Two
weeks later, there were no letters and no sister. Politicians who
disappointed Cobbett got short shrift. Frederick constantly disappointed him but was constantly forgiven, so that he would still write
years later, trying to persuade him to come to Botley where he
would be set up as a farmer or timber-merchant, 'This is your

home; and no other happy one will you find upon Earth.'[11]

Not surprisingly perhaps, the Cobbett relations took a dim view of what they saw as favouritism towards the Reids. Anne Cobbett, looking back on those days, tried to put the family relationship into perspective. 'Take it all together Papa had the kindest of intentions towards his and Mama's relations and a great deal of money was laid out upon them, first and last.' She admits he had a special affection for Frederick and Mrs Warner, his sister, but does not feel the Cobbett side had just cause for complaint. 'I do not know what more he could have done for the latter, than to put them in the way to do for themselves.'[12] The trouble was that they were bad managers, and Cobbett did what he could, much to his own wife's annoyance.

The relations were often a nuisance, and an expensive one at that. Meanwhile, he had his own growing family to contend with during the Botley years – a second daughter, Ellen, arrived in 1805, and a third, Susan, in 1807. As one would expect, Cobbett had decided views on the boys' upbringing. They were to be educated in a way that would enable them to think for themselves and earn a living, preferably on the land. He had a mistrust of conventional schooling, and many of his ideas would not have seemed bizarre to the trendiest of teachers working at the end of the twentieth century, with one important reservation: he put an immense emphasis on neatness and order. This was no more than a reflection of his own personality. His daughter reported that he was never seen around the house with so much as the cords of his knee breeches undone. Everything had to be done in an orderly and concentrated manner. If she was eating an apple and reading a book, she was told to put the book down and only return to it when the apple was finished. No one read a newspaper at breakfast in the Cobbett household. In any case, by the time breakfast appeared, the Cobbett day was already well advanced along its course.

> To teach the children the habit of early rising was the great object; and everyone knows how young people cling to their beds. This was a capital matter; because here were industry and health both at stake. The child that was downstairs first, was called the lark for that day, and, further, sat at my right hand at dinner. They soon discovered, that to rise early, they must go to bed early; and thus was this most important lesson secured.[13]

And early to Cobbett was early indeed – rising at 5 a.m. was considered quite normal. Once up and about, there was no formal structure to the day. Just being in the countryside, participating in its life, whether chasing game or tending crops, was as much a part of education as formal learning with books. In this, Cobbett struck

a remarkably modern note. It was his absolute conviction that, given
the right circumstances for education, children would positively
want to learn. This was clearly based on his own boyhood experience, when his own fascination for politics, history and literature
grew out of his father's regular readings.[14]

> What need had we of schools? What need of scolding and
> force, to induce children to read, write, and love books? We
> did not want to 'kill time'; we were always busy, wet weather
> or dry weather, winter or summer.

The days were busy indeed. Whenever Cobbett was at Botley
with time to spare, he was encouraging the children in outdoor
pursuits. They had garden plots; they kept rabbits, pheasant, hares,
dogs, donkeys, horses; they learned to use tools and shoot – even
Anne went out coursing with her father. The Cobbett girls were
encouraged as much as the boys. On wet days a long table was laid
out with books and educational prints, from Berwick's *Quadrupeds*
to the *Maison Rustique*. There was encouragement, but not compul-
sion, to read. Books were represented as practical tools in the business of life. William was anxious to grow melons in the garden, so
he was given a book, which he painfully struggled through, reading
it a score of times, until he was sure everything was clear and
understood. Only then did his father send him out to give detailed
instructions to the gardener. Cobbett's methods sound remarkably
like the idea of child-centred education introduced towards the end
of the twentieth century. And they worked. The young children
were remarkably self-sufficient and confident. Anne's bubbly little
letters have already been quoted, and the boys showed much of the
same freedom of expression. Because Cobbett laid down the law to
all and sundry in the *Register,* it is easy to see him as inflexible,
possibly despotic – but if he overawed his children they showed
little sign of it. When William was just nine, he went to stay with a
young friend and wrote enthusiastic letters home, very grammatical
letters even if the spelling is often wayward. What is even more
striking is their liveliness, full of animated accounts of what they
had all been doing, and certainly not showing any sense of undue
deference. He described an expedition to shoot partridge, ending it:

> Today we are a going to dine upon the partrigdes [sic] And
> wen you can get any more don't you say that I don't like
> them.[15]

Not the letter of a little boy intimidated by a famous, stern father.
And the father responded with due pride. It confirmed his view that
he had devised quite the best scheme that could be devised, no

matter what anyone – including the rest of the family – might say.

> All the meddlings and teazings of friends, and, what was more serious, the pressing prayers of their anxious mother, about sending them to school, I withstood without the slightest effect on my resolution.[16]

The Botley years were very much family years, when both parents devoted themselves to the children's welfare. They were never left with servants; one or other of the parents were always with them, or, in later years, one of the older children was put in charge. His main objective was to see the children happy, and from that everything else would flow. Cobbett loathed the idea of boarding schools, which at that time meant boys' boarding-schools. Schoolmasters were despots, who ruled by spying and punishments. Worse than that, the education they received did nothing to prepare them for an adult life.

> If boys only live with boys, their ideas will continue to be boyish ... It is, *at last*, only by hearing men talk and seeing men act, that they learn to talk and act like men.[17]

Schooling for girls was, if anything an even greater evil. Girls should be brought up by their mothers, and those who refused the obligation could only be doing so 'from love of ease or of pleasure'. Send them to school and heaven only knows what might happen.

> Is she to commit her daughters to the care of persons, with whose manners and morals it is impossible for her to be thoroughly acquainted; is she to send them into the promiscuous society of girls who belong to nobody knows whom, and come from nobody knows whither, and some of whom, may have been corrupted before, and sent thither to be hidden from their former circle; is she to send her daughters to be shut up within walls, the bare sight of which awaken the idea of intrigue and invite to seduction and surrender.[18]

Yet in spite of such protestations, the children did receive formal schooling. Their father had a busy working life, and although he had an assistant, John Wright, in London, he was frequently away from home. Anne, as the eldest, had her own part to play as her father's assistant, copying his letters, which she carefully noted were 'not amusing', all politics, field sports and plumbing. When there was spare time, she was sent three miles away to school at Bishop's Waltham. The boys, too, would receive formal schooling in due course.

The picture that emerges of the family at this time seems almost idyllic. Cobbett was hugely successful, combining his writings, which brought him fame and money, with a country life that offered genuine satisfaction. There were even local feuds to add spice to his life that he relished. At one time he piously noted that it was the duty of a father to take his children regularly to church, and if that was not possible the lessons should be read at home – and he went further, declaring that it was also the duty of a parishioner to be on good terms with the parson of the parish. He was scrupulous in following the first part of the argument: the second rule was followed for precisely as long as it took him to fall out with the vicar. The Revd Baker was an enthusiastic exactor of tithes, regardless of the financial state of the parishioners. He never failed to demand his due, and was, not surprisingly, unpopular in the village. He was subject to a hoax which played on his greed. He was told of a legacy in London, and all the locals began pestering him for payment of bills and minor accounts, so that he felt compelled to ride up there to sort out his affairs. There was no legacy, and on his return he found handbills posted all over the village, recounting the tale. He was not amused, and was ever after inclined to blame Cobbett for the affair. Whether he was behind it or not, he greatly enjoyed the whole business, and was not above adding his own verse, commenting on the greed of parsons.

> The magpie, bird of chattering fame,
> Whose tongue and hue bespeak his name;
> The first, a squalling, clam'rous clack;
> The last made up of white and black;
> Tender alike on flesh and corn;
> Greedy alike at eve and morn;
> Of all the birds, this prying pest
> Must needs be parson o'er the rest.[19]

Here, at least, Cobbett the opponent of authority was at one with the community in which he had made his home. In many ways, these were the happiest years of his life, for they combined cheerful domesticity with a period of great influence in the affairs of the nation.

11
THE SYSTEM

Cobbett had said that the war with France would restart, and so it had. The government had acted as if the peace would last, if not for ever, then at least into the foreseeable future, and had allowed the services, and the Army in particular, to decline. The *Register* had thundered against this mindless optimism since its inception, and had resolutely attacked Addington and his government. Yet however much Cobbett disliked the administration and however much he was tempted to crow over his own acumen – a temptation he rarely resisted – there was one aspect of his nature which came out at its strongest. Whatever changes of opinion he might have had and would have over the years, in one thing he was stalwart. William Cobbett was an English patriot. He had already shown the strength of his emotion in his great, oratorical pamphlet – and he had even sunk his distaste of the government and suppressed his ego to the point where he had allowed it to appear without his own name ever being mentioned. Now it seemed the country faced a dire threat. While the British government had been more concerned with purely domestic affairs, Napoleon had been preparing for war, amassing an army and a fleet of boats along the north coast of France. When war was declared, virtually everyone in Britain thought an invasion to be inevitable and imminent. Ex-Sergeant-Major Cobbett had no doubt at all as to where his duty lay:

> When the time comes, my intention is to go instantly *into the army*; talking wife and children to some tolerably secure place, for in such a crisis, that man will be best off who has a sword in his hand, and certainly he will be more likely to serve his king as a solider than as a writer, of which latter tribe there will be very few wasted when force, physical force, is become all in all things.[1]

This was a not a piece of idle bravado meant to impress his readers, but a heartfelt opinion expressed in a private letter to Windham, and there is no reason to believe that he would not have joined up the moment invasion became a reality, and why not? He was a man of considerable military experience, still only forty years old and full of vigour. One is rather more dubious about the fifty-three-year old Windham's protestation that he hoped to stand beside him. And Windham hinted, in any case, that Cobbett's talents might well be better employed than on the battlefield. In the event, the invasion never came, and Cobbett remained a prominent and indeed a leading figure in the literary tribe.

During the earlier phase of the war, when he had been in America, the war and Britain's interests had been an all-consuming passion. He was no less a patriotic supporter of the British forces, but there were now some very different circumstances to take into account. Much of the fire in the early writings fed on his hatred of what he had himself seen of revolutionary France, but now the war was being fought against a different enemy: Jacobinism had given way to Imperialism. Napoleon had been appointed Consul for life, and was already behaving as the emperor he would become, handing out principalities and kingdoms to family and favourites like prizes at a children's party. No one doubted the scale of his ambitions, and there was no need of the pen of a Cobbett to persuade the population as a whole that here was an enemy that must be resisted. In America, much of his time had been spent demonizing the French: now he could concentrate on other matters, in particular on the way in which the war was being conducted. He was no longer a somewhat solitary voice in a foreign land. Where before he had felt it essential to devote all his energies to an uncritical support of British policy in opposition to a largely hostile American press, he could now diversify. And he was able to do so from a position which was becoming satisfyingly solid financially, and which was developing in a way that would give him the maximum opportunity to deploy his own unique talents.

When Windham had funded the launch of the *Register*, its success was by no means assured. Cobbett estimated that when it was begun it had a modest sale of less than three hundred, yet within two years that had risen to over 4000 in spite of the fact that it was more expensive than the opposition.

> Those opponents are circulating their writings through sixpenny publications; on mine I put a price nearly double, rejecting, at the same time, the aid of those baits by which the needy, the grovelling, the idle, the foolish and the profligate are usually attracted; and appealing to the better qualities, the better feelings, to the sense, the reason, the public spirit, the honour and loyalty of the nation.[2]

Cobbett's politics may have been on the move but he was still

firmly believing in the idea of an élite. It is difficult to see the effect
of price without some sort of yardstick – and one which Cobbett
certainly knew was the rate set at Speenhamland as a reasonable pay
for a man and wife – six shillings a week. On that scale, the
Register would have cost a day's wages: he was not aiming his
works at the poor.

At this period, a great deal of the *Register* was taken up with
reports of procedures in Parliament. In 1804, he hived them off to
another journal, *Cobbett's Parliamentary Debates*, making an accurate verbatim report available for the first time. Like the *Register*,
in its first year it was printed by T.C. Hansard of Fleet Street,
London, who Cobbett described as 'the very best in London. A man
of letters, perfectly conversant in French, of great attention and
great means of despatch.' Had Cobbett hung on to the publication as
long as he did the *Register*, then it might have continued with his
name still attached, instead of coming down to posterity as *Hansard*.
But it was Cobbett's inspiration, and ultimately the credit for that
vital record of Parliamentary affairs remains his. Another area
where he felt a new journal would be valuable was in bringing to the
public a survey of informed opinion not just from Britain, but
France and America as well. It carried the rather cumbersome title
Cobbett's Spirit of the Public Journals. Begun in 1805, it did not
last the year. The notoriously insular British public showed a lamen-
table disinclination to hand over their cash simply to have the view
of a set of foreigners.

The three journals had the same aim: to inform the public about
the current state of the nation's affairs. He did not, however,
neglect the nation's past. In 1804 work began on the multivolumed
Parliamentary History of England, to be followed in 1809 by *State
Trials*. They were intended as standard reference works that would
be kept in print and sell steadily over the years. They were to be
good, reliable earners and much of the tedious work of researching
and writing them could be safely left to his assistant Wright.

Now Cobbett found himself in just the position he wished to be.
His finances seemed in good order – and would have been better had
he been able to resist the temptation to buy even more land and plant
it with increasingly experimental and exotic crops. He had cleared
the pages of much of the space-devouring news that had filled them
in the early days, opening up room for more expressions of opinion,
which meant the opinion of William Cobbett. Week in, week out,
year in, year out, he filled the *Register* with his own personality: the
Register was Cobbett. In its pages he harangued politicians and
lambasted whichever group had the current misfortune to have
incurred his displeasure. Laurence Sterne, that splendid purveyor of
eccentricities, had written:

So long as a man rides his hobby-horse peacably and quietly along the king's highway, and neither compels you or me to get up behind him, – pray Sir what have either you or I to do with it?[3]

That was not the Cobbett style. He galloped his hobby-horse full tilt, demanding attention. His insistence that whatever interested him should be of interest to everyone else was perhaps his most characteristic trait as a writer. It could have been intensely irritating, but he generally carried it off by pure vitality. Once one starts to read Cobbett and once one lets him grab the attention, then one is hooked, there is no getting away. So now he had space to expand, he could do what he most enjoyed: give the world the benefit of his opinion, and there was a great deal to give opinion about.

Yet even Cobbett did not work in isolation. His views were his own, but they were inevitably influenced by others, and particularly by men such as Windham and Sir Francis Burdett, who were steadily moving away from the old divisions of Whig and Tory and taking a more populist stance. They represented something new in Parliament, not yet fully formulated and certainly not formalized into anything that could be described as a separate political party. And that, of course, suited Cobbett very well indeed. The political world was in a state of flux, but with the outbreak of war it might have been expected that everyone would pull together in patriotic unity. Cobbett supported the idea of burying old enmities and uniting in a common cause. Let there be, he trumpeted, amid flourishes of capitals and italics, 'A ministry of men of *talents* and of *great public influence* collected from ALL THE PARTIES *that have hitherto existed*, taking as a bond of their union, an inflexible determination to resist the aggrandisement of France.'[4] Had that happened, Cobbett would have found himself in a most interesting position. He had already embarked on a severe roasting of the government for faults which he laid not so much at their door as at that of Pitt and the previous administration, as we shall be seeing shortly. But had the general coalition been formed, he would have been not just a lone voice, but – and this would have been intolerable – a voice sounding what would have seemed an unpatriotic tune. He was perfectly content to be patriotic to the point of jingoism in America, where he was surrounded by powerful forces that disagreed with him; he would have been a good deal less comfortable in criticizing a government that claimed to speak with a united voice for the whole of Britain. But the complex politics of the day made a grand coalition impossible.

It had been clear from the first that the Addington administration was a poor, weakly thing, fatally compromised by its feebleness in peacetime. It was not a government for what was certain to prove the far sterner tests of war. Equally, there seemed very little doubt as to who would be called on to form the new government: Pitt was clearly the first choice. On 10 May 1804, Addington handed over the seals of office and Pitt agreed to try to form a government. Now the complex juggling of factions began. One group was firmly excluded, not necessarily because Pitt wished it to be so, but because George III was adamant that Charles James Fox, the leading radical in Parliament, should have no part to play. He had opposed the war against revolutionary France, and the king took a bleak view of anyone who seemed in any way to support the party that decapitated monarchs.

In the event, the factions divided. Lord Grenville had joined forces with Fox in opposition, and he was not prepared to abandon his former ally now. It seemed to the Grenvillites that Fox was not being treated in an equable manner: he was not being excluded from government because his talents were not wanted but in response to what was in effect a royal veto. Pitt had no choice: he was absolutely reliant on the king and his supporters in the two houses – particularly as he did not have the trust of the Prince of Wales and his group. So there was nothing to be done but form an administration that would contain some of his own trusted men such as Castlereagh and Melville, the former Lord Dundas and a good many of the old Addington government. There was to be a government and an opposition after all, and Cobbett's friends were firmly placed among the latter. He could continue doing what he did best – attack. Even so, it looked very much like another Cobbett volte-face. He had, after all, been one of Fox's most vociferous critics, condemning him as an unpatriotic Jacobite. He had a simple, if somewhat disingenuous answer to that one: when Fox had opposed war with revolutionary France, Cobbett had opposed Fox; now that they were united in opposition to imperialist France, there was no quarrel between them. He blithely ignored every other political opinion on which they had disagreed just a year or two ago. It was part of a continuing pattern, by which he would cheerfully co-operate with old enemies when he found them to be supporting one of his causes of the day, and just as cheerfully drop old friends when they ceased to do so. One would not relish the post of whip for any party of which Cobbett became a member.

It is often confusing to a modern reader, accustomed to the modern political scene of more or less clearly differentiated parties with quite distinct agendas, to be faced with the complexities of the first decade of the nineteenth century. In an earlier age, it had been easier to speak in terms of Whigs and Tories – a division Cobbett categorized as 'court party' and 'country party' – but those categories were breaking down, and even when distinctions could be

made – new Whigs as heirs to the old Whigs – they did not necessarily help in understanding policy. It was a situation that made
formation of a coalition difficult, but always possible: parties could
unite on specific issues as easily as they could divide on others.

It was a background against which any political journalist who
specialized in single causes could thrive. Cobbett had one cause
which he had come to champion during the Addington government
and which could now be continued without interruption into Pitt's.
It was indeed an issue for which he had already declared Pitt bore
full responsibility: the system of funding and patronage, the deifica-
tion of money.

> The system of upstarts; of low-bred, low-minded sycophants
> usurping the stations designed by nature, by reason, by the
> Constitution, and by the interests of the people, to men of
> high birth, eminent talents, or great national services; the
> system by which the ancient Aristocracy and the Church have
> been undermined; by which the ancient gentry of the kingdom
> have been almost extinguished, their means of support having
> been transferred, by the hand of the tax-gatherer, to contrac-
> tors, jobbers and Jews; the system by which but too many of
> the higher orders have been rendered the servile dependents
> of the minister of the day, and by which the lower, their
> generous spirit first broken down, have been moulded into a
> mass of parish fed paupers.[5]

The system was not doing what Cobbett devoutly wished, bringing
the war against Napoleon to a speedy and satisfactory end; it was
doing what he very much did not wish, reducing the honest agricultural workers to pauperism.

The conduct of the war followed the pattern established in the
one so recently concluded. At sea, Britain was supreme, but at enormous expense in fitting out ships and keeping them at sea for
months on end, and in terms of human hardship, exemplified by the
miseries of the press-gangs. On land, the emphasis remained on
building up and financing dubious continental alliances – Britain's
own attempts at sending troops to Europe had been disastrous. The
one thing that could be said about the Navy was that it, at least, was
singularly successful – though for a time it did not seem that way.

One of the main policy objectives was to keep the French fleet
bottled up so that it could not provide support for the invasion fleet.
But in March 1805 a French squadron managed to slip out of the
Mediterranean and joined up with Spanish allies where it posed a
real threat to the British trade routes to the East and West Indies.
This combined fleet was reported as heading for the West Indies,
where it was pursued by the British under Nelson. It is difficult to

overestimate the enormous difficulties in making any sort of contact over the vast spread of ocean, or even receiving the most basic intelligence. In this case, by the time Nelson reached the Caribbean, the Combined Fleet was on its way back to Europe, and posing a much more potent threat. Nelson turned back to Gibraltar, and it is a mark of the strain of naval warfare at that time that it was his first step on land for nearly two years. The enemy had not passed the Straits into the Mediterranean. It could reasonably be assumed that the fleet was safe at Cadiz preparing for attacks in the English Channel – attacks that could well have succeeded had Nelson still been chasing shadows on the far side of the Atlantic. Nelson returned to England for consultation. The main objective remained to keep the Channel under British control. The French could either be blockaded at Cadiz, or – a far better option, encouraged to break out and engage in battle. The result is well known: the battle took place just south of Cadiz, off Cape Trafalgar. It was a victory of immense importance, and Nelson who had been a hero whilst alive was almost godlike in death.

Here was undoubted success, but did it do anything to bring the end of the war closer? Cobbett was not alone in arguing that blockade alone could achieve nothing. The war would only be won on land. Here alliances were made and broken with bewildering speed: today's ally could be tomorrow's enemy and friend again the day after. Buying alliances was a wretched and despicable way to gain victories, a view he maintained even after the war was over.

> The Pitt crew boast of their achievements in the war. Why! what fools could not get the same, or the like, if they had *as much money* to get it with? Shooting with a *silver gun* is a saying among game-eaters. That is to say, *purchasing the game*. A waddling fat fellow, that does not know how to prime and load, will in this way, *beat* the best shot in the country. And this is the way that our crew *beat* the people of France.

He was prepared to support the war, he was unstinting in his praise for the men who actually had to fight the war, shedding their blood for King and country – and implacably hostile to those who had the running of the war.

He saw Government policy as an entirely negative matter of avoiding defeat rather than actively pursuing victory. There was no lack of encouragement for the formation of militia at home, but little was done for the professional Army which was the only one that could carry the war to Napoleon. He had a special contempt for the money lavished on coastal defences, the system begun by Pitt which included the erection of the famous Martello towers to fortify the

coast and the construction of the Royal Military Canal to speed
communications. He only saw them at first hand many years later,
on one of his Rural Rides, but time had not dulled his anger:

> I had baited my horse at NEW ROMNEY, and was coming
> jogging along very soberly, now looking at the sea, then
> looking at the cattle, then the corn, when, my eye, in swing-
> ing round, lighted upon a *great round building*, standing upon
> the beach. I had scarcely had time to think about what it could
> be, when twenty or thirty others, standing along the coast,
> caught my eye; and, if any one had been behind me, he might
> have heard me exclaim, in a voice that made my horse bound,
> 'The MARTELLO TOWERS by——!' Oh, Lord! To think
> that I should be destined to behold these monuments of the
> wisdom of Pitt and Dundas and Perceval! Good God! Here
> they are, piles of bricks in a circular form, about three
> hundred feet (*guess*) circumference at the base, about forty
> feet high, and about one hundred and fifty feet circumference
> at the top. There is a door-way, about midway up, in each,
> and each has two windows. Cannons were to be fired from the
> top of these things, in order to defend the *country against the
> French Jacobins!*
>
> I think I have counted along here upwards of thirty of these
> ridiculous things, which, I dare say, cost *five*, perhaps *ten*,
> thousand pounds each; and one of which was, I am told, *sold*
> on the coast of Sussex, the other day, for TWO HUNDRED
> POUNDS! ... Here is a CANAL (I crossed it at Appledore)
> made for the length of thirty miles (from Hythe, in Kent, to
> RYE, in Sussex) to *keep out the French*; for, those armies
> who had so often crossed the Rhine and the Danube, were to
> be kept back by a canal, made by PITT, thirty feet wide at the
> most![6]

The policies of naval blockade and war by proxy were expensive,
and in Cobbett's view that expense was being borne by the ordinary
citizens of the country. Worse than that, the government, through its
patronage, its sinecures and placemen, was profiting and growing
fat on the system. All these expensive measures were paid for by the
funds, and these were financed out of taxation. And piling public
insult on public insult, the taxes were only paying off the interest
and doing nothing to slow the inexorable rise of the national debt.
The whole question was tangled, but Cobbett reduced it to a few
simple propositions. You cannot win a war by naval blockades,
therefore you must win it on the ground. You cannot win a war on
the ground by relying on the purchase and hire of foreign troops,
and you cannot win it with British forces led by men who owe their

position to influence and patronage instead of talent. But if the war cannot be won by such methods, why is it being conducted in such a manner? The only answer must be the self-interest of those in power, who care only for private profit and care nothing for the well-being of those who ultimately pay the bill through their suffering, the poor. If his arguments are accepted as valid, then he can be said to have united two powerful arguments against the government: they were not defeating the enemy across the Channel, and they were bleeding to death ordinary, hard-working citizens at home. Now he could combine patriotism and a plea for social justice with his attack on the funds and sinecures.

> Upwards of *six millions* a year are now raised upon the parishes to be dealt out in aid of those means by which the labourer obtains his bread; and of persons receiving this aid there are upwards of a million. *All*, all, the labourers, having families, are now *paupers*! This is a new state of things; a state of things which has been produced by the funding and taxing system, pushed to an extreme. Let us not be answered by the observations, that there must be poor, that there always have been and that there always will be, in every state of society in every country in the world. We know there must be poor; we know that some must be very poor; we know that some must be maintained, or assisted, at least, either by the parish or by voluntary alms; but is there any one who will deny, that this is a new and most deplorable state of things, which has rendered all the labourers, having families, paupers? The plain fact is, that a man with a wife, and with four children that are unable to work, cannot now, out of his labour, possibly provide them and himself with the means of living. I do not mean, that he cannot live *comfortably*, for, to comfort, such men have long ago bid farewell; but, I assert, and am ready to prove, that he cannot provide them, without parish aid, with a sufficiency of food, not to *satisfy* their cravings, but to *sustain life*. And, will any one say that this state of things is such as England ought to witness?[7]

The miseries of rural England could be contrasted with the shady affairs of those in power, and such affairs were given a very public airing in the Melville affair. Lord Melville, formerly Henry Dundas, was Treasurer of the Navy, one of those sinecures handed out to loyal politicians. Charges were brought by the Commission of Navy Enquiry of 1803 that the naval funds had been misused. It was not a case of outright theft or fraud, more a matter of using idle capital as a sort of interest-free loan. This was seized on by the more belligerent members of the opposition to demand Melville's removal from the government. It was by no means obvious how Parliament would react, and the turning-point in the debate came when Wilberforce, a man who prided himself on putting conscience before party, turned against Pitt and denounced Melville. The affair ended in a tied vote in the House of Commons, leaving the unhappy Speaker, 'white as a sheet', to cast the deciding vote. It went, as tradition demanded, in favour of the motion – and thus against Melville. It was a momentous occasion, and strengthened Cobbett's views that the whole system was corrupt from basement to attic.

Even the nature of the war and its implications began to take on new meaning when, in December 1804, Napoleon assumed the title of Emperor. In practice, there was no difference between the conduct of despotic First Consul and despotic Emperor, but it meant an ideological shift as far as Cobbett was concerned: Jacobinism had formally ended. He was quite ready to support the battle against a foreign despot that threatened his beloved country, but he was becoming increasingly convinced that all he really cared about in England was threatened by a despot a good deal closer to home. When Napoleon became Emperor, it removed a particular threat,

> but tends to excite apprehensions of a different kind, to make us fear that, by means of the immense and yet growing influence now deposited in the hands of the minister by the funding and bank-note system, we may, in fact, though not in name, become little better than slaves, and slaves, too, not of the king, but of the minister of the day.[8]

He saw that corruption was not an aberration but an inevitable part of the system, and he was unrelenting in attacking it wherever it occurred. In Melville it had been seen as affecting one of the great bodies of state. But every sinecure was evil, and he used one of his greatest gifts, the ability to bring complex issues down to simple language, to explain them for his readers. When Parliament discussed a bill for preventing grants of Places in Reversion, he told them precisely what it meant. The 'Places' were sinecures, a name derived from Latin for 'without care' – a name invented to disguise their true nature: 'for to call them, in plain English, *places without employment* or *nothing-to-do* places would naturally produce feelings, in the people, not very friendly to such a snug establishment.'[9] He then goes on to explain 'reversion', which meant no more than a guarantee of a place whenever it became vacant. The Lords rejected the Bill, and Cobbett simply listed the sinecures held by various noble Lords, and let his readers draw their own conclusions. He was not a man afraid of naming names and making enemies. In 1807 he wrote a pretended apology for accusing the administration of doing nothing, and fulfilling none of their pledges.

When we accuse Mr. Sheridan of having fulfilled none of his pledges, we uncandidly overlook the fact, that he has been settling his son in a place worth three thousand pounds a year, at home. While he is captain of a regiment serving abroad: is this doing nothing? Is it nothing for Mr. Grey to have made his father an Earl and himself a Lord? Did he do nothing while he was at the head of the Admiralty? Those who accuse him of that forget, surely, that he turned off Sir Charles Saxton, the Commissioner at Portsmouth, upon a pension for life, of six hundred pounds a year, in order to make way for his brother, the 'Honourable' Mr Grey; and that another brother of his, who has acquired his military fame I know not where, has been appointed to supersede General Baird in the command of the Cape of Good Hope. Is this doing nothing?[10]

The system corrupted everything it touched, from the great campaigns of the war to the problems of a local parish. The unhappy soldiers would find themselves led by men whose only claim to military excellence was wealth or powerful relations. All this had to be paid for out of taxation, and now voices were raised saying the taxes were too high, and landowners should no longer be required to give money to the poor – let them look to charities, not the farmer's shrinking purse. Cobbett would not accept such an argument for a moment. The placeman, the profiteers and fund-holders had forgotten that when they took up land they were taking on obligations with their holdings.

It is *not* the money of others, any more than the amount of tithes is the farmer's money. The maintenance of the poor is a charge upon the land, a charge duly considered in every purchase and in every lease.[11]

The poor had a right to help from the poor rates, and the farmer – and here Cobbett could speak as one himself – had an absolute duty to provide it. And what was more, no conditions should be attached, no demands for pauper labour.

His was a moral crusade, and he saw those who should have been among its leaders as being corrupted by just the same system. The church was contaminated by the system of patronage and plural livings, where parishes were handed out by rich landowners usually to relations or friends. This could result in abject compliance with every proposal of a powerful patron, exemplified in fiction by Mr Collins endlessly fawning on Lady Catherine de Bourgh in *Pride and Prejudice*. It could also result in a parson having a number of rich livings, far more than he could adequately serve himself. As a result, much of the actual parish work had to be handed out to impoverished curates. Supporters of the system argued that it would be quite impractical for parsons to pay curates a decent salary without reducing their own consequence and importance. Cobbett had the answer to that argument: there was only one way in which a parson could acquire real consequence and that was by performing his duty to the church:

> but alas! it is so much pleasanter to acquire consequence by riding a fine horse, by lolling in a coach, by strutting at a ball, by melting away at a music meeting, by eating frican-deaus, and by drinking claret.[12]

The fight against the system of privilege, funding and sinecures was to continue throughout his life. He saw it as a disease that ate into all that was good in the national body, and so felt under no compunction to dilute his criticism simply because the country was at war. On the contrary, there was all the more reason to bring it out and display it. Here was Parliament itself exposing fraud that diverted money meant for the Navy to private accounts. Here were incompetents in charge of whole armies on the basis of birth, not ability. Here was a war funded by the labour of the poor, who were reduced to even greater levels of degradation while the wealthy made fortunes simply by passing pieces of paper from one to another. Here were the old values of parson and squire degraded by luxury and greed. He poured out the same message over and over again, never shirking from naming the guilty, never worrying about what the powerful men he was attacking might do to take revenge. It was a great cause, but it was not in itself enough.

In the first half of the decade, Cobbett had his arch-villain firmly in his sights, William Pitt. When he died in January 1806, Cobbett was not hypocrite enough to pretend a false sorrow. He gave him what due he could: he was 'a great debater; a person of wonderful readiness and dexterity in conducting a contest of words ... But, that was *all*.'[13] It is not a verdict with which posterity can agree, but it sat with everything he had written and said over the last few years. There had been talk of a monument, and Cobbett had no doubt where it should be fixed, in the City of London where the 'blood-suckers' and 'muck-worms' had used the Pitt system to make their fortunes. But the system did not die with Pitt, and Cobbett could no longer personify his opposition to one demonized man. He had to think about the political world in general, assess his own position and decide what he stood for as well as what he fought against.

12

BIRTH OF A RADICAL

The death of Pitt brought an inevitable political realignment. A new administration came in, headed by Grenville, uniting the old opposition parties, including Fox among its members, with a sprinkling of Pitt men. So broadly was it based that it became known as the Ministry of all Talents. It was, in short, exactly what Cobbett had argued for a short time ago, and it was doubly welcome as Windham was given the vital post of Secretary of State for War and the Colonies. But by now Cobbett was less concerned about the progress of the war than he was about the wholesale demolition of the hated system. As was the case with every alliance he ever formed, his old friends of opposition days were to be judged not by what they had done in the past but by how they reacted to his own current fixation. One can understand his single-minded campaign against what he regarded as a great evil, while at the same time understanding how hopelessly unrealistic his expectations of instant reform really were.

The system was not something dreamed up in a moment by Pitt, but one which had developed step by step with the growing power of Parliament. The new men, with the exception of Fox, had all served in previous administrations at one time or another – had all, indeed, served under Pitt in the past. They had not achieved reform in the past, nor indeed had most of them wanted it, and they were unlikely to do so now. They were engaged in a major and very costly war, and the possibility of reducing taxes was quite simply not there. As for Cobbett's dream of a Merrie England of stout, independent yeomen, that was the most unrealistic fantasy of all. If it had ever existed in any form at all in the past, which is extremely doubtful, it was not going to come into existence in the future. The Industrial Revolution had happened and could not be reversed. That is not to say that the harsh effects of it on so much of the population were an essential part of the process and could not be removed, but the process itself had changed the world forever.

There were clearly fundamental flaws and terrible social injustices in the way the country was run, but it was wholly unrealistic to expect the incoming administration to do anything about them. They were the heirs, and in some cases the actual originators of the system – and a good many of them benefited from it. Cobbett had changed more perhaps than he himself realized. Where before he had cried out for king and country, he now offered a new definition of patriotism. The focus had moved.

> Amongst men who set a high value upon reputation, whether for talents or for courage, the renown of their country will be an object full as interesting as its liberties or its prosperity; but, amongst the mass of the people, freedom from oppression, and that happiness which arises from a comfortable subsistence, will always be the chief objects of attachment, and the principal motives of all the exertions which they will make in defence of their country.[1]

His trust in the strong and powerful had gone: they could not speak for the whole country, but would only try to protect their own interests. Cobbett and the *Register* would speak up for the great mass of people, the hard-working poor, the disenfranchised.

Soon Cobbett was attacking the new government as heartily as he had attacked the old, regardless of past associations. Windham, as a cabinet minister, could no longer contemplate continuing the old relationship. On 28 February 1806, he wrote in his diary that he had been to see Cobbett: 'Probably the last interview we shall have.' But Cobbett had already found himself courted by new friends. In October 1805 he had received this letter from Major John Cartwright:

> It was only lately I became a reader of your Weekly Register. Your energy, your indignant warmth against peculation, your abhorrence of political treachery, and your independent spirit, command my esteem. As a token of it, I beg to present you with a few essays written to serve our injured country, which has too long lain a bleeding prey to devouring factions, and which cannot be preserved, unless that public spirit and courage that were once the characteristics of England, can be revived.[2]

It was a letter guaranteed to make Cobbett warm to its author, combining praise for himself and an enthusiasm for change combined with a respect for older virtues. Cartwright had, in fact, been a radical campaigner for very many years. As early as 1776 he had written a pamphlet, *Take Your Choice,* which had argued for universal suffrage, annual parliaments, paid members and equal electoral districts. He was a realist, who did not expect to get everything done at once, but had a good rational argument for trying.

> On the old maxim of teaching a young archer to shoot at the moon in order that he may acquire the power of throwing his arrow far enough for practical purposes, I have always thought that a free discussion of the principle of Universal Suffrage the most likely means of obtaining any Reform at all worth contending for.[3]

He was then sixty-five years old, but still campaigning and always on the look out for recruits to the cause of reform. Cobbett, however, still had too many memories of American democracy to be an instant convert: his arrow was not yet aimed at the moon. 'Of universal suffrage I have witnessed the defects too attentively and with too much disgust ever to think of it in approbation.'[4] Cartwright, however, recognized the virtues of the Register, in that it was an independent voice that would, if nothing else, accurately report the views and speeches of the reformers: 'Cobbett's paper has a circulation and authority which nothing of the kind ever had.' And Cobbett, in his turn, recognized in Cartwright something which he had despaired of finding in the political world, a man of independence and principle, untouched by the System. He was 'a man having a mind which it is impossible to bewilder, and a heart of such integrity that nothing can shake.'

The letter from Cartwright represented the first step on the last leg of Cobbett's political journey. It had taken him a mere half-dozen years to make the transition from the Tory who had been proud to have been received by Pitt to becoming a leading member of the Radical movement, albeit a distinctly quirky one. In America he had held onto a dream of Britain as a staunch bastion of all the virtues, standing firm against the evil tide pouring out of France. Back home, his illusions had been slowly but remorselessly revealed as just that. His disillusionment was absolute, simply because he had expected so much, because he had been such a vigorous supporter of the regime. His was not a temperament made for compromise. Once he had been wholly in favour of the old order. It was inevitable that he would now be as wholly opposed to it. He became more and more convinced that neither the old aristocracy which he had so much admired, nor the new plutocracy he had always heartily despised would consider the welfare of the ordinary, working population of the country. They would only get justice when their voice could be heard directly in Parliament, and until that day came he would be their spokesperson.

He was, however, still deeply suspicious of political parties of whatever colour, and continued to declare his independence.

We have seen too much of *factions* to *belong* to any of them.
There is no comfort, and *solid* advantage, to be obtained by
linking oneself to a faction of any sort. If our friends can
accomplish any thing, it is well; but, they must not expect to
shackle me, who always have, and always will, do that which
I think best to be done in each case and circumstance that may
arise.[5]

He did indeed pursue an individual course. Cartwright who soon
took over the position previously held in Cobbett's life by
Windham, often pursued a very different agenda. His home base
was at the busy port of Boston in Lincolnshire, close to the industrial centres of the north. It is one of the interesting paradoxes of the
time that Cobbett, who loathed the Industrial Revolution, should
have been so closely allied to the brother of Revd Edmund
Cartwright, whose invention of the power loom had completed the
transfer of the textile industry from cottage to factory. Major
Cartwright was also a believer in the political clubs, on the pattern
of the Corresponding Societies, regarded in the 1790s by the authorities as dangerous seats of sedition and revolution. Cobbett was
himself unclubbable, and disliked the whole idea.

as to any *association*; any thing in the old style of the Whigs
and 'friends of the people', God forbid it should be resorted
to. *Clubs* never yet did good.[6]

Clubs could hold scoundrels as well as honest men: by far the better
way was to hold public meetings, be frank and open and appeal to
the sound common sense of all the people through reasoned arguments.

If Cobbett was not always in agreement with Cartwright – and he
was never totally in agreement with anyone – he found him and his
friends to be congenial company, with views close enough to his
own to make mutual help a pleasure. He soon came to know such
leading Radicals as Sir Francis Burdett, who saw himself very much
in the mould of Wilkes as man of the people, and Francis Place. If
anything could be said to show how far Cobbett had shifted in his
alliances, then it is the friendship with Place. Here was a man of the
town, not the country, a tailor who had organized his first strike
back in 1793 and was one of the leading members of the London
Correspondence Society, though it has to be said that he saw its
main role as one of educating the working class to take an informed
and active role in the political world, rather than promoting the
revolutionary aims adopted by other members. Cobbett, however,
was quite happy to support Place and the other Radicals both
publicly and in private. They had an independence he admired and

views which could, or at any rate, should convince others.

> The way to proceed is to leave Place and Adams and men of
> that stirling stamp; men of fair moral character, of good
> sense, and no ambitious views to take the lead, and to appeal
> to the nation in a plain unvarnished manner.[7]

In 1806, Cobbett experienced the political process at first hand.
A by-election was called at Honiton in Devon when one of the two
sitting members resigned to take advantage of the offer of a lucra-
tive sinecure, Teller of the Irish Exchequer. Cobbett spelled out just
what that meant:

> Perceiving that Mr Cavendish Bradshaw has, since by your
> voice he was constituted one of the guardians of the public
> purse, taken care to obtain a place by the means of which he
> will draw into his own pocket some thousands a year out of
> that purse, and this, too, at a time when the load of indis-
> pensable taxes is pressing his honest and industrious
> constituents to the earth.[8]

It was insupportable to Cobbett that such a wretch should be
replaced by another of similar persuasion. When no one came
forward, he offered to stand himself. His published address was
firm and to the point:

> Gentlemen, as it is my firm determination never to receive a
> farthing of the public money, so it is my determination
> equally firm, never, in any way whatever, to give one
> farthing of my own money to any man, in order to induce him
> to vote, or to cause others to vote, for me.[9]

This novel concept did not appeal to an electorate that had come to
regard voting as a substantial earner, recording their preference for
'Mr Most'. It was said that at the time local shopkeepers were
happy to let their customers run up substantial bills on the clear
understanding that they would settle up on polling day. He had
already made it clear that he was a reluctant candidate, and when
another candidate, Lord Cochrane, offered to take his place on the
same policies, he was only too happy to withdraw. He remained in
Devon, however, helping out with the campaign and discovering a
genuine talent for public oratory. He and Cochrane became, and
remained, firm friends.

Cochrane, like Cobbett, made it clear that he was offering no
bribes, and most of the electorate made it clear that he would not
receive their votes. When it was all over, however, he rewarded all

those who had voted for him with ten guineas apiece, to the extreme
chagrin of all those who had sold their votes to Cochrane's opponents for a good deal less. It was a good joke, and it is no wonder
that Cobbett warmed to such a man. He did not warm to the electoral system he had met at first hand, and he was as forcibly struck
by the beauty of the place, which epitomised everything he held
dear, as by the hideous system that was corrupting it.

> In quitting this scene, looking back from one of the many hills
> that surrounded the fertile and beautiful valley in which Honiton
> lay, with its houses spreading down the side of an inferior
> eminence crowned by its ancient and venerable church; in
> surveying the fields, the crops, the cattle, all the blessings that
> nature could bestow, all the sources of plenty and all the means
> of comfort and happiness, it was impossible to divest myself of
> a feeling of horror at reflecting upon the deeds which the sun
> witnessed upon this one of his most favoured spots.[10]

Cobbett made it clear that he had no wish to be a Member of
Parliament, though he characteristically added that 'it would be
contemptible affectation to pretend to doubt of my own ability to
discharge the duties of a Member'. He was even, he declared, rather
spoiling the effect of the earlier denial, prepared to stand if need be
for the City of Westminster. That opportunity came up rather sooner
than expected, with the death of Fox. He had been the nearest thing
to a radical in the Parliament, and he was one of the few important
figures who had earned Cobbett's respect. Just as he had baulked at
the notion of another self-serving systemite taking over at Honiton,
so now he was equally determined to help ensure that the indepen-
dently minded Fox was not replaced by anyone of less radical
views. The Whigs put up Sheridan, best known today as a great
dramatist, but known to Cobbett as a detestable purveyor and accep-
tor of sinecures. He had, however, been one of those who had
remained close to Fox, and it was generally felt that he stood a fair
chance of keeping Westminster for the more radical wing of the
Whigs. The Radicals had been too trusting. There was a back-room
deal going on between the Whigs and the Tories and at the last
moment Sheridan stepped aside and the Duke of Northumberland's
insipid son, Lord Percy, marched in unopposed. It was an election
with all the most blatant trappings of aristocratic patronage, where
liveried servants passed out bread, cheese and beer to the crowds.
Percy's stay, however, was brief, for the by-election was rapidly
followed by a general election.

This time, there were two seats to contest, and the usual deal was
made: Admiral Hood would stand for the Tories and Sheridan was
wheeled out again for the Whigs. The Radicals this time came up

with a candidate, who did not come with the most extreme Radical credentials, James Paull. He was a diminutive man who had made his fortune in India and returned to England in 1804 where he had entered Parliament for the very specific purpose of impeaching the governor general of India, Marquess Wellesley, brother of the more famous general, later to be the Duke of Wellington. Wellesley did as much as anyone to bring about the unification of India, but in doing so ran roughshod over friend and foe alike. To achieve his aim, Paull had got himself elected to a rotten borough on the Isle of Wight, and was soon a member of the Fox group, eager to embarrass Pitt. But when the coalition was formed, Wellesley was no longer needed as a target and Paull was told to drop the affair. He flatly refused and was dropped instead. So he was looking for a new seat. Cobbett was now openly associated with the leading Radicals of the day, for the campaign was financed by Burdett, and run by Place, with Cobbett himself providing the rhetoric. He began the first of a whole series of letters to the electors of Westminster, which were published in the *Register*, beginning with a denunciation of the shameful way in which the main parties were trying to tie everything up without the trouble of a real contest.

> To hear some persons talk of an election for Westminster, a stranger to the state of things would believe that the electors were the bondsmen, or, at best, the mere menial servants of a few great families.[11]

Westminster was no rotten borough, but one where journeymen and independent artisans also had the right to vote. He knew that they would be encouraged, probably ordered, to cast their votes for particular candidates, but he urged them to be bold.

> You are nearly *twenty thousand* in number. Your trades and occupations are ... full as necessary to your employers as their employment is necessary to you. If you are turned out of one house, there is always another ready to receive you; if you lose one customer you gain another ...[12]

And if they would not be rallied, then they should be shamed into independence: 'the artisans of a workshop, led to the hustings under the command of the master, are degraded to a level with cattle.'

If the Radicals suffered from one disadvantage, it was that the electorate were not greatly interested in tyrannies in India, but they came to see Paull as a doughty fighter and champion. 'He was game every inch of him: a real game cock,' as Cobbett recalled. Soon he was proving his popularity and the broadsheet ballads trumpeted the little hero of freedom.

> Let the place-hunting 'gainst our politics rant,
> Call us Jacobins, Traitors, and such idle cant;
> With our King we're determined to stand or to fall –
> So success to our cause – *Independence and Paull*!

In the event, to no one's surprise, he failed to win the seat, but he came a great deal closer than anyone had expected, polling just 300 less than Sheridan, 4481 to 4758.

Then, in 1807, another general election was called and this time the Radicals were prepared to fight both seats. Paull who had fought so well before was an obvious candidate and Burdett his reluctant partner. Burdett declared that there was no point in fighting the forces of corruption, which would continue to succeed until, in his words, 'corruption shall have exhausted the means of corruption', but he would stand anyway. Worse was to come, when he made it clear that he was even less enthusiastic about Paull, who he regarded as a bumptious little *arriviste*. Perhaps he was, but he was also notably fiery-tempered and promptly challenged Burdett to a duel. Both men were wounded, Paull so seriously that his candidature was withdrawn. In his place came Lord Cochrane, so Cobbett had the very agreeable task of working in support of two good friends. The unhappy Paull killed himself a year later. It was not, however, the best way to start a campaign, with a near lethal-brawl between the two main candidates. The Radicals were ridiculed everywhere, and in virtually the whole press, with the obvious exception of the *Register*. They followed their usual rule of offering no bribes and fully expected to lose, yet they both had notable victories. The inconceivable had happened – Westminster had fallen to the Radicals, and Burdett and Cochrane were carried through the streets by that crowd of artisans and journeymen to whom Cobbett had addressed his reasoned but passionate appeals. It was by any standards a great moment for the Radical movement, and a personal triumph for the unflagging abilities of Place and the literary skills of Cobbett.

Electioneering only took up a small amount of Cobbett's time in those years and there was no shortage of other topics to be aired in the *Register*. Having been a vociferous advocate of continuing the war against France in 1802, he was notably less interested in it once it was continued. Even his friends were confused by his apparent inconsistency, but that was largely because they could not see it through his eyes. Things which mattered immensely to others mattered not a jot to him. Overseas trade was a luxury, not an absolute necessity, and as overseas possessions were only good for promoting the former and creating strutting nabobs, they were not much use either. All that was needed to make a country great was a strong agricultural base and personal freedom. One can see a fine example of his thinking at this time in the case of the battle between the American ship, the *Chesapeak* and the British *Leopard*.

The ostensible reason for the encounter was the belief that the *Chesapeak* had British deserters among the crew. In reality it was just another move in the long-running battle to control the seas, and to prevent ships of neutral powers such as America trading with the French. The Americans were properly indignant at the attack on their ship, and many in Britain wanted the government to apologize and make amends before there was a damaging trade war underway. Not Cobbett. What was the worst that could happen, he demanded – that Americans would stop buying woollen cloth? And what would be the result of that? Cloth workers would leave the factories and return to the land, and a good thing too. The only ones who would suffer would be 'a few great merchants and manufacturers'.[13] But, said the critics, trade is needed to create national wealth and raise taxes, and one can easily imagine what he said to that argument. His views are economically naive, but certainly not inconsistent with the rest of his writings. He went on to support the Orders in Council, which decreed that all American ships bound for France should call first at British ports and pay dues. The Americans responded by an import ban on British goods. Again he argued that this meant nothing to Britain, but would more likely cause hardship to America, a prospect he viewed with enthusiasm: old wounds had not healed:

> I rejoice that it would prove the cause of great misery and ruin amongst their inhabitants; I feel great consolation that it would, in all human probability, cause the complete over-throw of their Federal Government.[14]

When he considered matters such as the wars in India, he was quite ready to praise the bravery of British soldiers and mourn for those who died, but he refused to celebrate the victories. The British should not be in India in the first place. 'There is no glory attending such conquests and their accompanying butcheries. We must be actuated by a shere love of gain; a shere love of plunder.'[15] The one area of the war where he was prepared to give unstinted praise was in the conduct of the British soldier, on the occasions when they actually went into battle. He had long said that the war could not be won at sea, but that the British Army could do the job. After Austerlitz and Jena, Napoleon had seemed invincible: the Peninsular War proved he was not. He was delighted by the British successes which seemed to prove his arguments, and he supported the Spanish people in their fight for freedom. For once, his jingoism was repressed, and he gave wholehearted praise to the Spanish themselves, and especially to the bravery of the people of Saragossa, where men, women and children fought beside the soldiers and withstood a siege of thirty-eight days followed by three weeks of street fighting. Here was nobility, not a squalid fight for material gains. The British government, on the other hand, was following no such glorious end. Their declared aim was the restoration of the Bourbon monarchy, a policy that Cobbett utterly rejected. Yes, he was in favour of throwing out Joseph Bonaparte, who had been placed on the throne by his brother, but that did not mean he was in favour of replacing him with Ferdinand.

He did not believe in fighting wars to remove one despot only to replace him by another, and he regularly pointed up the increasingly despotic behaviour of the government at home. The risk of a French invasion through Ireland was generally recognized, and there was a fear that the Irish themselves might turn on their rulers and favour the French. So the Irish Insurrection Act was passed in 1807, which gave the army almost *carte blanche* to search houses, impose curfews and arrest suspects. Cobbett put the matter simply. Whatever the threat, the Irish were supposed to be citizens like everyone else in Britain, with the same right to justice.

> How should you like it, I say? Pray do not answer me by talking about the necessities of such laws. What I want to know of you at present is how should *you* like to lead this sort of life?[16]

So, even here, his support for the war effort was at best half-hearted. He now seemed far more concerned with bringing corruption to light, in what seemed like a continuation of the campaign he had begun during his own time in the army. He found no shortage of material on which to exercise his talents. He had a deep distrust of the gentry and noblemen who were given command of regiments purely on the basis of their rank, and one of the regular butts of his complaint was the ineffectual Duke of York. In 1809 it transpired that Mrs Anne Clarke, referred to scathingly by one contemporary as a 'Babylonish person', had been offering commissions for sale in the army of which her lover, the Duke was Commander-in-Chief. It was a great scandal, and although the duke denied all knowledge of the sales he had to admit the liaison. At first the authorities had tried to deny the whole business, labelling it a Jacobite plot, which caused a typical Cobbett explosion of words 'Oh! the damned thieves! A Jacobinical conspiracy. Damned hell-fire thieves. The Duke must go.'[17] And go he did.

There are two ways of measuring the effectiveness of a man like Cobbett: the esteem in which he was held by friends and colleagues, and the hatred which he inspired in his enemies. By either reckoning, Cobbett was now at the height of his powers. The opposition was gunning for him. There was a rather feeble attempt to discredit him, when one of his farmhands, a boy of about sixteen or seventeen, ran away from the farm complaining of mistreatment. This looked a promising stick to beat him with, as he was constantly boasting of his own virtues as an employer, always paying the top wages, providing good cottages and keeping his farmhands on right through the year, unlike many others who turned them out once work was slack. As a result, he declared, he was 'better secured than anyone else. Those who have been long employed by me, not only like my employment, but they like me personally better than they like any other man in the world.'[18] Now handbills were rushed and headed, 'Cobbett the Oppressor of the Poor'. But he had a complete answer. The boy had been taken on under contract for a year, starting in winter when there was little to do and had decamped in the spring as soon as the hard work started. This sort of thing could be laughed off by a man who had been assailed by far worse pamphlets than this over the years.

> The best of it was, that, while these senseless creatures were plotting and conspiring against me, I was leading a life the most pleasing and undisturbed that could be conceived; I was walking over a very beautiful farm, and pleasure grounds. And, at the very moment that the placard was hoisted, I was in a farm-yard in Berkshire, taking and noting down the dimensions of a sheep-crib.[19]

But there were now powerful figures ranged against Cobbett who had more dangerous weapons than pamphlets at their command. The government had tried to hush up the Clarke affair, and those who did so were attacked in the *Register* with as much ferocity as the accused. The Chancellor, shortly to be Prime Minister, Spencer Perceval, was a favourite target. Cobbett had good reason to dislike him, since as Attorney General Perceval had been responsible for bringing the action against him in 1803. Now, with the heady whiff of corruption in the air, it was Cobbett's turn to be fired up for attack. Why should Perceval be so keen to deflect charges of corruption? Because he was himself deeply mired in the same cesspit, trebling his income as Chancellor through sinecures and handing out yet more to his brother. All of which was true. A prudent, man might have thought twice about taking on such a powerful enemy, particularly one who had already given him a drubbing in the courts. Cobbett was not prudent in much, and not at all once he was convinced he was writing in a just cause. He believed absolutely in the freedom of the press. It was not just a right to tell the truth, it was a solemn duty. This was even more the case when so many forms of expression were bought and controlled by the government. He set out quite clearly exactly what he meant by the freedom of the press: 'the acknowledged *legal* right, of freely expressing our opinions, be they what they may, *respecting the character and conduct of men in power*; and of stating anything, no matter what, if we can prove the *truth* of the statement.'[20]

He believed this, and acted steadfastly on the principle. But there were laws on the statute books which could make nonsense of such freedoms. In libel cases, if a statement can be shown to be true, then it cannot be libellous – though as Cobbett knew to his considerable cost, a court might choose not to recognize the truth. Seditious libel, however, was quite a different matter, for here the offence was bringing the king or his ministers into public contempt, and Cobbett had been bringing many ministers into contempt for a very long time. The law was seldom used, because it was notoriously difficult to get a conviction. No one was going to be able to claim that the Anne Clarke affair was somehow immune from criticism, simply because the government wished to cover it up. But ministers must have been confident that before long a case would appear, which Cobbett would have a much harder time in answering. His friends were aware of the situation, and urged caution: it was like warning a bull that no good would come of charging the matador's red cape.

13

NEWGATE

In 1809 a group of militia men in Ely had a grievance with their superiors over a matter of pay, the 'marching guinea' they were to receive for leaving home, so they refused to march until they were paid. Disobeying orders is a serious offence in the Army, for perfectly good reasons, but the Ely militia were scarcely frontline troops heading for battle. The charge brought against the ringleaders, however, was the far more serious one of mutiny. There was a hasty court martial and the men were sentenced to five hundred lashes apiece. It was absolutely inevitable that Cobbett would be roused. In the first place, he never lost the high regard he felt for the ordinary soldier, nor the contempt he felt for many of their officers. His own experience suggested that if the men were not getting their rightful pay, the answer could well be found in an officer's fat purse. Secondly, he knew the horror of flogging and had seen it carried out. At a later date, Parliament debated a motion that would have given judges the option of ordering imprisonment for mutiny, instead of 'corporal infliction'. Cobbett loathed such mealy-mouthed language, and he set out what he knew of the reality.

> Why not name the thing? *Flog is flog*, and *flogging* is the active participle of the verb to *flog*. *Flog, flogging, flogged.* That is the word; and, it means, in this sense of it, to whip the naked back (and, sometimes, *other parts*) of a soldier, with a thing called a *cat*; that is to say, with nine strong whipcords, about a foot and a half long, with nine knots in each, and which cords are fastened, like the thong of a whip, to the end of a stick about two feet long, With this cat-o'-nine-tails the soldier, being tied up to a thing for the purpose, by his hands and thighs, is flogged, out in the open field, or parade, while the regiment are drawn up round him.[1]

He knew, as well as any, that five hundred lashes was quite likely to prove a death sentence.

The sentence would have roused his indignation, but there was a third factor, which in his eyes made the whole affair infinitely worse. The 'mutiny' was suppressed by a squadron of Hanoverian cavalry, brought over from nearby Bury St Edmunds. The whole affair was bad enough in any case, but for honest English soldiers to be flogged while surrounded by Germans was insupportable. He had already denounced the policy of bringing German troops over and quartering them in England, and now he wrote more vehemently than ever. What he forgot, or more probably chose to ignore, was that these troops were loyal to the House of Hanover, and it was a member of the House of Hanover who sat on the English throne. To question the loyalty of Hanoverian troops to the English cause could be construed as questioning the loyalty to England of the Hanoverians. And that was precisely the construction put on the articles by Cobbett's opponents: he was approving a vile mutiny, disputing the findings of a properly constituted court material and, by implication, attacking the king himself. Cobbett had, with his customary recklessness, plunged in by writing that Napoleon had been condemned by using force to command loyalty among his conscript army. Was this really any worse?

> I hope that the loyal will, hereafter, be more cautious in drawing such conclusions, now that they see, that our 'gallant defenders' not only require physical restraint, in certain cases, but even a little blood drawn from their backs, and that, too, with the aid and assistance of *German* troops.[2]

It seemed at first as if he would get away unscathed, and as nothing much seemed to be happening apart from vague threats, his confidence was high.

> Be sure to tell Hansard, or any of them from me, that I hold the thing in contempt, that I am not more afraid of the rascals than I could be of so many mice. And, really, if we have an *honest* jury, it will be a famous thing altogether.[3]

He sounds very cheerful, but the threat was real, and there were other worries at home: Nancy was quite seriously ill. In a letter to his friend and doctor, A. Tegart, he described her condition in December 1809 after she had been ill for several weeks.

> On last *Sunday week* she took her first dose of the strong medicine, which has mercury in it, which made her feel very poorly. On the next Wednesday, a *St. Anthony's fire* began to assail her; it close up both her eyes; but, is now gone off again, after plaguing her a good deal. – Her legs are better. –

She has occasional *shooting pains* about her; but, the pain in her legs has gone off. – What I want, however, particularly to obtain information about, is, the *plaister upon the breast*. – She found it operating precisely in the same way as a *blister*. After that, there came, when the plaister was off, innumerable little pimples with heads full of water.[4]

The disease was ergotism, caused by a mould on bread. It constricts the blood vessels, and would have caused all the symptoms described. The treatment would certainly have made her feel ill, as mercury's main use until recent times was as a diuretic. It was a serious complaint, given a drastic treatment, so they must all have been very anxious. Happily, Nancy made a full recovery, but the threat of an action still hung over them.

Matters became even worse when a letter appeared in the *Register* for April 1810, under Burdett's name, complaining about the imprisonment of a Radical, John Gale Jones, and declaring that the House of Commons had acted illegally. The Speaker at once declared Burdett was in breach of privilege and ordered his arrest and instant incarceration in the Tower of London. The events that followed had more than a touch of farce. Burdett now averred that his own arrest was just as illegal as Jones's and promptly barricaded himself in his house, demanding protection from the City and his friends. Cochrane appeared with a barrel of gunpowder, though quite what he could have done with it is far from clear. Crowds gathered and it took the arrival of a whole troop of volunteers to persuade Burdett to march off to the Tower, where he stayed for the rest of the Parliament. It was an ominous sign of the determination of the government to attack the Radicals, however and wherever they could. The successful action against Burdett brought the dithering over Cobbett to an end: on 15 June 1810, with his printer, publisher and bookseller, he came to trial.

The case was to be heard before a special jury at the King's Bench under Lord Chief Justice Ellenborough, with the Attorney General himself leading the prosecution. The other three defendants pleaded guilty, but Cobbett pleaded not guilty and undertook his own defence. Perhaps he was mindful of how little lawyers had achieved for him in the past, particularly in the Rush case. But this was no ordinary libel action, with the threat of no more than a fine at the end of it. It could have been that he simply believed what he had often said, that special juries were little better than the paid servants of the government. Or, which would not have been out of character, he had supreme confidence in his own abilities. If the latter was the case, he was sadly mistaken.

Cobbett's performance in court was a sorry affair – introducing evidence, such as anti-flogging debates in Parliament, which the judge refused to allow in court, and often contradicting himself. Francis Place left a damning account of this pathetic spectacle.

> Cobbett made a long defence, a bad defence, and his delivery of it and his demeanour were even worse than his matter. He was not at all master of himself, and in some parts where he meant to produce great effect, he produced laughter. So ludicrous was he in one part, the jury, the judge and the audience all laughed at him.

He ended by declaring: 'I was thoroughly ashamed of him, and ashamed of myself for being with him.'[5] He was not to be seen with him again very often. Place felt that had he behaved with dignity, Cobbett would have been held up as a heroic victim of government persecution: instead he merely appeared as a buffoon. In fact, public opinion did rally behind Cobbett, but by then Place had done with him: from then on, he saw as little of him as he possibly could.

After the verdict, Cobbett retired to Botley to await sentence, having already heard the judge's summing up in which he referred to 'a most infamous and seditious libel'. He could only have expected the worst, and as if to confirm his suspicions, he was treated with rough contempt. Instead of a note being sent informing him of the date he was to appear in court, the tipstaff came in person without warning to carry him back to London.

The sentence was as bad as anything he could have imagined. He was fined a thousand pounds, sentenced to two years in Newgate, and had heavy bail conditions imposed on him after release – should that day ever arrive. Newgate was a notorious hell-hole where disease and filth took their toll, and which few survived. The news was sent down to the family at Botley.

> The tears of the postman, a rough and hardy fellow, who had lost an arm in the military service, prepared my daughter for the news. The three boys were in the garden hoeing some peas. My daughter called the eldest to tell him what had been done. He returned to the others, and they hearing their sister cry, asked him what was the matter. He could make them no answer, but, pulling his hat over his eyes, took up the hoe in a sort of wild manner and began to chop about, cutting up the peas and all that came in his way.[6]

Nancy was distraught, as well she might have been: she was pregnant again, her husband had been sent to gaol, debts were mounting and she was to be left to manage as best she could. Yet her first concern was for William. Against everyone's advice and Cobbett's own wishes, she insisted on seeing him in Newgate. He did not want her to see him just then, for he had already taken steps to get himself out of 'the company of felons'.

> By great favour I finally obtained leave to occupy two rooms in the jailer's house, paying for them twelve guineas a week, and it required eight more to fee the various persons, and to get leave to walk an hour in the leads of the prison in the morning: so that here were £2,080 during the two years besides the £1,000 to the good old King. These direct losses were, however, trifling compared with the indirect. I was engaged in the publication of two works, called 'The State Trials' and 'The Parliamentary History'. There had been a great outlay for these works; several thousands of pounds were due to the paper-maker and the printer. These works were, as far as regarded me, ruined ... Almost exactly ten years after landing in England, having lost a fortune in America, solely for the sake of England, I was sent to prison in that same England. It was quite impossible for me to banish reflections of this sort from my mind.[7]

Cobbett was inevitably despondent, and began to think of ways to provide for Nancy and the children if the worst should happen. It might seem odd that, given the important connections he had now made in England, including men of wealth and influence such as Sir Francis Burdett and Lord Cochrane, he did not turn in that direction for help. He never gave an explanation, but he was well aware that Place had already turned against him, and, although he would not have liked to admit it even to himself, he must have known that he had behaved recklessly in writing the Ely piece and foolishly in conducting his own defence. He had managed to bring the whole Radical movement into disrepute and had made the task of criticizing the government, especially in their conduct of the war, doubly difficult. He looked instead to America and the Quaker James Paull, a man of whom, he wrote 'I have never conferred a favour to the amount of the value of a pin.' He at once received a reply which instantly removed one major anxiety.

> Give thyself no trouble about Nancy and the children. If thee should die, which I hope thee will not for years to come, thy dear family shall find a home under my roof, and shall be to me and all of us as our own kindred.[8]

His immediate problem was working out how family life at Botley could continue in his absence. He knew very well that Nancy had taken a dim view of many of his ventures – he had even gone so far as to ask Wright to keep the publication of *The Spirit of the*

Journals a secret. She was bound to consider it as a foolish gamble, and one certain to lose money. 'I cannot blame her anxiety,' he wrote, 'but, as I cannot remove it, it is better not to awaken it.' In this, at least, she would have shown sound common sense, and preserved her husband from at least one of his many expensive failures. She was similarly distrustful of some of his more exotic farming notions. Now, nothing could be kept from her. She must have the running of the farm. Even more painful to Cobbett was the thought that he would no longer be able to have a direct involvement in the day-to-day education of the children. In time, they established a system for running their separate lives.

Anne was a great comfort to him in Newgate, often helping out as copyist and general factotum. Nancy had a regular routine of riding round the farm on her little pony, passing out the orders to the men and checking on the work done. William was the connecting link between his father and the rest of the family. He sent regular reports to Newgate, and referred all decisions there. He would send in a sheet of paper, with all the questions neatly set out down the left-hand side of the page, leaving a space on the right for answers. Nothing seems to have been too trivial to bring to the absentee farmer for a decision. Here, for example, is a note from 20 October 1811.[9]

> What is to be done about the heap of earth opposite our wall, in the river? are you going to write a note to John Cleaver to ask him to take it away? It will undermine wall.
>
> I am afraid we must let alone. We cannot compel *them* to move it. We had better get some stones to throw in against the wall.

At other times there were detailed instructions sent with orders that they should be read out to the farmhands. Everyone had to do their bit, even the two younger boys, John and James – John was just ten when the sentence began and James seven. They rode out each day, and wrote their reports for their father.

William Cobbett rarely strikes one as a sentimental man, and though he often spoke of his love of his children, he usually did so as part of one of his improving essays, so that it seems more a necessary part of an argument than any real, deeply felt emotion. When he was forcibly separated from them, however, his real feelings showed through, particularly in the letters he sent to the younger boys. He imagined what they might be doing down at Botley, and spelled it out in little illustrated stories. He shows the two boys on their ponies hunting rabbits and up a tree with lanterns catching jackdaws in drawings full of a simple charm. Another is almost a strip cartoon, showing John and James out in the rain and coming home wet. They arrive back to find their angry aunt at the gate, shaking a fist at them. It is plain that the father is doing his best to cheer up the young boys and make light of the appalling situation in which they all found themselves. They in their turn did their best to please the prisoner with their letters and regular hampers of farm produce. Even so, it was not possible for everything to go on as before, and Cobbett reluctantly had to agree to a certain amount of formal schooling for his young family. They also found time for some informal education, including dancing lessons, which brought humour into dull Newgate as the boys showed off their steps.

> They put on their pumps and danced the best part of the day; and laughed till their jaws ached, and so did I. John has got all the capers, and he skips and twists himself about like a grasshopper, I would have the girls of the Village get themselves in order for dancing, for these fellows will soon be ready to hand them about.[10]

Things were bad, but the family coped. There were, however, to be still more misfortunes and calamities before the sentence came to an end. There was pressing anxiety about Nancy's pregnancy. He had always been with her during her labour, but could not face the idea of a child being born in gaol. It was left to Nancy, already under immense stress, to resolve this dilemma.

> My wife, who had come to see me for the last time previous to her lying-in, perceiving my deep dejection at the approach of her departure for Botley, resolved not to go; and actually went and took a lodging as near to Newgate as she could find one, in order that the communication between us might be as speedy as possible; and in order that I might see the doctor, and receive assurances from him relative to her state. The nearest lodging that she could find was in Skinner-street, at the corner of a street leading to Smithfield. So that there she was, amidst the incessant rattle of coaches and butchers' carts, and the noise of cattle, dogs, and bawling men; instead of being in a quiet and commodious country-house, with neighbours and servants and everything necessary about her. Yet, so great is the power of the mind in such cases, she, though the circumstances proved uncommonly perilous, and were attended with the loss of the child, bore her sufferings with the greatest composure, because, at any minute she could send a message to, and hear from me. If she had gone to Botley, leaving me in that state of anxiety in which she saw me, I am satisfied that she would have died; and that event taking place at such a distance from me, how was I to

Newgate, Wednesday, January 23. 1811.

My dear Johnny,

     You asked Papa the other day, whether he did not think that the Dogs better not be kept in the Stable. I told you a great while ago, that the Dogs should always sleep there at nights. —— I hope you are all well. —— As you are so very impatient about your Plans, I will draw them. —— Why don't you write to me sometimes? I hope you will write to me about how many Birds you have shot.

     This is a Plan of you and James shooting rabbits. James is on his Jack ass, shooting, and you are galloping on them Don Fernando Septimion.

     This is a Plan of you and Jemmy, catching Magpies in the morning. You are up in the Tree, and James is tying the Birds, (Magpies) up, at the bottom of the tree.

     Uncle Tom is coming here next Saturday week; and Mama is going to ask him to get us a Terrier. —— You and Nancy are coming up here, with Dean, in just 21 days; you will most likely come on the 15. of next month, it being the first day after shooting season.

         God bless you.

Papa says you must be kept keep all the Plans   Wm Cobbett.   I send you.

                       (and bring them up with you.

Cobbett's letter to his son John, written in Newgate and showing the boys out rabbit shooting and catching magpies. (The Warden and Fellows of Nuffield College, Oxford)

Newgate, *Jan*. 2? 1811.

My dear Johnny,

Mamma loves you and James don't get your feet wet. And Mama says that she will not let you go out at all if you do.

This is a Plan of you and James coming home dripping wet; and Aunty standing at the White Gate, and shaking her fist at you; and you saying to James, "I'm afraid we shan't have a morsel of our jackets left". — I beg you to be aware of getting your feet "Wetted" again, for if you do, you will look as ugly as you are now, coming home with James behind you, and not so pretty as you are riding the Jackasses, and shooting Birds, and hunting Rabbits. — And now, look at yourselves, coming home dripping wet, looking like old man of four score, and Aunty shaking her fist and saying, "Upon my word, you shan't have a morsel of dinner all this day, that you shan't."

This is a Plan of all three of us Rabbit-Hunting. — And don't you see how much better you look like you are now, than when you are slouching home in the wet and dirt, and Aunty threatening you that you shall not have a bit of dinner?

Now I am going to draw a Plan of the Dear little Girls, playing with the

A second Newgate letter. This time the boys are trudging home in the rain to be scolded by their aunt and rabbit hunting with their dogs. (The Warden and Fellows of Nuffield College, Oxford)

contemplate her corpse, surrounded by her distracted children, and to have escaped death or madness myself?[11]

Cobbett would not have been Cobbett if he had not taken this personal tragedy and made it a part of his political crusade. It was all a part of the government's plot to ruin, break and even kill their hated critic: 'that amiable body may be well assured that I have taken and recorded the will for the deed, and that as such it will live in my memory as long as that memory shall last.' This was more than rhetoric: the sense of injury that he felt over the committal to Newgate never left him, nor the bitterness towards those who put him there.

He was not helped in this most difficult time by his brother and his family. Not only were they still in a financial muddle, but they had decided that Cobbett's nephew Tom should have a good career, based on learning a profession by taking a premium apprenticeship, and who better to pay for it than his jailed uncle? That pushed family loyalty beyond the limit.

As to my poor Brother, I will write to you about him tomorrow and will tell you what I think you had best say to him I was afraid that his family would be a bad race, and as to his son Tom, he ought to be horsewhipped to work – *Premium* with Charles! Do you not think he has cost us enough? No, no, I shall see him off clothed, and then let him make his way in the world or starve.[12]

Through all of this, his own immediate family was the greatest comfort he had. What a contrast there was between nephew Tom's life style and that of his own son, William. The boy's reports of progress on the farm were a constant delight: 'One really fancies that one sees the things he is describing; and the kindness of his disposition, towards every living creature, breathes through every sentence that he writes.'[13]

Before his imprisonment, his financial position seemed generally sound, sound enough to withstand his somewhat wayward management of his affairs. He had put his complete trust in Wright, and they worked together on what seemed a very *ad hoc* basis. Wright appears never to have had a fixed salary, but drew money as it was needed, hopelessly muddling cash for necessary expenses with his own pay. A young barrister, Thomas Bayly Howell, had been brought in to edit *State Trials*, and he not unreasonably suggested that he might take a share in the profits, and if that was agreed he would need to see the accounts. Cobbett thought this a great joke, which he shared with Wright.

Only think of having another person invested with a right, a *legal* right, to make us account, us whose accounts the devil himself would never unravel. No, no; you and I were never made to have our accounts unravelled by anyone but ourselves.[14]

Now, however, matters stood very differently. Cobbett was in urgent need of money, and the old system of casual payments was no longer adequate. An unravelling was necessary to find out exactly how matters stood. Wright did his best, but when the figures were produced it was clear that things had gone badly wrong. It came as a terrible blow to Cobbett to find that the money he was absolutely relying on was simply not there. He exploded into denunciations of Wright, all the more vitriolic for his deep sense of betrayal. He had been his confidante, a man with whom he had entrusted his affairs. Now he accused him of appropriating the huge sum of £12,000 – four times the estimated extra expenses of his time in prison. Wright strenuously denied the charge, though he reluctantly admitted that he had taken out £500 as an unauthorized advance. In the event, the matter went to arbitration by a Lincoln's Inn lawyer, who found that Wright in fact owed £6,500. It was a vindication of Cobbett's claims – and a damning indictment of his managerial incompetence. But what was the use of vindication? The money had gone and there was no getting it back. This was even worse than the £2000 fine.

Wright had to go, that was obvious and money had to be raised. The only publishing assets that were readily saleable were the reference works, the *Parliamentary History, Parliamentary Debates* and the *State Trials*. All these went to Hansard. Wright, as far as Cobbett was concerned, was proved a double-dyed villain, yet Hansard kept him on as editor of the *History* and *Debates*. There are a number of explanations, but the most plausible suggests that the man considered the financial débâcle to be at least as much the fault of the owner's muddied and muddled way of running affairs as it was his editor's. Howell continued with the *Trials*, and just as Hansard's name lives on in politics, so does his in the legal world. Needless to say, the whole world would have had to collapse before Cobbett would even contemplate selling the *Register*. In fact, he decided to increase his income by publishing it twice a week instead of weekly: a decision that, if it did nothing else, ensured he never got bored in Newgate. His pen was never idle and on his own reckoning, he wrote and published 364 political essays and letters during the two years. The venture, however, was not quite the success he had hoped, and the *Register* reverted to its former weekly appearance.

The other obvious way to raise money was to sell Botley. His hard-pressed family, doing their best to cope with the farm, might have been expected to greet the idea with enthusiasm. Nancy, however, was far from keen. She had supported her husband with great fortitude, but she was by no means a happy woman. She did not, as far as we can tell, hold any deep political convictions, but she believed in conventional values. In the heady days of the return to England she had been treated as a lady, greeted and feted by some of the country's most important men and women. Had her husband done as he had been pressed to do and taken some form of official paper and supported the government, she would have been riding in her carriage, not trotting around the countryside on an old pony giving orders to labourers. But he had turned away from his old friends and joined the Radicals, and she was well aware that her neighbours in the country regarded them as little short of murderous revolutionaries. Of all those who tried to follow Cobbett's changes of direction, none found it harder than his wife.

She retained a hope that he might yet settle down to a more conventional life, though it must have been a faint one. There was, however, another, more compelling, reason for keeping the land, and she marshalled the family in her support. And in this argument, even Cobbett's best friends would have to concede that she had a point. Anne describes that time.

> Mama was afraid that whatever money there might be over and above paying the mortgages Papa would speculate with in printing his writing or something or other. She talked in such a way to Mr Crabtree that I know he went to Sir F.B. and said that Mrs Cobbett thought it would be worse for Papa to get rid of his land. He told her he wd. do so. Of course we did not know any better, but I remembered afterwards of the letter I wrote by Mama's desires to Papa imploring him not to sell the place.[15]

She was reluctant to go along with the scheme, for she was, of all the children, closest to her father in spirit and opinion. Later she was to regret the decision even more. She wrote a little note, which sits oddly with Cobbett's own enthusiastic appraisal of Botley (p.94). One cannot help but feel that she was the clear-eyed one. Cobbett was no man for half-measures: he was always as violently in favour of one thing as he was – rather more frequently – violently against another. There is a sad air of bitter truthfulness about her assessment.

> If he had sold off Botley and never gone back to it I think things might have become better with us. It was an unfortunate choice of a place for him at the first, surrounded with

Nabobs from India, and there being no small gentry except Army or Navy people: and there were Dock Yards and Barracks Departments close by us, and whole hosts of people depending upon Govt favour. It was like getting into a hornet's nest. He had no society there whatever, none but friends who came from a distance and staid in his house.[16]

In many ways, life for the family was harder than it was for Cobbett himself, coping, and coping very well, with problems they had never had to face before, constantly worrying about money, but not able to do anything directly for themselves. He, on the other hand, was lodged in comparative comfort, and he was not neglected by his old friends and associates – with the notable exception of Place. It appears a somewhat bizarre situation to modern eyes. Here was a man convicted in wartime of a most serious offence against his country, and yet the street outside the gaol rang to the sound of hooves and carriage wheels as lords and gentry called to pay their respects. He was even visited by a senior judge of the sheriff's court, Francis Maseres, who pointedly showed his disapproval of the court's verdict by always arriving in wig and gown. It all went a long way towards supporting Cobbett's own view of himself as martyr to the vindictive treatment of a currupt government, most of whose members were more deserving of imprisonment than William Cobbett. And as there are few things more satisfying to a radical opposition than a martyr to their cause, he was soon attracting the attention of groups all over the country. It was very flattering.

I was visited by persons, whom I have never seen before, from one hundred and ninety-seven cities and towns of England. Scotland and Ireland; the greatest part of whom came to me as the deputies of some society, club, or circle of people in their respective places of residence. I had the infinite satisfaction to learn from the gentlemen who thus visited me, that my writings had induced those who had read them to think.[17]

But nothing could compensate him for his loss of freedom. He was an active men, pent up with limited opportunities for exercise. He did his best to keep up the routines of life. He still got up early every morning, regularly exercised with dumb-bells and tried not to eat too much for fear of getting fat. What really made him miserable was the enforced stay in town, two whole years with no glimpse of his beloved countryside; a fine view over sooty roofs was no compensation for the lack of good air, the walks over the fields and the song of birds. And what made his misery doubly bitter was the absolute conviction that he was innocent. Physically he

came out unimpaired: emotionally, he was damaged for ever. It was
Anne, as was often the case, who saw it all most clearly.

> Papa's health did not suffer in Newgate, but his temper did.
> He left it an altered man, in many respects. Miss Mitford says
> that he never talked politics in society, never broached them
> at least. After Newgate he talked little else. He was so *angry*
> at being so ill used, and there was the loss of so much money
> and the bad, ungrateful behaviour of Wright and the rest of
> that set ... it all wounded him very deeply.[18]

It touched all he did, and all his relationships, and even Anne had
to add wistfully, 'he was never cross to *me* before.'
When his release finally came, he left prison a hero.

> On the 9th of July 1812, a great dinner was given in London
> for the purpose of receiving me, at which dinner upwards of
> 600 persons were present, and at which Sir Francis Burdett
> presided; that dinners and other parties were held on the same
> occasion in many other places in England; that, on my way
> home, I was received at Alton, the first town in Hampshire,
> with the ringing of the Church bells; that a respectable
> company met me and gave me a dinner at Winchester; that I
> was drawn from more than the distance of a mile into Botley
> by the people; that, upon my arrival in the village, I found all
> the people assembled to receive me; that I concluded the day
> by explaining to them the cause of my imprisonment, and by
> giving them clear notions respecting the flogging of the Local
> Militia-men at Ely, and respecting the employment of German
> Troops; and, finally, which is more than a compensation for
> my losses and all my sufferings, I am in perfect health and
> strength, and though I must, for the sake of my six children,
> feel the diminution that has been made on my property (think-
> ing it right in me to decline the offer of a subscription), I have
> the consolation to see growing up three sons, upon whose
> hearts, I trust, all these facts will be engraven.[19]

Anne also wrote her account of those days. She had spent so
great a time in Newgate helping her father that she seemed almost
as much a prisoner as he was, and now was looking forward to
sharing his triumph as she had shared his misery. But at Alton on
the way home, where there was a great public breakfast organized
by a friend, James Baverstock, she was taken away 'from the
company of so many gentlemen' for a solitary sedate breakfast with
Mrs Baverstock. She was absolutely furious and never forgot the
prudery that had taken from her what should have been one of the

great moments of her life. She also provides a more colourful account of the return to Botley.

> Parson Baker refused the keys of the Church so that the people could not ring the bells which they wished very much to do. However, they sufficiently testified their respect to Papa, and their pleasure at his return, without the assistance of the Church. For a party of young men, I should think about a hundred, or a hundred and fifty, accompanied by a band of music which they had hired themselves for the purpose, met him about a mile out of Botley, on the new Winchester road, where they insisted on taking the horses out of the carriage, which they did, and, with colours flying and the band of music marching before them, they brought him into Botley.[20]

This did nothing to improve Cobbett's opinion of political parsons – nor of his old adversary Parson Baker. At the end of that tumultuous day, Anne too had her moment to savour and remember.

> Mama had ordered four hogsheads of ale, one at each of the public houses, in the morning, but she had no idea of what was to be done. Papa arrived here about eight o'clock, and after we had drank tea about nine, the band came and stationed themselves on the lawn, where they continued playing for some time, after which we called them into the Hall, and I gave the young men and young women of the village a dance. Mr Walker and your humble Servant opening the Ball.[21]

Newgate represents one of the great turning-points in Cobbett's life, so that one has to address the question: was he as innocent as he claimed? There can be no doubt at all that the government sincerely hated Cobbett, loathed the *Register* and would have been heartily glad to have silenced both for all time. Their motives for the prosecution were certainly vindictive, but that is not quite the same thing as saying that the court was wrong in bringing in a guilty verdict. The facts are that the Ely militia had refused to obey orders at a time of war. They may have had good reason and they were not directly involved in any actual fighting, but no army could really expect to tolerate such actions. Cobbett had two arguments: the first that the punishment was out of all proportion to the crime, an argument that seems self-evidently justifiable today, and one which was scarcely less so then. His second argument – objecting to the role of German troops – was altogether different, and smacks of xenophobia. The Hanoverians were allies in war, not a bunch of foreigners who happened to be around at the time. There was an implicit suggestion, to say the least, that there was something basically unpatriotic in having them in England at all – and that could certainly be taken as undermining the united front that was being formed against Napoleon. Cobbett's judgement had been poor. He was used to attacking with any weapon that came to hand: this time he chose the wrong one. He saw the issue as the freedom of the press to criticize the government of the day; but such absolute freedom has never existed and newspapers and journals have always provided a good living for lawyers as well as editors and writers. He chose to ignore the law as it stood and acted as if there were no legal limitations to what he could write. Having conceded that, his punishment, like that of the soldiers he so vigorously defended seems out of all proportion to the severity of the crime. It was meant to ruin him. It would have ruined a lesser man. It seemed only to confirm Cobbett in his new Radical views and made him an even more powerful enemy of the old regime.

14

AN ANGRY MAN

Whatever the government may have expected, or at least hoped, prison did nothing to diminish the severity of the attacks in the *Register*: if anything, it strengthened them. Nor was the impact reduced because they were written in prison by a convicted criminal. Instead Cobbett wore his insignia of punishment as badges of pride, signing each piece with the address 'State Prison, Newgate' and in the last piece he wrote before release, he cocked a final snook at his tormentors, ending it this time 'State Prison, Newgate, where I have just paid a thousand pounds fine to the King; and much good may it do his Majesty'. It was a typical piece of Cobbett bravado, leaving the reader with the vague notion that the issue was not so much a crime committed, as some sort of personal quarrel between equals – himself and George III. Even his enemies had to admit, William Cobbett was a bonny fighter.

One of the causes dearest to his heart was developed over a number of years, but was finally worked out to his own satisfaction during his time in Newgate: the question of paper money. In his autobiography, he detailed the steps by which he had come to his present position. He saw a system that began as a convenient way for rich men to settle large debts, by exchanging notes, generally not less than twenty pounds, which were secured by the backing of a bank. But once notes came as low as one pound, they went into general circulation, and there were so many of them that there was no realistic chance of them all being converted into gold or silver. There was also – a point which he preferred to ignore – no realistic chance of everyone wanting to convert them to specie. He was sure, however, that it was all a plot to finance the national debt and to make large profits for speculators. However, he persevered in his search for enlightenment, turning first to the man generally regarded as the leading economic theorist of the day, 'that old Scotch tax-gatherer, Adam Smith'. It has to be said that Cobbett had a deep suspicion of both Scots and tax-gatherers, but he protested that he came to the works with an open mind. But he could 'make neither top nor tail of the thing'. If there was nothing to be gained from commentators, then he would look at the source, and set out to read all the Parliamentary papers on the national debt, loans and the funds – 'and disgusting as this would have been to almost any other man upon the face of the earth, to me it was pleasant.' 'He reached the conclusion that the whole thing was a plot to increase the power of Parliament, which in the process would destroy the small farmer and pauperize the labourer. Then he read Paine, and all was clear (p.90).

He took Paine's dogma to heart, and although he was still critical at this stage of many of Paine's ideas, he had come an immense distance from the time in America when he had reviewed his scurrilous biography.

> How Tom gets a living now, or what brothel he inhabits, I know not, nor does it much signify to any body here or anywhere else. He has done all the mischief he can in the world, and whether his carcass is at last to be suffered to rot in the earth, or to be dried in the air, is of very little consequence.[1]

They were words he would regret even more deeply later, when they would be turned against him, but for now he was content to see some virtue in the man. He was, however, sure that he himself could do a good deal better in spreading the word on the evils of paper money. Paine had made himself unpopular – he was, of course, one of the most popular and influential writers of the eighteenth century, but one can ignore that and return to the main argument – unpopular because of his 'gratuitous and rude assault on the Christian religion'.[2] The people, however, would listen to Cobbett: 'My manner of attack on the accursed system of funding had its charms in its boldness and originality.' The result was a series of letters begun in Newgate and eventually published in book form,[3] which became a best-seller – 150,000 copies were bought, an immense number given the comparatively small reading public and the somewhat arcane nature of the subject.

The House of Commons had set up a Bullion Committee, which proposed that the government should agree to exchange all notes for gold over a two-year period. Cobbett attacked the proposal, though he might have been expected to support a scheme to end paper money. He saw the whole thing, however, as inextricably tied to the National Debt. As long as that remained in existence, any change to gold at the old rates would simply be rewarding the fund-holders, speculators and general parasites. The debt must be paid off and the fund-holders' clutches eased before anything could be done. To those economists who declared that what he was proposing would not just end the paper money system but would ruin the banks, he

offered only cheerful assent. His reply was absolutely typical: it was
not high finance that made a country great and the people happy, but
the eternal values of the land.

> No: the corn and the grass and the trees will grow without
> paper-money: the Banks may all break in a day, and the sun
> will rise the next day, and the lambs will gambol and the birds
> will sing and the carters and country girls will grin at each
> other and all will go on just as if nothing had happened.

He was convinced that the paper money system would collapse
and, when it did, that the government would collapse with it. He
was equally convinced that there would be no real change until it did
collapse. It created a web of self-interest that kept out all reforms
and reformers. This for Cobbett was the great issue of the age, so it
is no surprise to find that he regarded the work in which he spelled
it all out as 'the best of my life'. Paradoxically, it was being shut up
in Newgate that gave him all the time he needed to polish and refine
these ideas.

Newgate itself helped to continue and accelerate the changes in
attitude exemplified by his new views on Paine. There was no doubt
that his treatment at the hands of the law in America coloured his
whole attitude to that country, but all that seemed quite mild
compared with that he had received in his own homeland. So his
position towards the Americans softened. His view of the war also
changed, though he himself would have denied the fact, and in one
sense he would have been right to do so, for in one essential he was
always consistent. He was no internationalist: everything he wrote
and said was purely in the national interest, and had no other
concerns. In fact, he went further, and said that it was not Cobbett
but the government that had altered its policies.

> Not only did the people of France and of Europe see England
> at the head of a league against the French before the name of
> Napoleon was known to us; but they saw us, after he became
> known, and after he became chief of the nation, make peace
> with him, make a treaty of *friendship* with him, and heard us
> say, that we liked *him better than we did the republican
> government*.[4]

He also saw the war as having quite different aims now than those
it had at the start. The defence of Britain was no longer the only
cause, the war was also being fought, for example, to restore land
to the House of Hanover – a cause for which Cobbett could hardly
have been expected to show much enthusiasm given that it was criticism of the Hanoverians that had sent him to prison. And dominat-

ing much of his thinking was the conviction that the war was adding to that National Debt which was the root cause of all the country's calamities. So it was that he was to be found arguing an opposite case to the one he had put with great vehemence only a few years before. He had been an enthusiastic supporter of the Order in Council (p.123), had supported the right of the Navy to stop and search American ships and control American trade. Now he took precisely the opposite view, on the sensible grounds that circumstances had changed. France had dumped its restrictive trade legislation and as the British orders were issued in response to them, there was no reason to keep them. Where before he had seen America in need of British goods, he now saw a prosperous nation growing ever stronger, more and more reliant on its own resources and rapidly developing manufacture. Now a strong America was being provoked to the point of war, a war that would only add more miseries to the British poor and achieve nothing. It seemed to everyone else that there was a contrariness in Cobbett that must be a part of his nature. In 1801, when the whole country had rejoiced in peace, he had called for the continuation of the war: a decade later when there was immense patriotic fervour calling for war and victory, he wanted to start talking peace. He could reason as much as he liked, but it did seem odd, and there were very many who felt that the change was as much in the man himself as in outside circumstances.

No one can doubt that he had changed, and that these changes were more than a reaction to changed circumstances. Yet equally, no one can deny that he was often right. He said the Peace of Amiens would be temporary and so it was; he announced that unless the government did something to come to terms with America there would be a wholly unnecessary war. The government dithered and tinkered and finally rescinded the Orders, but too late: the Americans had declared war a few days earlier. What, however, was new was Cobbett's growing anger at the state of the people, and those he held responsible for it. He was more and more convinced that nothing would be done until the whole corrupt old order was swept aside, and that could only be achieved by reform. The man who had once scornfully tossed the democrats a bone to gnaw, looked very much as if he was about to sit down and share their meals.

For Cobbett in Newgate the real enemy of Britain was not to be found in France or America, but in the government in London. He was now quite ready to praise America, or was if it gave him a chance to lambast the British government. He spoke up for 'the enlightened states of the minds of the whole populations' brought about by universal education, democratic institutions and low taxes. Here was a country whose men could advance by hard work alone, and had no need of influence. Others would find it a hard place to succeed, and that included the full ranks of Cobbett bogey-men: 'sinecure-placemen, pensioners, grantees, venal news-paper writers and reviewers, puffers, parasites and quacks in every department.' He later threw in lawyers, clergymen and big-bellied farmers for good measure.[5] Again we can see the extent of the changes in his thinking in his response to events. When he had first returned to England he had shown nothing but contempt for the rioters demanding cheaper bread. In 1811, a much more widespread movement appeared: Luddism. Few movements have been more misunderstood or more misinterpreted. The name has come down to us as a synonym for mindless opposition to progress, but that is not how the movement began.

It all started with the framework knitters of Nottingham and Leicester. The knitting frame was no new invention. The Revd William Lee of Calverton near Nottingham had first come up with a design for knitting hosiery by machine at the end of the sixteenth century. What was new was the collection of knitters into ever larger workshops, where pay was controlled by their masters. When the knitting frame was first introduced, its use was controlled by Acts of Parliament, which were undoubtedly couched in terms of a pre-industrial age of craftsmen and apprentices. Nevertheless, the laws had not been changed. When the knitters were faced by an illegal increase in the use of child labour and with that an inevitable fall in wages, they looked to the law for redress. The law turned them away. Strikes were ineffectual, as adult workers would have been replaced by children, so the knitters took direct action, breaking, or threatening to break, the machines of all employers who refused them their legal rights. It was an attack on employers, not on the machines from which they all gained their livelihood. And it was highly organized.

> The practice of these men was to associate in parties of from six to sixty, according as circumstances required, under a supposed leader, that was stiled *General Ludd*, who had the absolute command of them, and directed their operations; placing the guards, who were armed with swords, firelocks, etc. in their proper places, while those armed with hammers, axes, &c were ordered to enter the house and demolish the frames; and when the work of mischief was completed, he called over the list of his men, who answered to a particular number, and he then gave a signal for their departure, by discharging a pistol, which implied that *all was right*.[6]

Luddism was unquestionably illegal, but it seemed to the poor and dispossessed to be the only form of protest that offered any real hope of justice. It soon spread to other industrial areas, simply because all industrial workers found that the law, whatever the statute books might say, would always be used against them, never in their favour. A particularly blatant case occurred in Scotland in 1812. The Glasgow weavers had a legal right to a certain minimum wage, which their employers refused to pay. So they took their case to court, and won – won, that is, insofar as the justices agreed that their case was just and they were legally entitled to the wage they claimed. But the court absolutely refused to make their judgement binding on the employers, so rates remained untouched. The weavers went on strike, and now the forces of justice were roused at last; the strike leaders were arrested and brought to trial and imprisoned. Having seen what legal means would achiever it is little wonder that many turned to illegal. To large sections of the populace, the Luddites were heroes.

> No more chant your old rhymes about bold Robin Hood
> His feats I do little admire.
> I'll sing the achievements of General Ludd,
> Now the hero of Nottinghamshire.
> Brave Ludd was to measures of violence unused
> Till his sufferings became so severe,
> That at last to defend his own interests he roused,
> And for the great fight did prepare.
>
> He may censure great Ludd's disrespect for the laws.
> Who ne'er for a moment reflects
> That foul imposition alone was the cause
> Which produced these unhappy effects.
> Let the haughty the humble no longer oppress,
> Then shall Ludd sheathe his conquering sword;
> His grievances instantly meet with redress,
> Then peace shall be quickly restored.[7]

Cobbett would not condone violence, but at least he could now sympathize with the conditions of those for whom violence seemed the only answer. He employed a heavily ironic tone, when comparing the crimes of the poor with the harsh justice they received.

> Far be it from me to attempt to justify people in the commission of unlawful acts. I do not wish to justify the woman, who according to the newspapers, committed *highway robbery* in taking *some potatoes out of a cart at Manchester*, and, who, according to the newspapers, was HANGED FOR IT. I do not pretend to justify her conduct. But there is, I hope, no harm in my expressing my *compassion for her*.[8]

His anger was reserved for those who had driven the poor woman to theft: the government then headed by his old adversary, Spencer Perceval. He was certainly not among those who mourned when John Bellingham, a man with a personal grievance against Perceval and the government, casually walked up to the Prime Minister in the House of Commons, and shot him dead. There was uproar in the country and many saw the event as signalling if not a revolution, then a great change that would bring new men into power. In the taverns of London toasts were drunk to Burdett, Cobbett and the Radicals. The authorities decided on a quick trial, sentence and execution. Within a week of the event, Bellingham was walking to the gallows in front of a huge crowd, and in view of Cobbett's window at Newgate. He described the scene in the *Register*: the crowds standing in the pouring rain, filling all the surrounding streets as Bellingham was led out, then bursting into impromptu shouts – 'God bless you! God bless you! God almighty bless you!' Cobbett drew the moral for his readers: they were not cheering a murderer, but applauding an act of justice against a man who had caused immense suffering throughout the country. Rebellion and revolution had never seemed nearer, but the moment passed. Nothing really changed: Perceval went, and Lord Liverpool took his place. When Cobbett emerged from prison, he found a political world not greatly changed from the one he had left behind two years ago.

Once the euphoria of release had abated, it was time for new assessments. The first wave of Luddism was slowed in 1813, when an exceptionally good harvest reduced prices and reduced the clamour of the hungry. It was to prove no more than a pause before the waves of violence rolled out again with even greater intensity. Cobbett responded by ever more sympathetic pronouncements, and closer identification with the poor. It was time not only to speak up for the working poor, but to speak directly to them. The *Register* was beyond the reach of the poor at 1s. $0\frac{1}{2}$ an issue of which fourpence was tax, and that represented a whole day's pay for many agricultural workers; so he decided to cut out all the lengthy official bulletins and the correspondence and trim it down so that it could all be printed on a single broadsheet. The first obvious advantage was that a broadsheet was not subject to the newspaper tax. As a result, the cheap *Register* could sell for twopence. Another advantage also soon appeared. The new sheet could concentrate on matters that directly affected the poor. He started with an 'Address to the Journeymen and Labourers'.[9] It began with a rousing endorsement of the poor, who for a long time had been accustomed to hear themselves spoken of as ignorant and undeserving at some times, and as a dangerously vicious mob if they objected.

FRIENDS AND FELLOW COUNTRYMEN,
Whatever the Pride of rank, of riches or of scholarship may
have induced some men to believe, or to affect to believe, the
real strength and all the resources of a country, ever have
sprung and ever must spring, from the *labour* of its people;
and hence it is, that this nation, which is so small in numbers
and so poor in climate and soil compared with many others,
has, for many ages, been the most powerful nation in the
world: it is the most industrious, the most laborious, and
therefore, the most powerful. Elegant dresses, superb furniture, stately buildings, fine roads and canals, fleet horses and
carriages, numerous and stout ships, warehouses teeming with
goods; all these, and many other objects that fall under our
view, are so many marks of national wealth and resources.
But all these spring from *labour*. Without the Journeyman and
the labourers none of them could exist; without the assistance
of their hands, the country would be a wilderness, hardly
worth the notice of an invader.

As it is the labour of those who toil which makes a country
abound in resources, so it is the same class of men, who must,
by their arms, secure its safety and uphold its fame. Titles and
immense sums of money have been bestowed upon numerous
Naval and Military Commanders. Without calling the justice
of these in question, we may assert that the victories were
obtained by *you* and your fathers and brothers and sons in co-
operation with those Commanders, who, with *your* aid have
done great and wonderful things; but, who, without that aid,
would have been as impotent as children at the breast.

His arguments were by now familiar enough. He sympathized
with the plight of Luddites and others, but nothing would come of
such methods: what was needed was an end to the present system.
There was nothing wrong with machines as such – if more can be
produced, more can be sold – provided the people are not taxed into
pauperism. What was absolutely new was the implicit suggestion
that the workers were at least as valuable to society as their masters:
without them, there would be no masters and no society. They not
only had a right to a fair share of the wealth they helped produce,
but they had an equal right to a voice in the running of the society
they helped create.

The Address struck an immediate chord – over 40,000 copies
were sold and caused consternation in the establishment. And they
were right to be flustered. Here was something genuinely new, a
newspaper available to all, a voice speaking to all people. If he had
achieved nothing else in life, then this one act of producing a
genuinely popular newspaper would have earned him a place of high

honour. It was *The Courier* which first called the publication 'two penny trash', a title which Cobbett promptly gleefully accepted. *The Times* (circulation 5000) derided the rival and Cobbett, but nothing could stop the trash's growing popularity. Having failed to ridicule it out of existence, the authorities tried to force its failure. *The Times* announced that anyone selling the paper in the streets could be arrested for not having a licence; employers threatened to sack anyone found reading it, publicans were warned that they could lose their licences for even having it on the premises, and magistrates in Shropshire went furthest of all by having a seller actually flogged, all of which only served to increase Cobbett's fame and popularity. He extended his argument to the troubled land of Ireland. In April 1816, Robert Peel, Chief Secretary for Ireland, refused to hold an enquiry into poverty in Ireland on the grounds that everything that could be done had been done, and if the people were poor it was due to their being 'in a state of depravity which baffled description'. This was the undeserving poor all over again, and Cobbett addressed his words as many others were to do later, to the Americans and asked them to consider their own, successful Irish *immigrants*.

> Does the salt air change their nature while they are crossing the seas? What is there in Pennsylvania or New York to subdue and keep down this ferocious disposition: this disposition to combine against 'all law'? Not a single bayonet! Nothing but the constable's staff! How will Mr Peel account for this?[10]

He then dealt with a case cited by Peel to prove the depravity of the Irish. A magistrate had been killed in broad daylight. No one would testify. Even a man condemned to death and offered a pardon refused to speak, and it was his own wife who begged him to remain silent. Cobbett as always, condemned the crime, but placed a quite different interpretation on the woman's actions.

> What in all the world can have placed people in such a state as to induce a woman who dearly loved her husband to beseech him to lose his life on the gallows rather than incur the disgrace of giving evidence against an enemy of the government? ... What must have been the causes of hatred so deep?

It was an attitude very like that he now showed to the Luddites.

However much he might be turning his attention to the new poor of the industrial world, his heart remained in the country and with country people. The poverty that had once been localized, spread throughout Britain, even touching the rich lands of the south east.

> Nothing struck me so forcibly as to find that this was the case
> in the adjoining parish of Tichfield. A parish rich in its soil,
> in its woods, in its wastes, in its inhabitants, consisting of
> many gentlemen of fortune, and of numerous opulent and
> most excellent farmers, and of a neat little town, not
> surpassed in point of appearance by any in England. And yet,
> in this parish, decent, honest, able, and well-behaved labour-
> ers, and those in great numbers, too, were compelled to
> become paupers.[11]

If in all this he sounds the very pattern of a radical, even socialist,
thinker, one has to remember that his goal was often very different
from that of his new associates. Where they dreamed of a new
society, he saw reform as a means of bringing back an older, better
world. And he was still very much the enthusiastic advocate of the
old country ways.

> It is all very well in the way of a joke, to ridicule fox-hunting
> 'Squires and Parsons; but, if the matter be well considered,
> we shall find that these gentlemen are as usefully employed in
> this way as they would be in any other. By following this
> sport, they set an example of adventurous riding to those
> beneath them.

And went on to show that rugged country sports were as good for
the yeoman as they were for the squire.

> A regiment of soldiers all of whom can *ride* and *box* and *shoot*
> must be much more formidable than a regiment of men who
> only know how to dance and sing and act plays.[12]

It might seem perverse, when writing about this stage of
Cobbett's life, to concentrate on home affairs, when Britain was
engaged in one of the greatest wars of its history. But this reflects
Cobbett's own preoccupations. One has the feeling that he almost
regretted that the war was going well. It gave him one less stick
with which to whack the government. And things were going well,
due rather more to horrendous misjudgments made by Napoleon
than to any great virtues on the part of his opponents. He set off on
his disastrous campaigns in Russia, and returned with his army
broken and demoralized. Wellington's campaign in Spain was
proving immensely successful. The European alliances had always
been determined more by self-interest than principle, and now there
was a general feeling that Napoleon's days had ended, Russia,

Prussia, Austria and Britain turned their full forces on the weakened
enemy, with the inevitable result. The peace that saw Napoleon
exiled to Elba seemed to be the end of the matter. Then came the
brief return that brought the true finale at Waterloo. Here was a
cause for celebration far more potent than the Peace of Amiens: no
compromise, but a decisive victory, with an English commander as
the hero. The rejoicing was immense. This time, Cobbett had no
arguments to raise against the coming of peace, but he was wholly
incapable of sharing in the general rejoicing. His own description of
hearing the news of Waterloo shows how far sunk he was in disillusionment. He learned of it from a band of gypsies: 'The blackguard ruffians of men had laurel boughs in their hats; the nasty
ferocious-looking women, with pipes in their jaws, and straddling
along like German trolls, had laurel leaves pinned against their
sides.' He asked one of the men what it was all about.

> he informed me that they were hoisted on account of the
> 'glorious victory obtained by the Duke of Wellington over
> Boney'; that they were furnished them by a good gentleman,
> whose house they had passed the day before, between
> Andover and Botley, and who had given them several pots of
> ale, wherein to drink the Duke's health. 'And to be sure,'
> added he, 'it is glorious news, and we may now hope to see
> the gallon loaf at a groat again, as 'twas in my old father's
> time.' I left this political economist, this 'loyal man and friend
> of social order', to overtake his companions; I went home-
> ward with a mind far from being as completely made up as
> that of the Gipsey and his black-coated and white-wigged
> benefactor.[13]

If Cobbett was ruthless in exposing mediocrity, he was no less
willing to laud greatness. He despised the meanness and pettiness of
many of the men who were now crowing over Napoleon's downfall.
At the time of the exile to Elba, he wrote with moving simplicity of
his sadness not for what was, but for what might have been. If only
Napoleon had remained faithful to the old Republican ideals, he
could have achieved so much. Here Cobbett publicly conceded that
post-Revolutionary France was a better place than it had been under
the monarchy. Napoleon could have carried the process on to the
whole of Europe, but he fell instead, tempted by the old tawdry
dreams of empire and royalty. In 1815, he spelled it out in full in
an open letter to Castlereagh, and he leaves no one in doubt who he
considers the greater man. Castlereagh may be the victor, but he has
no control over posterity.

Do what you will; if you were to thumbscrew him, flog him,

and, at last, cut him to mince-meat, you could do away not
one jot of his military renown; his battles, his victories, his
conquests, his mastership of all the old families of the continent, are recorded in a way never to be forgotten; they form
a portion of the knowledge of mankind; they occupy a seat in
all men's minds; and, as to his *fall*, why, we all fall at last;
only the far greater part of us fall with little more noise than
is occasioned by the fall of a bullock, whereas his fall is the
subject of conversation amongst ... *all the people of the
civilised world*.[14]

He ended in his best flamboyant style, which sets down in a few
short sentences not just his regard for the fallen hero, but the new
spirit that was animating William Cobbett. Who could have imagined that they would be reading a eulogy for 1789 from the pen of
Peter Porcupine? One newspaper, the *Courier*, had declared, 'The
play is over: let us go to supper'. Not so, he says, this is no time
for supper, for the bill has to be paid, that huge debt and the interest in it – 'forty-five millions a year for ever to pay for the play'.
That is no cause for celebration. And do not think for a moment that
anything has finished.

The *first act* is, perhaps, closed. But, that grand revolution
that bright star, which first burst forth in the year 1789, is
still sending forth its light over the world. In that year, feudal
and ecclesiastical tyranny, ignorance, superstition, received
the first heavy blow; they have since received others; and in
spite of all that can now be done in their favour, they are
destined to perish.

The real war, the only war that mattered, was the war against the
system of corruption at home. The battles against Napoleon were at
best a distraction, at worst an attempt by those in power to keep
what they had and gather ever more of the nation's wealth into their
own coffers. This was the war in which he was enlisting, and in
which he would be a leading campaigner for the rest of his life.

15

REFORM AND REPRESSION

The years immediately following his release from Newgate were doubly difficult for Cobbett. He was in a mess financially, and he was in the process of redefining his whole political philosophy. His first priority had to be getting back on a firm financial footing that would keep himself and his hard-pressed family from bankruptcy. He had played the squire at Botley, and now the time had come to retrench, but even when he did so he could not quite rid himself of old habits. He resolved to take a smaller house, but it still had to have the best garden in the country, regardless of cost. Nancy might plead prudence all she wished, but she could never persuade him that certain things were luxuries, not essentials – the gardens and the farm were very much in that category. He intended to be sensible.

> When I left prison in 1812 I thought it prudent to quit so large a house as my own at Botley was, and to lessen all my expenses I therefore took the place of a Mr Kempt, which had a neat little gentleman's house on it, and the best gardens in the country, having nearly three quarters of a mile of high walls, for fruit trees.[1]

He meant well, but what was to be done when faced with these oh-so-tempting walls.

> I laid out more than £150 in purchasing and planting the walls and gardens with all the finest sort of peaches, nectarines, apricots, plums, cherries, pears and apples ... The vines against the walls, which bore nothing scarcely before I went to the place, I made by my management bear half a ton of grapes.

Need one say that the success of his gardening meant as much to him as any victory in a public debate? The boy who had walked to Kew was still present in the figure of the great political radical.

I mention these things to show what pains I took with these gardens, where I grew as great a weight of melons as was grown in any 20 gentlemen's gardens round the country; where I had very large watermelons, which I never saw in England except in my gardens. In short, I never set myself down in any spot in my whole life, without causing fruits and flowers and trees (if there was time) and all the beauties of vegetation to rise up around me.

Nancy was all too aware that the interests of the family coffers was not always at the top of the list when decisions had to be taken involving money. Cobbett relished the role of landowner and community leader. It pleased him immensely that the boy who had followed the plough could give orders to his own ploughmen. It was vanity, but to his everlasting credit he never deserted the cause of those who still worked the land as lowly labourers. But the knowledge of where he had begun made it especially pleasing to him to be able to do real good in the community. He worked with immense energy for the bill to get a turnpike road built that would link Botley to Winchester. When it was completed, it proved a real boon and soon began to show a profit. But when the Treasurer offered Cobbett £70 as his share, he loftily turned it down, preferring to play the part of the great benefactor. Nancy noted, somewhat tartly, that the turnpike trustees had been careful not to offer her the money.[2] Anne was the most level-headed and observant of all the family, and it was she alone who saw the darkness that had come into her father's life – 'the black ox', as she put it, that had trodden on him. The farm and the gardens were a barrier against the realities of a hard world, in which he often felt a lone crusader, and he felt just as isolated in the country, if anything even more so, for here there were few who shared his radical views: 'He took to farming for *something to do*. He was so entirely *by himself* at Botley.' He wrote always with such an air of supreme self-confidence, that one does not think of him as being vulnerable. Yet those few words of Anne do seem to put him in a new perspective. As one looks at his life up to this point it seems to be one of endless change, of moves from place to place, from opinion to opinion; a succession of friendships formed and lost, alliances made and broken. His wife always stood firm at his side when the worst disasters fell, but there was no escaping the fact that their views of life and society were steadily moving apart. Friends such as Sir Francis Burdett had stood by him through the Newgate years, but now, as Cobbett was becoming steadily more radical, Burdett was drifting away in the opposite direction. Paradoxically, Cobbett's views were now far closer to those of Place, yet it was Place who had rejected him at his darkest time. His most trusted aide, Wright, had been proved, at least to his satisfaction, to be no better than a swindling rogue. Who was his friend? In whom could he trust? Anne wrote many times of his anger, but there seems also to have been a sad emptiness somewhere at the heart of his life. He would never acknowledge it, never give in to self-pity. The nearest he came to doing so was when he looked back at this time towards the end of his life.

> My imprisonment gave me, as to money matters, a blow not easily recovered. The Peace came, too, in about twenty months afterward, which was greatly injurious to me as a farmer, and at the same time as a writer; for, in its fit of drunken joy, the nation in general laughed at me.[3]

He did not want to face such bleakness, so he filled every hour with activity. At Botley, it was the farm; in London, new ideas and new alliances. His steady move into the heart of the Radical movement brought him a new colleague and friend, a man as bold and idiosyncratic as himself, Henry 'Orator' Hunt. Another leading Radical, Samuel Bamford, who, it has to be said was no great friend of Hunt's, left a memorable portrait of Hunt in action on the platform.

> His lips were delicately thin and receding ... His eyes were blue or light grey – not very clear nor quick, but rather heavy; except as I afterwards had opportunities for observing, when he was excited in speaking; at which times they seemed to distend and protrude; and if he worked himself furious ... they became blood-streaked, and almost started from their sockets. Then it was that the expression of his lip was to be observed – the kind smile was exchanged for the curl of scorn, or the curse of indignation. His voice was bellowing; his face swollen and flushed, his gripped hand beat as if it were to pulverise; and his whole manner gave token of a painful energy, struggling for utterance.[4]

If one were to direct a play based on the life of William Cobbett, and was dramatizing one of his more rhetorical passages, that would do very well as a pattern for the actor playing the role. They were alike in other ways. They were both big men of commanding presence, and both countrymen – though Hunt was the gentleman-farmer by birth rather than inclination.

They first came to know each other in both roles: Hunt farmed land near Andover in Hampshire, which gave them an immediate point of common interest. And they were soon exchanging political ideas as readily as they were exchanging notes on the price of barley

and treatments for fowl pest. Cobbett, who, in public at least, was
an advocate of strict sexual morality, was prepared to overlook the
fact that Hunt had left his wife and was living with another woman.
Their official collaboration began when Cobbett supported Hunt in
the Bristol election of 1812 and continued afterwards with Hunt
drawing heavily on articles in the *Register* for his speeches. It was
not, however, the easiest of relationships, for Hunt was a good deal
more extreme in his views than his friend ever was – and was
prepared to take any risks and face any dangers in the names of
Radicalism and Reform. Cobbett had seen himself as a one-man
campaigner, a lone champion of the oppressed, daring to say out
loud what others were too scared to whisper. Hunt was louder and
bolder. Cobbett, who may have felt the need for a certain caution
after his earlier experiences, was now encouraged to try and match
him. He went into battle, and no opposition was too great or
impressive for him to face. How many politicians at the end of the
twentieth century would dare to write a paragraph such as this about
the royal family?

> Of all the objects which the Borough-mongers would most
> dread, next after free elections, would certainly be a king of
> sound understanding, good talents, aptness for business, and
> really desirous to promote the honour and happiness of the
> country. And, it must be confessed, that, in this view of the
> matter, they could hardly have been more fortunate than they
> are in the Guelphs, not one of whom, since their being pitched
> upon to fill the throne of England, has ever discovered symp-
> toms of a mind much more than sufficient to qualify the
> possessor for the post of exciseman.[5]

And having disposed of the Crown, he moved on to the Church. Pitt
had left office because of George III's refusal to accept any discussion of Catholic emancipation, or so most commentators would
agree. Not Cobbett; he had a far more sinister theory of conspiracy
and greed.

> The rejection of 'Catholic emancipation' was attributed to the
> '*conscientious* scruples' of the king; and by others to his
> '*obstinacy*'. The poor old man had no more to do with it than
> had any one of the little land turtles in the American woods.
> It has always been foreseen, that, if the Catholics are
> 'indulged', as it is impudently called, any further, they will
> next demand an 'abolition of tithes,' and the Church demesnes
> would follow of course. This is property, altogether, worth
> more annually than a fourth part of the *rent* of all the Land
> and Houses in Ireland. And to whom does this property

belong? Why, to the nobility and a few commoners who own the seats in parliament. Three fourths of the Church Livings are their own *private* property. The rest, and the Bishopricks and other Dignities, they, in fact cause to be filled with their own relations, or by those who serve them, or whom they choose to have appointed. If, then, we find them in real possession of a quarter part of the rental of the kingdom of Ireland, by the means of the existence of a protestant Church, is it wonderful that they do such abominable acts as they notoriously do, in order to support the Church?[6]

Here was keeping up with Hunt with a vengeance. But he would not go as far down the radical road as Hunt was prepared to march.

The Radical movement covered a broad spectrum. At one end were the moderate reformers, such as Burdett, at the other were men such as Thomas Spence. He began as a schoolmaster in Newcastle, but soon devoted himself exclusively to politics. At the heart of his theories was a plan for the nationalization of all the land. Other reformers, notably Place, regarded him as idealistic, unworldly and innocent to the point of naïvety. But he was persistent, and even persecution and two spells in gaol did not deter him, and he pursued his aim with great determination and attracted a small but dedicated following. A group was formed with neither real power nor influence, under the cumbersome name of the Society of Spencean Philanthropists. This was not a group whose ideals were likely to impinge on Cobbett, nor, one would have thought, on the landowning Hunt, but they did, and in a cataclysmic way.

1816 was a year of great distress, exacerbated by atrocious weather. All the Radicals, of whatever persuasion, looked for some form of relief for the sufferers: Cobbett's recipe was in its standard form. There was no need for charity, a word which did not cover poor relief, which was a right: what was needed was a reduction of taxes to revitalize the economy. Meetings were held throughout the country, one of which was organized by the Spenceans at Spa Fields in London. Hunt and Cobbett discussed whether they should attend and Hunt agreed to go to speak on Reform but with no intention of speaking in favour of land nationalization. Cobbett stayed away. It turned out to be a sensible decision, though it was to make no difference in the long term. The meeting went off well enough, with Hunt making one of his impassioned speeches, though there were alarming signs of trouble in the evening when a number of food shops were attacked and bricks were chucked at the *Morning Chronicle* offices, but hardly a riot. At a second meeting on 2 December there was a far greater disturbance, fed by all kind of wild rumours, including one that radical forces had taken over London and the revolution had begun. This was nonsense. As E. P. Thompson wryly noted, the 'revolutionary groups' of the time were guilty of hopeless amateurishness: 'they plotted with home-made grenades and pikes but were unable to erect, in the London streets, a single defended barricade.' This did not stop the authorities screaming treason and revolution.

A secret committee of the House of Lords described the Spa Fields meeting as part of a long conspiracy to overthrow the government, and put part of the blame for the riots on seditious publications, circulating 'at the lowest price'. The names of Cobbett and Hunt had been bandied around at Spa Fields and their health drunk in taverns all over London, and no one doubted that among those seditious cheap papers, the *Two-Penny Trash* held a prime place. The leading Spenceans were arrested amid hysterical reports of immense conspiracies stretching back for many years. It is doubtful if anyone believed that the little band of Spenceans would overturn anything, let alone a government, and Cobbett ridiculed the accusation. 'Now, when your laughing fit is over, let me ask you, whether you ever heard of a *Plot* and *Insurrection* like this before? What an eight years' Plot! A *good* Insurrection!' But ridicule alone was not enough to hold down the mounting anger of the government and their determination to stamp out radicalism. They huffed and puffed that the real object of Reform was

> to infect the minds of all classes of the community ... with a spirit of discontent and disaffection, of insubordination, and contempt of all law, religion, and morality, and to hold out to them the plunder and division of all property as the main object of their efforts.[7]

Cobbett might ridicule but it was clear that there was to be a concerted effort to tie men like Hunt, Cobbett and Place into the same group as the wildest revolutionaries and bundle them all ways to enter political darkness.

These were poisonous times. There were armies of spies and some of the rioting of the time was fomented by *agents provocateurs*. As political clubs sprang up around the country, the spies infiltrated and reported meetings, such as that held at Leicester in October 1816.

> Some one said, We are met to get shut of some of these fellows ... Another answered, 'Let them die in their garters.' Another said, 'Send them to the Tower.' Another said, 'Wait only *two* years' ... Standing armies loudly condemned ... A man named Riley made a motion that 100 copies of Cobbett's *Register* be purchased every week ... It was carried by a show of hands.[8]

Cobbett's name was prominent everywhere, and the importance of the *Register* universally recognized. He was himself as well aware as anyone of his central role in the Radical movement, and was quite certain that he was the prime target for his opponents in the government. If at times he might have seemed almost paranoid, it has to be remembered that he had recently had all too personal experience of what a government could achieve. At first, however, the establishment were content to try and turn his fire with broadsides of their own.

Early in December, Mr Becket, the Under Secretary of State to Lord Sidmouth, said, in answer to a proposition for silencing me in some very atrocious manner, 'No: he must be written down.' Accordingly, up sprang little pamphlets at Norwich, at Romsey, at Oxford, and at many other places, while in London there were several, one of which would not cost less than two thousand guineas in advertising and in large and expensive placards, which were pulled down, or effaced, the hour they were put up, and which were replaced the next hour as one wave succeeds another in the sea. At last, after all other efforts of this kind, came 'Anti-Cobbett', written 'by a Society of Gentlemen', amongst whom, I was told, were Canning, Mr Gifford, and Southey. Not content with advertisements in three hundred newspapers; not content with endless reams of placards, the managers of this concern actually sent out two hundred thousand circular letters, addressed to persons by name, urging them to circulate this work amongst all their tradesmen, farmers, work people, and to give it their strong recommendation; and this they were told was absolutely necessary to prevent bloody revolution.[9]

Argument alone was not winning the battle, so the government turned to the law. Lords Sidmouth and Castlereagh pushed a bill through Parliament which stated as its dubious presumption that 'a traitorous conspiracy' did indeed exist and must be squashed. It decreed that anyone who supported such a plot could be imprisoned on a warrant without bail and without trial. The upholders of law and order had just removed one of the great pillars on which justice rested: Habeas Corpus was no more.

This was followed by a rush of 'gagging acts' which were designed to stifle virtually all criticism. Cobbett was not greatly exaggerating when he wrote that they gave 'absolute power to the Ministers, to take any man that they please, native or foreigner, to put him into a jail that they please, and any dungeon that they please, to treat him there in any manner that they please, to deny access to him by any human being, and to keep him to that state just as long as they please.'[10] They were so written as to cover all forms of dissent from political clubs to newspapers, but Cobbett saw them as aimed primarily at himself and the *Register*. The question now was what was to be done. The first option was: publish and be damned. He could not realistically contemplate that choice, which would have inevitably seen him back in Newgate. Some commentators have suggested there was something cowardly in his backing away from the fight. He explained his own position in a little allegorical story.

A few years before, being at Barnett Fair, I saw a battle going on, arising out of some sudden quarrel, between a Butcher, and the servant of a West-country Grazier. The Butcher, though vastly superior in point of size, finding that he was getting the worst of it, recoiled a step or two, and drew out his knife. Upon the sight of this weapon, the Grazier turned about and ran off till he came up to a Scotchman who was guarding his herd, and out of whose hand the former snatched a good ash stick about four feet long. Having thus got what he called a long arm, he returned to the combat, and, in a very short time, he gave the Butcher a blow upon the wrist which brought his knife to the ground. The Grazier then fell to work with his stick in such a style as I never before witnessed. The Butcher fell down and rolled and kicked; but, he seemed only to change his position in order to insure to every part of his carcase a due share of the penalty of his baseness. After the Grazier had, apparently, tired himself, he was coming away, when, happening to cast his eye upon the knife, he ran back and renewed his basting, exclaiming every now and then, as he caught his breath: 'dra they knife wo't!' till at last the Butcher was so bruised that he was actually unable to stand, or even to get up; and yet, such amongst Englishmen was the abhorrence of foul fighting, that not a soul attempted to interfere, and nobody seemed to pity a man thus unmercifully beaten.[11]

Cobbett was going to play the grazier: 'Nobody called the Grazier a coward because he did not stay to oppose his fists to a pointed and cutting instrument.'

The government made informal overtures to Cobbett, hinting that if he gave up the *Register* and retired to Botley he would be guaranteed freedom from prosecution and compensated for loss of earnings. This would have suited them very well. Had he withdrawn and accepted government pay, he would have been totally discredited: no better than the other placemen and pensioners he had ceaselessly attacked. There was another option: to get out of England, where he faced certain imprisonment, and continue the fight from abroad, or to conclude his own metaphor, 'to combat Corruption while I kept myself out of the reach of her knife.'

Cobbett had by now left Botley and was living permanently in London when he broke the news to the family.[12] 'Mama was asked to come in, and as soon as she was in the room, Papa, his two hands on her shoulders, sd 'Nancy, I must go to America'. She said, 'Billy, I'm glad of it', for terror was beginning to seize upon every body.' The family was to be split again, for Nancy and the three girls and younger boys, the latest addition to the family, Richard, born in 1814, were to stay in England. Cobbett, with William and John, set off for Liverpool on 22 March 1817, and five days later they boarded ship for New York.

When he had last crossed the Atlantic, returning to England in triumph, he had succeeded in quarrelling with his fellow passengers. That much at least had not changed. He was disgusted by salesmen on board carrying goods with insignia that flattered Americans at the expense of the British. There was a man carrying samples of decorated cloth from a Manchester manufacturer.

The British crown was represented as stricken down by the beak of the American Eagle, which was waving its wings over it in triumph. Could you, taking the motive into view, imagine anything more base than this, on the part of the English manufacturer? Another ruffian, a crockery-ware man, had furnished engravings on them representing an old crazy lion, all skin and bones, with an American standing with his foot on his neck.[13]

Cobbett, however, was not going to allow anything to disrupt his routine, whether it was disagreeable passengers or alarming weather.

In all respects that can be named our passage was disagreeable; and, upon one occasion, very perilous from lightning which struck the ship twice, shivered two of the masts, killed a man, struck several people slightly, between two of whom I was sitting without at all feeling the blow.[14]

Through it all he was always first to rise; then washed and dressed, he called out his sons and together they cleaned their own cabins. When the boys suffered from seasickness he nursed them. With only one tumbler of water a day to wash in, they still managed to keep themselves clean and their cabins as fresh 'as one of our fields at Botley'. As a result they arrived in New York on 5 May fit and ready for a new life. What was not yet clear was where he would go, what he could do and how he could continue the fight. It was all very well talking about a long stick, but this was a very long stick indeed. However one looked at matters, there were difficulties ahead, and difficult decisions to be taken. Could he really make a contribution to political debate, when there would necessarily be a gap of weeks between an event occurring in Britain, the news reaching America and comments being sent back to England for publication? More importantly, was this to be a temporary exile or a permanent move, and how long would the family have to remain apart? These questions were not all satisfactorily resolved.

16

LIFE IN AMERICA

In many ways it must have been a immense relief to be back in America, free for a time at least from immediate political pressure and quite free of the fears of persecution. Much as he regretted being driven out of England and forcibly divided from his wife and five of the children, Cobbett was generally in a benign mood. From the first, everything pleased him. He soon left New York and set off down Long Island, arriving at a country inn, then some thirteen miles from the city although today it would be just beyond the district of Queens. Here he found everything to be a delight, and nothing pleased him better than the food. If he watched his diet in Newgate, for fear of getting fat, there were no such inhibitions here.

> We had smoked fish, chops, butter, and eggs for breakfast, with bread, crackers, sweet cakes; and, when I say that we had such and such things, I do not mean that we had them for show, or just enough to smell to; but in loads. Not an egg, but a dish full of eggs. Not a snip of meat or of fish, but a plate full. Lump sugar for our tea and coffee; not broke into little bits the size of a hazelnut, but in good thumping pieces. For dinner we had the finest of fish, bass, mackerel, lobsters; of meat, lamb, veal, ham, etc. Asparagus in plenty, apple pies (though in the middle of May). And for all this an excellent cider to drink, with the kindest and most obliging treatment, on the part of the Landlord and Landlady and their sons and daughters, we paid no more than twenty-two shillings and sixpence a week.[1]

He had to add a little moralizing, noting the unfailing goodwill of the landlady and the trust in the honesty of their neighbours, which allowed doors to be left unlocked. He put it down to 'good government ... which took so little from the people in taxes that they had the means of happiness fully left in their hands.'

This was only a stopping place until he found a farm to rent, Hyde Park, at nearby North Hempstead. It was a good house but in need of a great deal of repair and he was made warmly welcome by his new neighbours. He even found a Mr and Mrs Churcher to take on as servants, who had come out from Hampshire, and their soft country accents almost convinced him he was back home: 'only the fine sun, the fine roads, the fine fruits, and the happy labourers told me that I was not.' All that was needed to make this place a paradise was to have it settled entirely by Englishmen, and to have all his family to share in it. The boys saw his contentment, but did not share in it.

> The Governor and I are just this moment come in from before the House, it is 10-clock, we have been looking down the beautiful Avenues of High trees before the House, and He wishing he could see little Dick trotting down them–We have been landed just one month today, four weeks, and I declare it seems to me four years.[2]

The boys were also a good deal less enthusiastic about the American way of life and their neighbours than their father was. William tried the local debating society, but was decidedly unimpressed by the level of argument, declaring with all the assurance of an eighteen-year old that they were one and all 'dull dogs'. He was rather more taken with the trotting races, which provided good entertainment, and with horse-racing in general, though he was highly critical of the American jockeys' riding style, leaning back in the saddle. In fact, neither of them found much to enjoy, and were becoming increasingly disillusioned with the farming life as well. One can sympathize with them. They were working on the farm for no pay–though the father had made over the proceeds of the book he was working on. They did not any longer enjoy the life, and were already thinking of making professional careers for themselves, and both were, in time, to become lawyers. It was a great disappointment to Cobbett, and one of the first signs that he could not keep up his role of family dictator for ever.

He, however, remained in good humour. He found rich farms and labourers with full bellies. He had his criticisms, and could not refrain from comparing what he saw with the very best to be found in England: post and rail fences were a poor alternative to thick-set hedges; there were flowers a plenty, but none as fine as those to be found in a Hampshire meadow, and though the birds were as beautiful they did not sing as well. He would not have been Cobbett if he was not sure there were ways in which matters could be improved, notably by attending to the advice and following the example of William Cobbett. Much as he admired the farms, he was quite shocked by the gardens. He followed his English practice of establishing good vegetable plots with highly satisfactory results.

A print entitled 'Transatlantic Luxury' showing Cobbett writing to Hunt from his Long Island farm (The British Museum)

'How I have got this broccoli I must explain in my *Gardener's Guide*; for write one I must. I can never leave this country without an attempt to make every farmer a gardener.'[3] He was especially gleeful, when he ignored his neighbour's advice on how things were done in America, and followed his own ways. They left their fowl out all year, but he decided to convert the coach house into a hen-house, and the hens showed their appreciation by snuggling cosily in there during the winter, and providing a clutch of chickens as early as March. Cobbett crowed as loudly as his own rooster: '*Young chickens* – I hear of no other in the neighbourhood. This is the effect of my *warm fowl-house!*'[4]

He also brought his old hobby-horse out for a canter in the New World. He had a long-lived and deep distaste for the potato, which he regarded as being foisted on the poor in place of a more wholesome diet. In America it was naturally in common use, but he insisted on regarding this as an inexplicable quirk of fashion, and drew the unliterary comparison with a taste for Milton and Shakespeare. Give Cobbett his due: when he disliked something he never kept his opinion to himself nor feared ridicule. *Paradise Lost* was 'barbarian trash' and 'outrageously offensive to reason' and 'if one of your relations were to write a letter in the same strain, you would send him to a mad-house and take his estate'. Shakespeare was even worse, always immoral and often lewd. Cobbett would have been an appropriate subject for a twentieth-century stream-of-consciousness novel, for one thing inevitably led to another, and he would find nothing incongruous in starting with a discussion of a vegetable plot and ending with literary criticism.

There were also more direct criticisms of the American life-style, and he was particularly outraged by their habit of 'tippling' – 'You can hardly go into any man's house, without being asked to drink wine, or spirits, even *in the morning* ,,, There is no remedy but the introduction of *beer*.'[5] He had to note, however, that his attempt to convince others of the folly of their ways met with no great success.

> My driver, who is a tavern-keeper himself, would have been a very pleasant companion, if he had not drunk so much spirits on the road. This is the *great misfortune* of America! As we were going up a hill very slowly, I could perceive him looking very hard at my cheek for some time. At last, he said: 'I am wondering, Sir, to see you look so *fresh* and so *young*, considering what you have gone through in the world'; though I cannot imagine *how* he learnt who I was. 'I'll tell you,' said I, 'how I have contrived the thing. I rise early, go to bed early, eat sparingly, never drink any thing stronger than small beer, shave once a day, and wash my hands and face clean three times a day, at the very least.' He said, that was *too much* to think of doing.

Yet it seems that for every critical comment he made at this time he was ready with a word of praise. Shooting, for example, was a subject on which he could rhapsodize. In America there were not the same private estates, but everyone could shoot what they liked, where they liked with no game laws to hinder them and no game-keepers to haul them in front of the magistrates. And what game there was! – 'Think of it! A hundred brace of wood-cocks a day!'[6]

Cobbett had spent so long in criticizing everything around him, that it is a pleasure to share with him his delight in the New World.

> And then, to see a free country for once, and to see every labourer with plenty to eat and drink! Think of *that*! And never to see the hang-dog face of a tax-gatherer! Think of *that!* No Alien Acts here. No long-sworded and whiskered captains. No judges escorted from town to town and sitting under a guard of Dragoons.[7]

He could still attack his old enemies with as much vigour as ever, but now he had something positive to say as well. He was no more reconciled to Church of England parsons than he had been before, especially not to Baker of Botley, and he was still opposed to compulsory titles. Now, however, as he addressed a letter to old friends back home, he could bounce out a cheery message, that he was living in a land with no titles.

> But, my Botley neighbours, you will exclaim, 'No *tithes*! Why, then, there can be no *Churches* and no *Parsons*! The people must know nothing of God or Devil; and must all go to hell!' By no means, my friends–there are plenty of Churches.[8]

The difference here was that the church was amply supported by those who chose to do so.

> Why cannot you reverence God, without Baker and his wife and children eating up a tenth part of the corn and milk and eggs and lambs and pigs and calves that are produced in Botley parish! The Parsons in this country, are supported by those who choose to employ them.

There is a sense of ease about Cobbett in America, a feeling that this was one of the few occasions in his life when he could really relax. On the whole, he was perfectly happy on his Long Island farm, and when he did travel it was to see old friends and to immerse himself in a society with which at this stage in his life – though one could not expect him to remain in such a happy state – he felt perfectly at home. He went back to once-despised Philadelphia. It was here that he had once been roughly handled, but it was also here that he had found his truer friends who had been willing to offer unqualified support during the bleak Newgate years. He found people after his own heart, honest and unpretentious, sober and industrious.

> Here I am among the thick of the Quakers, whose houses and families pleased me so much formerly, and which pleasure is all now revived. Here all is ease, plenty, and *cheerfulness*. These people are never *giggling*, and never in *low-spirits*. Their minds, like their dress are simple and strong. Their kindness is shown more in acts than in words. Let others say what they will, I have uniformly found those whom I have intimately known of this sect, sincere and upright men; and I verily believe, that all those charges of hypocrisy and craft, that we hear against Quakers, arise from a feeling of *envy*:

envy inspired by seeing them possessed of such abundance of
all those things, which are the fair fruits of care, industry,
economy, sobriety, and order, and which are justly forbidden
to the drunkard, the glutton, the prodigal, and the lazy.[9]

Even disasters did not disturb his equanimity. There was a fire in
the house and he set up camp in the grounds, in a sort of makeshift
tent lined with old newspapers. He wrote on a table made out of a
slab of mahogany supported on timbers so green that they put out
shoots and leaves. He slept out in the open on home-made palliasses
and on the whole thoroughly enjoyed himself. It was a curious time
in his life, and one on which he never dwelt in a direct fashion. So
one is reduced to speculation. There is a great deal in what he did
write about this time which strikes that careful note that had not
really been heard since he had visited the old farmstead in Canada.
Cobbett's restlessness and belligerence seemed often to define his
whole character, but there were times when he seemed to yearn for
a calmer, more settled life. Canada was certainly one such time, and
here was another, but it was at best an interlude, at worst a fantas-
tical dream. There was no chance of his reverting to his other
persona, that of William Cobbett, untroubled farmer and son of the
soil. Too many things had happened in his life. But underlying
much of his American writing is a sense of longing for that other,
simpler life. There was an inward battle between famous William
Cobbett, leader of political opinion, and plain Billy Cobbett, farmer
and landowner. For a time, at least, it seemed that the latter might
be winning through, but it was not to be. The pleasures of the
simple life were constantly at odds with the anger and the passions
of the political world, and were losing the battle. Paradoxically, it
was in America that he was most alone. His sons were already tiring
of agriculture, but he still had at least a notion that he might make
a new life. Nancy and the children came over, and it is not known
whether this was intended to be a short visit, a long stay, or the start
of a permanent shift. In the event, they only remained for a short
time, leaving only James behind with his father. It must have been
obvious that the Cobbetts were not going to be permanently resident
in America.

One of the frustrations of writing about the family is the lack of
direct evidence about Nancy's views. It is especially annoying when
one comes to crucial points such as this, when one is reduced to
deduction and speculation. Nancy's early experiences of America
had not been happy ones, for there was no denying they had
suffered badly in their court cases, and the time there had been
coloured by personal tragedy, with their death of their baby. They
had left America harassed by the courts and creditors, and returned
to England to be praised and lauded by the rich and famous. One

should always remember that she was not courted by William Cobbett, famous author, but by Sergeant Cobbett of the 84th. All she would have expected was a life not very different from that of her mother. Instead, she had been swept along by his immense energy and drive, and had been faced, in bewildering succession, by triumph and tragedy. The low points had come when she was reaching the end of the first stay in America, the deliriously happy highs had appeared when they had returned to England. Why should she want to go back to the start, making a new life in an alien land? Why could they not regain the days of their triumph? She looked at America, viewed the ramshackle farm, and she and her brood headed for home.

And what of Cobbett in all this? Could he really have regained the Arcadia he had lost and, reluctantly, discarded in Canada? It does not seem likely. He was enjoying the best of worlds for a time. He had his farm and was luxuriating in the lush ease of a comfortable life in the open air, where he needed nothing more than a roof over his head, even one made out of old newspapers, and good food in his stomach. At the same time he still had the *Register* as an organ for preaching, teaching and even more enjoyable lambasting his enemies. It could not last: each month he was away removed him further from the mainstream of political life. Had Nancy wanted to stay in America, would things have been different? There is no answer, only hints. Cobbett was still a man of obsessions, and it is impossible to imagine him letting them go. Yet, at the same time, there seemed a calmness about his everyday life that had not been there for some time, and was not to be repeated until he went on his Rural Rides. He even found time to sit back and admire the beauty of young American women – a habit which Nancy had firmly suppressed on their previous visit. In any case, whatever he might have wished, there was no real chance of his staying on. That, however, did not mean he could not make the best of his time there. He had leisure to write, without the nightmare of constant deadlines. Some commentators notably Daniel Green,[10] have seen these years as a time for rehearsing tired old arguments, a time of diminished powers. I cannot agree. These are the days when he was at liberty to spread himself, and he used that liberty to produce a series of sustained arguments, systematically demolishing the theories built up by his own opponents. At the end of his American period he set out his own philosophy of literary merit. The standard he set was, admittedly, one well designed to put himself in the front rank, but it succinctly lays out just what he thinks writing can and should do, and in this time he triumphantly met his own criteria. The piece itself, combining rational argument with vituperation intended to wound, is a fine example of what he judged to be successful writing. A sophisticated critic would dismiss it as simplistic, but Cobbett had

already fired two barrels at point-blank range into the same critic's
face before he got to the main fight.

> I know well that those who carry on the trade of critics are a
> base and hireling crew, more corrupt, perhaps, than any other
> set of beings in the world. The only critics that I look to are
> the public; and my mode of estimating a writing, is by the
> *effect* which it produces. If there be two writings, having the
> accomplishment of the same object in view, that writing
> which soonest and most completely accomplishes its object, is
> the best of the two. I listen to nothing about *style* as it is
> called; or anything else. As the man, who soonest and best
> weaves a yard of cloth, is the best weaver; so, the man who
> soonest and best accomplishes an object with his pen, is the
> best writer.[11]

The argument is fatuous. If followed to a logical conclusion, the
bigot penning inflammatory rhetoric to move a rush to – shall we –
say attack the home of a publisher who opposed a popular peace
treaty is a better writer than one who eloquently and reasonably
pleads for tolerance. But Cobbett believed in the need to write for a
purpose, and if that meant dispensing with nuances and eloquent
flourishes, then that was fine by him. And that is why so many of
the most memorable examples of his prose show him on the attack,
mercilessly ripping in with blows, regardless of the niceties of rules
and regulations. His métier was akin the single-stick fighter,
hammering away until the blood ran an inch thick, not that of the
cowardly foreigner armed with the delicate feint and thrust of a thin,
lethal blade.

During the American period, he found time to turn all his formidable powers against his most hated enemies, and there were few he
regarded with greater scorn than the Revd. Thomas Malthus. The
Malthusian argument was by no means absurd then – nor, indeed, is
it absurd now – stating that population was expanding more rapidly
than the means of feeding it, a process which would ultimately end
in disaster. It could be countered much as Cobbett's arguments
against paper money could be countered, by pointing out that there
was no logic in extrapolating a trend forever into the future. In the
one case, prosperity might be such as to provide funds to cover the
national debt; in the second, improvements in agriculture could well
be significant and produce sufficient to feed all families. What is
interesting is in seeing how one man set up what he saw as a sound
scientific argument, only to be attacked by the other on very different, socio-economic grounds. We think, today, that the notion that
a scientific theory might be conditioned by social factors is a brand
new idea. Cobbett was saying the same thing at the start of the last

century. He also added another factor which seems sadly lacking from much modern debate: passion. He set the emotional temperature high before he began any arguments.[12]

PARSON:
I have during my life detested many men; but never any one so much as you. Your book on Population contains matter more offensive to my feelings even than that of the Dungeon Bill. It could have sprung from no mind not capable of dictating acts of greater cruelty than any recorded in the history of the massacre of St Bartholomew. Priests have, in all ages, been remarkable for cool and deliberate and unrelenting cruelty; but it seems to have been reserved for the Church of England to produce one who has a just claim to the atrocious pre-eminence. No assemblage of words can give an appropriate designation of you; and, therefore, as being the single word which best suits the character of such a man, I call you *Parson*, which, amongst other meanings, includes that of Boroughmonger tool.

Now everyone knew how things stood, and the reader could look forward to the literary equivalent of a bare-knuckle scrap. Cobbett rehearsed the more obvious arguments against Malthus: he was positing as a natural law a theory that said the poor were growing in number, and their numbers must be reduced or they would starve. But, says Cobbett, it was not the case in Britain. The problem was not one of a lack of resources but of some having a very great deal indeed, while others had far too little. It was not a problem of nature, but of society that pandered to the greed of a few at the expense of the many. The natural law was the one that gives men and women the drive to get together and have children.

Your muddled parson's head has led you into confusion here. The *law of nature* bids a man *not to starve* in a land of plenty, and forbids his being punished for taking food wherever he can find it. Your law of nature is sitting at Westminster, to make the labourer pay taxes, to make him fight for the safety of the land, to bind him in allegiance, and when he is poor and hungry, to cast him off to starve, or to hang him if he takes food to save his life! That is your law of nature; that is a parson's law of nature. I am glad, however, that you blundered upon the law of nature; because it is the very ground on which I mean to start in endeavouring clearly to establish the *rights of the poor*.

I have quoted the passage at length because it seems to exemplify

Cobbett's ability to be direct and forthright, to set matters out in a way that all his readers could understand. It shows a typical literary device of repetition for emphasis – 'That is your law of nature; that is a parson's law of nature.' He goes on to elaborate his views, but very near the beginning he sets out the main thrust with great clarity. Something else comes through the whole piece, that anger which his daughter said never left him for long after Newgate. His was a passion that could easily overflow into quite crude invective, which is no doubt very reprehensible, but makes for immensely lively reading. That was surely the source of much of Cobbett's success: the passion which smokes off the page. And it is this passion which keeps us reading today. Here he is at his most vituperative, attacking not just Malthus, but the whole of the church and its clergy.

> The bare idea of *a law* to punish a labourer and artisan for *marrying*; the bare idea is enough to fill one with indignation and horror. But when this is moulded into a distinct proposal and strong recommendation we can hardly find patience sufficient to restrain us from breaking out into a volley of curses on the head of the proposer, be he who he may. What, then, can describe our feelings, when we find that this proposition does not come from an *eunuch*; no, nor from a *hermit*; no, nor from a man who has condemned *himself* to a life of *celibacy*; but from a *priest* of a church, the origin of which was the incontinence of its clergy, who represented views of chastity as amongst the damnable errors of the Church of Rome, and have, accordingly, fully indulged themselves in carnal enjoyments: what can describe our feelings, when we find that the proposition comes from a priest of this luxurious, this voluptuous, this sensual fraternity, who, with all their piety, were unable to devote their own vessels to the Lord!

There are interesting signs here of things to come, including the idea that he would develop later that the Church of England was little better than the illegal supplanter of the older Church of Rome. At this time, he was still totally opposed to most of the nonconformist sects, largely because he was disgusted by the hypocrisy of men like Wilberforce, who preached Methodist morality while supporting a government that allowed poverty at home to go unaided – and punished those who spoke up for the poor.

He was, as we have seen (p.169), still favourably disposed to the Quakers, but he increasingly saw much of organized religion as being at the service of the oppressors. These were ideas he would work out later. For the time being, he had other literary projects in hand. As well as his political works he had started writing his promised guide to gardening for Americans,[13] and an English grammar,[14] the proceeds from which were to go to his sons in lieu of the pay they had not received on the farm. It was written for boys such as he had been, born poor and who needed to read and write well if they were to rise in the world. He understood his readership and knew that a little humour and a little politicking would help make the lessons more palatable. So, for example, he defined the use of the word 'moderate', or rather its misuse: 'Amongst a select society of empty heads, "moderate reform" has long been a fashionable expression; an expression which has been well criticized by asking the gentlemen who use it how they would like to obtain *moderate justice* in a court of law, or to meet with *moderate chastity* in a wife.' One is rather reminded of some of the definitions in Johnson's Dictionary. Cobbett was not in awe of the great lexicographer, and even pulled him up on bad use of the language. Johnson somewhere wrote that he spent a day 'in viewing a seat and gardens', where he should have written 'a seat and its gardens'. Parts may have been amusing, but there was a good deal of nitpicking as well. He certainly would not have been in agreement with Johnson on the value of a classical education.

> The cause of the use of this false appellation, 'learned languages' is this, that those who teach them in England have, in consequence of their teaching, *very large estates in house and land*, which are public property, but which are, by abuse, seized on by, and used for the sole benefit of those teachers, who are the relations or dependents of the all-devouring aristocracy.

Though both might have agreed with Cobbett's assertion that a knowledge of Latin and Greek 'does not prevent men from writing bad English'.

At the same time, he was musing over the man he had so roundly dismissed during his last stay on this side of the Atlantic, Tom Paine. Having first been impressed by his views on paper money, he had become very close to him in other ideas as well, and was considering writing his own life of Paine. He now felt that the reformer deserved a better resting place than 'a little hole under the grass and weeds of an obscure farm in America'. In February 1819, he wrote an article published in Britain which proposed that Parliament should pass an Act authorizing his body to be brought back to England and buried with all the honour due to one who had opposed Pitt and the System. It was hardly a serious suggestion, and his readers would have seen it as a typical piece of Cobbett Rhetoric. Yet seven months later he set out with friends to that obscure farm at New Rochelle, just north of New York. There at dawn they took up Paine's coffin and brought it back to New York. Cobbett was due to return to England and Paine was to travel with him. He was aware that some would, to say the least, find this piece of grave-robbing offensive, and would attack him. He wrote a little doggerel for himself, mocking those who would certainly soon be the mockers.[15]

> An old Monk and a Jew
> Made a devil to do
> About raising the bones of Tom Paine;
> But they could not agree,
> As you'll presently see,
> How to make the offender be slain.
>
> Says the Monk, I'll continue
> To have him burnt alive,
> Who has cruelly thus robb'd the maggot
> Says the Jew, I've no doubt,
> We can stone his soul out:
> But talk not of flames and of faggot.

He was soon to find must how many people thought his actions downright ludicrous. He certainly would not have enjoyed being the butt of a poetical joke himself, particularly one that was a good deal better written than his own doggerel and hit harder home – Byron's famous verse sent to Moore:

> In digging up your bones, Tom Paine,
> Will Cobbett has done well;
> You'll visit him on earth again,
> He'll visit you in hell.

Cobbett's plans for returning to England were somewhat delayed by one of those episodic outbreaks of yellow fever that afflicted New York at the time. 'The yellow fever rages to a great degree. We keep out of town, about $3\frac{1}{2}$ miles.' The *Amity,* on which he had planned to sail had been laden with cargo from the storehouses which 'were the very seat of contagion'.[16] The ship was, however, being cleared out of a 'clean' port to avoid quarantine regulations in Liverpool. Cobbett made the deception known to the authorities, and waited for another ship. He eventually sailed on the *Hercules* on 30 October 1819, taking Paine with him, but leaving James behind to wind up Cobbett's business affairs. It was a heavy burden to lay on the teenage boy, and he was left in the fever-infected district, with only the Churcher family as company. His father very soon had cause to regret his decision, for the ship had scarcely left for

England before his son became dangerously ill, Cobbett wrote with obvious deep affection, no doubt strengthened by remorse:

> My dearest little son,
>
> My heart seems lead within me! My dear, kind, good child, God almighty bless you. You dear health is all I can now think of. Pray, think for nothing in comparison with *that*. Get you good clothes, good fires, good warm bedding.... .
>
> I know that Mrs Churcher is devoted to you as well as to all of us; and I have done all in my power to show how grateful I shall be for her attention *to you*. I have told her that *all* I care for on this side the water is *your health*. My dear, dear child, if you were to die, I should die. I always loved you in a peculiar manner; and your dutiful, affectionate, sober, and thoughtful deportment, which alone with me, has made an impression in my heart never to be effaced.[17]

Nevertheless, the rest of the letter still directs him as to what he should do about butchering pigs and advises on how to treat a badly behaved employee. A Cobbett was expected to behave like a Cobbett, even if he did have the fever. Meanwhile, William Cobbett was returning to England and what was to prove one of the most hectic periods of his life.

HOME AGAIN

The period of Cobbett's absence in America had been one of immense turbulence in Britain. The Gagging Acts had done what they could to remove all criticism of the government, but though they had succeeded in uprooting one particularly thorny specimen, other native species were flourishing. New Radical publications were led by the *Black Dwarf*, with William Hone's *Reformists' Register* and T. Sherwin's journal rather curiously entitled *Political Register*. The *Black Dwarf* was notably more radical than Cobbett's *Register,* and the editor, T. J. Wooler, had taken issue with Cobbett even before he left over the matter of political clubs. The latter had never changed his mind about the question of the great virtue of public debate and the dangers of secretive clubs and societies. Wooler was adamant that clubs were essential in establishing organizations just as their opponents used their clubs for the same purpose. He argued, forcibly and convincingly, that the government opposed the radical clubs precisely because they were effective, and took Cobbett to task for aiding their common economy.

> Sir, you are playing very mischievously with the cause of reform, by thus giving its opponents your sanction to the worst arguments against it.... . The man who would *divide* the public, in effect *destroys the public mind*.[1]

With Cobbett gone, the other periodicals continued the fight, never changing their tone to fit the demands of the new Acts – and not being prosecuted either. He would not have been too surprised at that, since he had claimed from the start that the whole of the legislation was aimed directly at him, and certainly when the Acts were passed, the *Register* was far and away the most influential publication the Radicals had, and arguably the most important paper of any party of any persuasion. Yet it did look very much as if Cobbett had been overhasty, and the new journals thrived at the expense of the old *Register* and its absentee owner. He continued to

attack the Gagging Acts and the Spy System from a distance, and in
the latter case was even prepared to admit that he had been wrong,
a rare occurrence in his writings. Whatever his views on the government, he had still not been prepared to believe that they would
employ men to infiltrate workers' organisations where they would
then act as *agents provocateurs* to incite violence as a way of entrap-
ping the leaders. Now, however, he was able to point out that he,
who throughout the early Luddite actions had called for peaceful
protest, had been vilified and banished – and why was that? Because
the authorities did not want to argue a case but preferred to beat
their opponents down – the machine breaking must go on: 'Those
were the things, which these ruffians wanted to see continued;
because against acts like these all good men would say, that *force*
would be employed.'[2]

Matters in Britain steadily worsened as the government hysteria
mounted, seeing armed conspiracies and revolutionary plans in
every dispute and demonstration. There were insurrectionary forces
and men who saw actual revolution as the only means of redress for
the poor. The leaders moved from district to district, wholly
unaware that one of the principal figures and the most enthusiastic
proposer of violence was the man who was to become famous under
the name, 'Oliver the Spy'. The one genuine attempt at armed uprising was led by Jeremiah Brandreth and began at Pentridge, in the
industrial area of Derbyshire, and the man at Brandreth's side
throughout the planning was Oliver. There seems little doubt that
the authorities could have stepped in before a rather pathetic band of
ill-armed men marched off, convinced that there was to be a general
uprising involving hundreds of thousands of men. It never
happened, and the inevitable fiasco occurred, with Brandreth and
twenty-five others accused of High Treason, which was the result
the government wanted. By the time the case came to trial, Oliver's
past was widely known – though his true identity was still a secret
– and his role as instigator was generally accepted. But that was not
the case brought out in court. Instead the defence lawyer, Cross –
not the prosecution but the defence – laid it all on Brandreth being
an innocent subverted by 'the most mischievous publications that
were ever put into the hands of men'. And what were these revolutionary tracts? Cobbett's *Address to the Journeymen and Labourers*.
There was an explosion of anger across the Atlantic against those
who would put the blame on Cobbett and the injured author for once
did not even add his usual caveat of deploring acts of violence. And
that in spite of the fact that on this occasion an innocent man had
died, shot by Brandreth. Cobbett had never been angrier.

THERE was not a man amongst them who did not know, and
well know, that it was OLIVER, who was the immediate

cause of the rising in Derbyshire. There was not a man amongst them who did not know, that the discontent was created by the tyrannical Bills, and that it was worked into a rising by OLIVER. And yet, they could *unanimously* pass an address, which ascribed it to me and to others, who had taken an active part in the cause of Reform; they could, thus, unanimously, vote this, which originated in the false and base mind of LAWYER CROSS, whose *defence*, to make the thing complete, is complimented by that wonderful patriot, SIR SAMUEL ROMILLY, who, as if that were not enough, called the Derby men, *poor, ignorant creatures*. Faith, SIR SAMUEL was deceived; for the Derby men knew very well what they were about; they were betrayed; they were deceived; but they knew what they were about very well, and all the grounds upon which they proceeded. They knew well, that according to law as well as reason, *Resistance of Oppression* is a RIGHT, and not a CRIME. They *might* be wrong, as to whether oppression did, or did not, exist; but, in their *doctrine* they were perfectly right. Their measures, too, were efficient, had they not been *betrayed*. Even here their humanity was the cause of their defeat. OLIVER was suspected, and so strongly suspected *that a rope*, as I have been assured, *was ready prepared for his neck*; and, he would have carried intelligence to the Devil at once, instead of to LORD SIDMOUTH.[3]

The whole affair was, in its way, a triumph for the government. They were able to do what they had wanted to do, deal firmly with an actual revolutionary. At the same time they went some way to discredit constitutional reformists by associating them with violence, and so were able to justify the harshness of the law. But whatever gains they might have made in swinging public opinion away from the Radical movement were lost at St Peter's Fields, Manchester on 16 August 1819, in what was to become known as the Peterloo Massacre. The main outline of the events is well known. A well-publicized meeting had been called to hear speakers led by Hunt on the subject of the reform of Parliament, a not unreasonable subject for discussion in what was by now one of the most powerful industrial towns in the country. Manchester was totally unrepresented in Parliament, while a rotten borough might send two members, representing no one at all. That this was a gross injustice was the great and logically unassailable argument of all the Radicals. For many years it needed only the sight of the most infamous of all the rotten boroughs to send Cobbett into a rage. Some years after Peterloo, he was riding towards Salisbury when he reached Old Sarum, which had once been a prosperous town with a hilltop castle, but of which

J. R. Smith's portrait of Cobbett in Newgate. (Museum of Farnham)

Cobbett's return with Paine's bones was much ridiculed. Here the Americans dance to see him gone, while the radicals wait to greet him under the banner of riot. Napoleon, in exile, looks on bemused. (British Museum)

Cobbett looks down scornfully on the mob at the Coventry husting (I. R. Cruikshank). (British Library)

Nancy Cobbett in around 1830. (Museum of Farnham)

Queen Caroline by James Lonsdale. She is shown holding the letter written for her by Cobbett. (Guildhall Art Gallery)

A sketch of Cobbett painted opposite the title page of the English Grammar of 1824. (Mrs Janice Robinson)

Cobbett in the clothes he wore for the 1831 trial. (Southampton City Heritage Services)

Dancing display for visitors in the school room at New Lanark with the 'thinly clad girls' that shocked Cobbett. (New Lanark Conservation Trust)

The 'accursed hill' of Old Sarum painted by Constable around 1830 when Cobbett passed it on one of his Rural Rides. (V&A Picture Library)

A typical chop-stick pausing for a midday snack. (Bodleian Library, Oxford)

A chopstick sharp-ening his scythe. (Bodleian Library, Oxford)

Normandy Farm, Ash, where Cobbett died. (Museum of Farnham)

there was now nothing left as the whole population had moved to a new site centuries ago, the city of Salisbury.

> I resolved to ride over this ACCURSED HILL. As I was going up a field towards it, I met a man going home from work. I asked him how he *got on*. He said, very badly. I asked him what was the cause of it. He said the *hard times*. 'What *times*,' said I; 'was there ever a finer summer, a finer harvest, and is there not an *old* wheat-rick in every farm-yard?' 'Ah!' said he, '*they* make it bad for poor people, for all that.' '*They*?' said I, 'who is *they*?' He was silent. 'Oh, no no! my friend,' said I, 'it is not *they*: it is that ACCURSED HILL that has robbed you of the supper that you ought to find smoking on the table when you get home.' I gave him the price of a pot of beer, and on I went, leaving the poor dejected assemblage of skin and bone to wonder at my words.[4]

There was a rational case to be made, and the organizers of the meeting wished to argue it rationally. They went to immense trouble to ensure that there was no violence by getting the main delegates together in advance to drill them so that they could march in an orderly fashion to the meeting place, following their own home-made banners. This they did under the eyes of the local magistrates. But it was only when Hunt rose to speak that they gave the order to arrest him. A troop of mounted yeomen, middle-class part-time soldiers, was sent into the huge crowd, by then estimated at nearly 100,000 men, women and children. Then, when it was obvious that the yeomen were hopelessly disorganized, a band of hussars was sent in to clear a way. There was no way for such a crowd to make an easy passage for the troops: those close to hand had nowhere to go to get out of the way. So infantry and yeomanry set about them with sabres. There was now a wholesale panic and between the thrusting, slashing blades and the crush of the crowd, nine men and two women were killed and uncounted hundreds injured.

The facts are not in dispute: questions of responsibility have been argued about ever since. The very orderliness of the marching contingents, intended to show that the working people of the area could behave responsibly, is said to have alarmed the magistrates, who read a military significance into the event. Did they see it as the start of a revolution begun by unarmed 'troops' who had brought their wives and children with them? Attempts were quickly made to blacken the names of those who died. Home Office papers recorded that one of the women who had died was a dangerous character on the grounds that someone thought they had heard her curse at a curate.[5] It was said that the magistrates had acted on their own and that there was no responsibility that could be laid at the government's door. But Lord Sidmouth sent a letter to the magistrates and militia, praising them for their prompt action in the 'preservation of the public tranquillity'.

The government badly misjudged the public mood. Even *The Times* was moved to doubt the morality of Peterloo–a view not unconnected with the fact that their reporter had been taken as an agitator and roughly treated. It was left to the poet Shelley to sum up the disgust and bitterness of many with his famous couplet.

> I met Murder on the way–
> He had a mask like Castlereagh

He continued the poem[6] with an openly revolutionary call to the masses:

> Rise like lions after slumber
> In unvanquishable number,
> Shake your chains to earth like dew
> Which in sleep had fallen on you –
> Ye are many – they are few.

It sounded more reasonable after Peterloo. The Radicals were no longer bloodthirsty insurrectionists but heroes of the poor. Hunt, released on bail, returned to London to ecstatic crowds. If ever there was an opportunity for Cobbett to wield his pen in a popular cause this was it. But, sadly, he knew nothing of it until his ship arrived in Liverpool on 21 November 1819.

He returned to a situation which was in many ways very different from the one he had left behind. New Radical leaders were coming forward, the old slipping into obscurity. Sir Francis Burdett was the most notable of those who fell away from the cause. He was the most moderate of moderate reformers, and the more he saw the pace of change quickening, the less he enjoyed the sight. He looked for a little change, a tinkering with the mechanism of government, not the construction of a whole new political machine. When the Gagging Bills were being debated in Parliament, he remained silent and left the House before he could be called on to second a motion of Lord Cochrane's opposing them. This naturally dismayed his Radical colleagues, including Cobbett in America. But he was in a difficult position, for Burdett had lent him substantial sums to help pay off his debts. He decided to leave personal matters aside, and joined in the attacks on his old friend. This seemed most ungrateful to Burdett, and when Cobbett wrote to him about the debts in November 1817, he chose to misconstrue it. It looks very much like an opportunity was seized to show Cobbett in a bad light, for he quoted part of the letter out of context. Cobbett had written to say that he could not, for the moment, pay off many of his English debts, as his finances had been ruined by a despotic government's unjust actions. But in Burdett's case he made it absolutely clear that 'no pains shall be spared by me to obtain the means of paying it as soon as possible'. This unequivocal statement was totally ignored, and Burdett widely publicized the fact that Cobbett was refusing to pay his debt to him. It was clear in 1817 that Burdett was moving away from the cause of reform, and the two men would have soon found their political opinions irreconcilable, but the affair of the debt meant that instead of a seemly disagreement, there was a rancorous, and very public, row. The result was that, on his return, Cobbett found himself wholly aligned with what many saw as the extremists of the reform movement. He was soon to discover what those who had stayed behind already knew, that the public support he would find would be immense, and that the official opposition he would encounter would be more bitter than anything he had previously experienced. The welcome he received was a great encouragement to him.

> After twenty-one days' sailing over a sea almost as smooth as the beautiful Long Island Lake, I arrived at Liverpool, on a Sunday evening, in November 1819. We were not permitted to land until Monday about two o'clock. There had been a great multitude assembled on the wharf the whole of the day; and, when I landed, I was received with cheers and with shakings of the hand, which made me feel that I was once again in England.[7]

His first plan had been to head to Manchester, but the authorities had no intention of allowing him anywhere near that town, where the memory of Peterloo was still so fresh, so he turned for Warrington. There a crowd gathered, and he gave a short address, and in return they gave him a memorably warm reception. 'My hand yet reminds me of the hard squeezes I had from them; and how great a favourite of mine a hard squeeze of the hand is!' He continued on to Coventry and when he left on 1 December he was followed by a large crowd, and he drew up at last when he was a mile from the city centre.

> Having drawn the chaise up in a suitable position, and having placed myself upon the outside of the chaise on the footboard, I found myself surrounded by several thousands of persons of both sexes, the females forming a very beautiful battalion, many of them with children in their arms, in one part of the circle, not mixed among the men, while other

persons were running towards us, not only along the track of
the chaise from the city, but in all directions over the fields
and meadows. This was not a meeting. There had been
nothing done to call it together. It was spontaneous, it was
collected of itself, by the mere sound of my name. Never did
I behold any spectacle in my whole life that gave me so much
pleasure as this.[8]

He finally came back home to Botley, and an equally gratifying
reception as described by Anne.

The men took the horses out of the chaise and brought them
home, filling the air with most tremendous shouts, which
must have grated the Parsons' ear, who was one amongst the
throng. He had been for several days previous poking about
in the village, telling the people they would do very wrong in
doing such honour as they intended to P's [Papa's] return. He
told them they would draw the devil into Botley for *beer*, and
they civilly told him they would 'dra him out for nothen'. But
one man 'told me to us head' (so Punch says) that so far from
expecting beer from Mr Cobbett they would rather give him
some if he should want it. When Papa got out of the chaise at
our door, poor Jurd burst into tears, and I could have cried
too to hear the hearty cheers the men gave.[9]

It was all most gratifying, but a good deal less pleasant was the
roasting he received in the government press. Quite what he thought
he was going to do with Tom Paine's bones is not at all clear. He
probably envisaged some great ceremonial burial attended by
speeches from all the Radical leaders. The Radical leaders simply
found the whole affair embarrassing, as caricatures appeared everywhere and the newspapers reworked old arguments against him and
added a few new ones. One newspaper editorial must have stung
him very hard, for he cut it out and kept it – not something he
normally did when he was mocked and opposed. The piece began by
reminding readers of the William Cobbett who had previously
arrived from America:

Supposing him sincere, he was welcomed by eminent and
honourable men. Forfeiting all pretensions to political consis-
tency and personal truth, he, however, soon apostatized from
the opinions he held before, merged at once into the very mire
of Jacobinism.[10]

Now, even worse, he had come back with 'his remains whose living
he had treated with the utmost scorn'. The piece concluded that

'nothing so horrible and insane' had ever happened before. Bitter criticism, but all the more damning because it was largely true, and the best that Cobbett could now hope was that the Paine affair would be soon forgotten. In that, he was to be disappointed.

Cobbett had three main objectives at this time. He wanted to re-establish the life-style he had enjoyed before the American interlude, and that meant settling back into Botley. He absolutely insisted on the whole family joining him there, a gesture of solidarity to show that they supported his aims. Everything there seemed to be just as he hoped, with the farm 'in very neat order' and his beloved trees thriving: 'The American trees are of finer growth than any that I ever saw in America of the same age.'[11] There was, however, one problem that would have to be addressed immediately, if they were all going to come back, refurbish the big house and live in it. They would need money. He had debts, and everyone suddenly seemed very keen to collect, and his main source of income was again under threat.

The cheap *Register* had been a huge success, rather too much so as far as the government was concerned. Lord Liverpool, with his two principal ministers, hustled legislation through Parliament that December, a group of laws that became known only as the Six Acts, more infamously self-serving than even the gagging laws had been. There were laws against mass meetings, magistrates were given new rights to search private homes, the already severe laws on seditious libel were made even fiercer and the defence against them made more difficult. But the one that would most grievously affect Cobbett was a brand new newspaper tax, to cover any publication of two sheets or more, or one costing less than sixpence that contained news or political comment. That sweeping definition certainly included the cheap *Register* which had a fourpenny tax slapped on it. That took the price up to sixpence, three times the old price. It was a measure blatantly designed to silence Cobbett, and, for once, his view that the government was aiming legislation specifically at himself was wholly justified. His reaction was absolutely typical of his self-belief and confidence. Assailed by creditors, his income drastically reduced – he estimated the new tax cut the circulation of the *Register* to less than a quarter of what it had been – he started a new daily, *Cobbett's Evening Post*. It began on 29 January 1820 and was a disaster. People would pay to read William Cobbett, but the William Cobbett who was given the running of the *Post* was the son not the father. The latter suddenly found he had other matters to demand his attentions. The third aim he had set was to regain his position among the leading Radicals of the day, and now the opportunity seemed to have arrived.

The first day of publication of the new paper was also the last day of the reign of George III, and his death brought an immediate

General Election. Cobbett announced that he was to stand for Coventry, where he had been received with such enthusiasm. He was, as always, determined to avoid all bribery, but was facing a far less scrupulous opposition. He was, in any case, faced with huge expenses. A bizarre electoral law allowed all freemen of Coventry who wanted to vote to charge the expense of going to the polls to the candidate they supported. A Coventry man living in London was thus entitled to send Cobbett a bill for £15 for the privilege of having him vote for him. By the end of the election, the bill could have run to thousands but Cobbett persevered. He tried to raise election funds through the *Register* but met with only partial success. He had managed to choose a borough which was almost uniquely expensive to fight, and one which was notoriously corrupt. But he was determined to fight what Anne, with a good deal of justification, called 'this horrid election'. Everything that could go wrong did.

He set off with Anne on 28 February and arrived the next day at Dunchurch, just south of Rugby. There they received alarming news.

> A band of rich ruffians had leagued together against me. They had got together a parcel of men, whom they made partly drunk, and whom they gave orders to go out, meet me at a bridge about a mile from the city, and if I refused to return to London, to fling me over the bridge.
>
> While we were deliberating on what course to pursue a gentleman arrived with intelligence, that the enemy had drawn up, rank and file, in the city; that they were marching off with fourteen banners waving over their heads, and with drum and music in their front; and that they had not reached the outside of the city, when our friends sallied forth upon them, took away their banners, staved in their drums, dispersed them in all directions, and set off to meet me.[12]

That seemed a hopeful beginning, but the threat of violence had not been removed, only temporarily set aside. He was forced to travel bare-headed, standing on the footboard of the chaise, through the cold, damp day, as a result of which he lost his voice. This was, to say the least, bad news for an orator. All through the campaign, the violence reached appalling levels. The house of the Serjeant family, where the Cobbetts were lodging, was repeatedly attacked and his supporters assaulted whenever they were incautious enough to go out alone. But all that was nothing compared to the start of the poll itself on 8 March. Cobbett seemed quite well placed at the end of the first day, but that brought out the worst of the violence on the second day.

On Thursday the savages came well fed and well supplied, all
the day long, with gin and brandy, brought out to them in
glass bottles, and hauled about from one to another. I, that
day, saw about twenty of my voters actually torn away from
the polling-place, and ripped up behind, and stripped of their
coats. During the afternoon, several fresh bands of savages
arrived from the country; so that, by the hours of closing the
poll, an immense multitude of these wretches, roaring like
wolves, and foaming with rage and drink, were collected
round the Booth.

As I went out of the Booth I had to pass through bands of
savages; and I was scarcely among them, when they began an
endeavour to press me down. I got many blows in the sides,
and, if I had been either a short or weak man, I would have
been pressed under foot and inevitably killed. However, the
crowd took a sway toward a row of houses, standing on a
pavement above the level of the area of the open street. With
a good deal of difficulty I reached the pavement keeping my
feet. I had to fight with my right hand. I had to strike back-
handed. One of the sharp corners of my snuff-box, which
stuck out beyond the bottom of my little finger, did good
service. It cut noses and eyes at a famous rate, and assisted
mainly in securing my safe arrival on the raised pavement.
Just at this time one of the savages exclaimed: 'Damn him!
I'll rip him up!' He was running his hand into his breeches
pocket, apparently to take out his knife, but I drew up my
right leg, armed with a new and sharp gallashe over my boot,
and dealt the ripping savage so delightful a blow, just between
his two eyes, that he fell back upon his followers. For this I
should certainly have been killed in a few moments, had not
Mr Frank Serjeant made shift to get along, by the side of the
houses, to the spot where I was. Getting to me, he turned
round, saying, 'Follow me, sir!' and, beating back three or
four so as to make them press upon others behind them, the
whole body turned about, while he with thumps on some, with
kicks bestowed on others, set the body on a sway toward the
house, at which we arrived safely.[13]

Cobbett refused to be provoked by the violence, but in the end there
was a concerted attack on Serjeant's house.

They first dashed in the upper-room windows; next they
pulled down the shutters of the ground-floor room. Then they
broke into the house passage by forcing the door; and while
the main body were entering in front, others were (as we
could see from the window of our room) scaling a wall to get

into the house in the rear. I, who was very ill with a cold, was
sitting in my bedroom with my daughter Nancy. Some gentlemen came running up for our poker and tongs. One or two
took station at the top of the stairs; while I fixed the bedstead
in a way to let the door open no wider than to admit one man
only at a time, and stood with a sword. I had pulled off my
coat, and was prepared to give with a clear conscience as
hearty a thrust as was ever given by man.

The attackers had been repulsed in what in Cobbett's own account
sounds an heroic affair. Anne's plainer account sounds as if it might
be nearer the truth.

It was a frightful time to us even in the house for at one time
a savage mob burst in, calling out for the 'miscreant' to kill
him. We were in the bed-room and heard the noise, and we
pushed the bedhead against the door and hid the fire-irons.
Down stairs they were so frightened that Mrs Serjeant ran
down into the cellar with the knives.[14]

The intimidation was ugly but effective and Cobbett came bottom
of the poll. It had cost him a great deal physically and financially,
and at the end there was nothing to show for it. Cobbett and Anne
retired to Meriden, but were even driven away from there; and were
finally forced to return to London.

To Cobbett, the whole affair was quite clear. The mob was paid
by his opponents, kept more or less permanently befuddled with gin
and given every encouragement to be as violent as they wished.

The ferocity of the Savages, this day, was such as I thought
human beings incapable of. I have seen parcels of drunken
soldiers. I have seen gangs of furious and drunken sailors. I
have seen roaring mobs in London. I have seen whole bands
of Indians, drunk with rum. But, never did my eyes behold
any thing in human shape so furious, so odiously, so diaboli-
cally ferocious, as those bands of villains, hired, paid, fed,
drenched by the Rich Ruffians of Coventry.[15]

There were other factors at work as well, and the affair was not
without the ironies that so often surface in the Cobbett story. Back
in 1791, the 'Church and King' rioters of Birmingham had seen
Joseph Priestley's house destroyed and he himself had fled to
America. There he had been fiercely attacked for his 'atheism' and
Painite Jacobinism. Now the press had been daily denouncing
Priestley's denouncer for just the same crimes. And the evidence
they brought forward was the box of bones carried back from

America. The mob could shout 'Atheist' and 'Jacobin' at Cobbett, as they had once done at Priestley.

Cobbett and his daughter made their dejected way back home. He was ill, and stayed only for a short time in Botley before returning to London to start putting his literary career back together again. There was an urgent need to do something, for his creditors were becoming ever more insistent. He was ready to make every sacrifice to pay off his debts, but others counselled taking advantage of the law and becoming officially bankrupt. It is certainly difficult to see how he could sensibly have hoped to pay off the massive debts, which amounted to £28,000. The family, often inclined to bicker when things went well, were always stalwart when threatened from outside. James was as indignant and fiery as his father himself, though he was notably more sensible when it came to deciding what should be done.

> He has been so ill-used by several persons, to whom he owed money, that he will shortly be compelled to *surrender himself*, and to yield up all the property he has, though he could so easily clear off all the claims upon him, and though he is anxious to do it to the last farthing. But, the spiteful villains, urged on, no doubt, by the Government, will not give him anytime at all, and, therefore he must take the usual protection of the law, and be either a *bankrupt* or an *insolvent*; and we all insist that he ought to do it as well as other men who do it and live well on the *reserve* whereas he will *reserve nothing*; he will *give up all*; and rely on his and our future exertions for support.[16]

Anne, as always, was keen to take up the fight, and typically confident that the family would pull through as it always had: 'we can all work and work well, and cheerfully too.'[17] Meanwhile as the bankruptcy formalities went ahead, and their assets were frozen, they had to endure a miserable existence in Lambeth – 'a small, dirty place in a dirty road', according to Anne. There they lived in conditions as near to real poverty as they had ever known, on a diet that seemed to consist merely of cauliflower and salad. As the bankruptcy came through and was made official, and it was clear that the terms were reasonable, a new lightness of spirit fed through them all. The event which had seemed so traumatic had happened, and far from being broken they could look forward to a new start.

> This country is full of traitors and villains; and Papa has been deceived by them all – He is, however, now *free* from them all; and he will do well for him and ourselves, in spite of all that can be done against him ... Mama never looked better

or prettier in her life, and as she sees a prospect of Papa's being in a state of tranquillity as to all embarrassments her mind is more at ease than it has been for years. While all the rest of us are at work she and Dick must prattle together and amuse one another.[18]

They seem to have been thinking of a return to America, but in the event there was no need. For Cobbett found exactly what he needed to boost his morale – a new cause to fight. He had declared that he would never have got through the difficult period without Nancy's help, and now, for once, here was a cause of which she heartily approved – not the plight of workers, but the problems of the Queen.

QUEEN AND COUNTRY

Royal scandals, then as now, excite immense popular interest, and no affair has ever been as scandalous, nor conducted with such blistering public acrimony, as that of Queen Caroline. The story ran for years. It began back in the 1780s when Prince George, bloated, dissolute, gluttonous, but with, it has to be said, a certain panache notably absent in the other Hanoverians, secretly married a widow, Mrs Fitzherbert. To marry a commoner was bad enough, but she was a Catholic and for the heir to the throne this was not just unwise but actually illegal. So that matter quickly came to an end. But by 1795 the Prince was so deeply in debt that he was forced into a marriage with his cousin, Princess Caroline of Brunswick. It was like many dynastic marriages, arranged with no thought at all for the personal preference of the parties. George's character had not changed over the years and Caroline seems to have been one of those genial bouncy girls with a good heart but a poor head. They stayed together just long enough for Caroline to give birth to a daughter, Princess Caroline, at which point the Prince suggested that they might both be happier if they led separate lives. And so they did.

The Prince's life-style after marriage was every bit as flamboyant as it had been before, and it was largely tolerated because people liked the show and the pomp that surrounded him. Stylish immodesty was more interesting than dour conformity. It was well known that the affair with Mrs Fitzherbert had not ended, but she was only one among many young ladies who received the royal favours. It might have seemed a bit rich in the circumstances for George's faction to start accusing Caroline of immorality but in 1806 they suddenly sprang the charge that she had given birth to an illegitimate child. A 'secret' commission which everyone seemed to know about dismissed the claim as totally baseless, but the affair did nothing to improve relations between the pair. Caroline certainly had her own circle of friends, including a number of personable young men, and the rumours of infidelity continued. It all remained in the realm of rumour and innuendo until Cobbett published details

of the whole story in 1813, and publication brought immense
sympathy for Caroline and condemnation of the Prince.

Caroline could have stayed in England, but by then she had had
enough and, with war in Europe at an end, she left for the continent,
where she had a more or less open affair with a gaudy Italian,
Bartolomeo Bergami. Then George III died, and she became officially Queen of England. But her husband would have none of it,
declared she was no queen and demanded a divorce. The government promptly backed their new king and set in motion what was,
in effect, an attempt to do his bidding without so much as even the
pretence of even-handed justice. Reports were sent back from Italy,
discussed in secret and decisions taken without the Queen being
given any right of reply. Castlereagh in the Commons and Liverpool
in the Lords declared that the case was proved that she had an adul-
terous relationship with Bergami and introduced a Bill of Pains and
Penalties which declared that she was no longer wife to George IV
and no longer Queen. A Bill, however, is not an Act, and Caroline's
case was taken up by Cobbett.

He could have had many reasons for rushing to Caroline's
defence. The blatant injustice of the proceedings was bound to touch
a chord with a man who had himself been so badly treated by the
same government. He had a genuine and hearty dislike for the king
and everything he stood for, and it would have done no harm to the
Radical cause to have a friend at court. There were many ready to
come forward with advice to Caroline, some urging her to reach a
settlement and get what she could from a deal; others arguing that
she should stay and fight for her full rights. Needless to say,
Cobbett was foremost among the latter.

> The humble individual, who hopes that the goodness of his
> motives will apologize for his addressing this paper to the
> Queen, most deeply regrets that her Majesty cannot be truly
> and fully informed of the sentiments of the people respecting
> her Majesty's case. He ventures to inform her Majesty, that it
> is the universal hope that she will not suffer herself to be
> induced to accept of any *compromises*; but, that she will insist
> on the full enjoyment of all her rights; that being the only
> thing which can completely put to silence the calumnious
> aspersions of her indefatigable and implacable enemies.[1]

It was his advice that she eventually decided to take.

The government had made much of Caroline's affair with
Bergami and he persuaded her that the best way to fight back was to
make the whole story of George's own far more numerous affairs
public. A letter was published in *The Times* under Caroline's name,
but the secret author was Cobbett. On publication, the Cobbetts

were understandably nervous, but they were soon to enjoy a comic
interlude, which Anne recounted with relish. A friend arrived with
the paper, 'and read it out with great feeling. Papa and I affecting
wonder and admiration the while. He the writer, I the copier.'[2] The
letter had a great effect, and public opinion was kept firmly behind
Caroline, not least by a series of well-argued pieces in the *Register*
pointing out the weaknesses in the government case. He was called
to the Court and the family understandably preened itself over the
honour, though Anne brought her own sense of humour to the
account.

> Papa has been to court and kissed the Queen's hand, and a
> very pretty little hand he says it is. We made the gentleman
> dress himself very smart, and powder his head, and I assure
> you he cut a very different appearance to what he used to do
> on Long Island with the straw hat slouched over his eyes.

The Queen was, by a chaplain's report, suitably impressed.

> Well now, if that is Mr C no wonder such fine writing comes
> from him, he is the finest man I have seen since I came to
> England, aye, aye, if there be only a few such men as that to
> stand by me, I shall not care for the Lords.

But Anne could not resist adding.

> All of which the Govr says is nothing more than bare justice
> for he says he saw no man there anything to compare to
> himself; you know the gentleman has by no means a
> contemptible notion of his person.[3]

By November it was all over, and the government was forced to
bow to public opinion. It was a hugely popular result, and as Anne
wrote to her brother, '*her* triumph is *ours*'. And indeed it was, a
triumph for the whole Radical movement, and an overwhelming
demonstration of the real power of public opinion, even against this
most repressive government. Anne, ever prepared to be optimistic,
was now almost overwhelmed by enthusiasm for the present and
hope for the future. Even John, usually more cautious, was full of
it all.

> The Governor's power is monstrous now, and they all feel it.
> He has pointed out their difficulties to them and they plainly
> see that they can do nothing without giving the people all they
> want.[4]

It was true, everything was going well, even when his old enemies the libel lawyers were back at work. All through the Caroline affair, Cobbett had been attacking her legal adviser, Henry Brougham, who had proposed compromise. He had, as usual, gone way over the top, and had written what even Anne called 'a furious libel', and he was once again in court conducting his own defence. The action went against him, but instead of the £5000 Brougham had demanded, the jury awarded forty shillings.

But there were still family matters to be sorted out. Nancy wanted James back from America, largely because she was worried he might take an American wife. Anne wanted him back for other reasons, to take over the running of their affairs.

> *you* are at all events so far unlike the Govr as to look after the needful, and not feel so great a disgust to ugly figures as to run a risk of being robbed of money rather than face them.[5]

It was very frustrating for Anne, who had worked so hard for her father, done so much to help him, and yet had to be content with a subsidiary female role. In this letter she let her real feelings show.

> the boys are sore about my grumblings that the money is not sufficiently looked after. Papa says very candidly that he cannot take up his time or turn his thoughts to the keeping accounts, and the boys, who have the same dislike, think they have as good an excuse for not looking after these matters. Not so. If I were a man, I would take it upon my own shoulders, very soon, and I know the Govr would feel mightily obliged to me.

Anyone reading the family papers can only agree. She had wit, style and flair, matched to the true Cobbett enthusiasm and obstinacy. In another age, she would have been a formidable figure, but was destined to be always kept in a subsidiary role. The best she could hope for was reflected glory, though she deserved far more. She was fond of her mother but they had little in common. Nancy remained rather primly conservative, while Anne was as enthusiastic in pressing for parliamentary reform as her father. Whether she also secretly wished not just for male suffrage but for female suffrage as well is not known, but she could point to her own career as an example of why it was deserved. She was aware of her own worth, often scathing about her brothers, and quite dismissive on the subject of her younger sister. She described Ellen as 'monstrous slow to move, and who says it is because she is so big.'[6] And that as far as Ellen was concerned was that. But even though she felt that there was more she could have done, she was always willing to

throw her energies into what needed to be done. And that meant
fighting causes old and new – and addressing the perennial problem
of refilling the family coffers.

In January 1821, the scattered family was fully reunited in hired
rooms at Brompton, with 'three shillings and a few halfpence' and
money had to be borrowed to pay for the paper to print the *Register*.
But somehow the money was found for yet another move, this time
to a house in Kensington, with a large garden, pigs, five cows, and
a pigeon house of which 'Dick was the grand pigeon master'. The
Register began to thrive again and Cobbett rode high on the popularity that followed on from the Caroline affair. Now he turned all
his attention to one of the great problems of the day, the distressed
state of the farm labourers. It was a subject he had never really left
and never would.

The main thrust of his argument had not changed a great deal
over the years. The country was worn down by the high level of
taxation, most of the money going to causes of which he heartily
disapproved. It went to pay for the ever-increasing costs of government itself. It paid for the huge amount of interest that went out
each year as a result of the national debt, without reducing the debt
itself by so much as a penny. It went to pay for the standing army,
still in place even though the war had ended, with its incompetent
aristocratic officers and troops stationed all around the country, not
to meet the threat of foreign invasion, but to keep down the people
who clamoured for reform. And last, but enjoying a special place in
the Cobbett demonology, were the tribes of pernicious placemen
and holders of sinecures. Nothing would be done to restore prosperity, while the country staggered under this deadweight. To these
old arguments was added the new factor that had appeared in 1819,
when Robert Peel had presented his Bill to make all paper money
translatable into gold between 1820 and 1823.

When Peel first introduced his Bill, Cobbett declared that it
could only lead to ruin, and if his prediction proved wrong then his
enemies were at liberty to place him on a gridiron and roast him.
Now he brought the gridiron out to taunt the government, using it
as a masthead decoration on the *Register*.[7]

> Please to look at the head of this Register; look at the Motto;
> look at the *Gridiron!* and then please to pay attention to what
> I am about to say.
>
> The time is now come; it is actually arrived, when I am
> called upon to *begin* to do justice to *myself*; and, not only to
> myself, but to many thousands of zealous and faithful
> *Disciples*, who have long adopted my political opinions, and
> many of whom have had to endure no small quantity of
> reproach, injustice and persecution on that account. Our day

is, at last, come; and, please God, we will enjoy it.

He then proceeded to repeat the words he had written in America in 1818, when the proposal for a gradual change from paper to gold was first put forward.

> if the paper be drawn in *gradually*, the approach of the misery and ruin and uproar will be gradual; but they will *approach*. The want of employment will come on gradually and gently; but *it will come*. The convulsion will be the end of the scene; but there will *be a convulsion*. Ruin and starvation will come by degrees; but ruin and starvation *will come*.

The gridiron was to stay in place and Cobbett was to hammer home the same message, year in, year out. He not only saw the country heading for ultimate ruin, but argued strongly that the process was already well under way. It is notoriously difficult to quantify the distress of the age, but there are statistics which suggest strongly that things were worse for a great many. For example, records were kept of vagrants counted passing along the Great North Road. In the early years of the century there were around 500, but in 1820 the numbers had risen to 7000.[8] The government, whether it agreed with Cobbett's pessimistic view of the economy or not, had in any case a ready-made justification for poverty, which they were always poised to promote: poverty was not a result of political mismanagement, but part of the divine order of things. Here was a new object for Cobbett's derision. He had a particular loathing for the Methodists who preached servility on earth, with the promise of rewards in heaven. And no one was more deeply loathed on this account than William Wilberforce. His argument was that the poor should be taught 'that their more lowly path has been allotted to them by the hand of God; that it is their part faithfully to discharge its duties and contentedly to bear its inconveniences.'[9] To Cobbett, this was cant, an excuse for the rich to stay rich, while the poor starved, on the dubious grounds that this was a plan devised not by men but by God himself. As a later hymn of 1848 put it

> The rich man in his castle,
> The poor man at his gate;
> God makes them high or lowly
> And ordered their estate.

Cobbett was not going to have God blamed for the actions of men. What the poor wanted was good food, a roof over their heads and warm clothes, and they were not going to get them through

Methodist sermons and 'stupid and indignant things, called Religious Tracts'. He produced his own version to counteract them, what he called his sermons, the first of which appeared in March 1823, and were then collected together in book form.[10] There were predictable attacks on old targets, such as plural livings and the clergy who neglect their duty. He proved to have as good a command of biblical rhetoric as any ranting preacher.

> The Prophet Zechariah, in the words of a part of my text, has, manifestly, such a result in his eye when he cries, 'Woe on the shepherd that *leaveth* his flock.' And the Prophet Ezekiel, in the other parts of my text, clearly means to impress the same thing on the minds of the priests. What, indeed, can be more just, than that *woe* should fall upon those, who '*eat the fat* and clothe themselves with the *wool*', but who feed not the flock.

He also put out positive messages in direct opposition to the Wilberforce line of the duty of the labourer to meekly comply with whatever his employer decides. Cobbett turned the argument round – labour was not just another commodity to be bought and sold.

> It is altogether personal. It is inseparable from the body of the labourer; and cannot be considered as an article to be cheapened, without any regard being had to the well-being of the person who has to perform it.

Whatever the duty of the poor might be in Wilberforce's religion, there was a more compassionate one argued in Cobbett's, one that placed a duty on the rich not to show charity, which he heartily despised, but to display justice. At the same time as the Sermons began to appear, he also began publishing a monthly part-work that eventually became *Cottage Economy*.[11] Its lengthy sub-title set out the practical use to which he hoped it would be put: 'Containing Information Relating to the Brewing of Beer, Making of Bread, Keeping of Cows, Pigs, Bees, Ewes, Goats, Poultry and Rabbits, and Relative to Other Matters Deemed Useful in the Conducting of the Affairs of a Labourer's Family.'

It is an absolutely typical Cobbett piece of writing. He never for a moment saw it as simply a set of useful hints on practical husbandry, though these were a very important part of the work – and few things made him happier in later years than to meet a cottager he had helped to a better life. Just as important, however, was the political message that poverty was a fundamental wrong which should not be tolerated in a just society.

A nation is made powerful and to be honoured in the world, not so much by the number of its people as by the ability and character of that people; and the ability and character of a people depend, in a great measure, upon the economy of the several families ... There never yet was, and never will be, a nation permanently great, consisting, for the greater part, of wretched and miserable families.

He should not be thought of as a sort of nineteenth-century advocate of the welfare state, for that he certainly was not. He put great stress on individual responsibility. 'I despise the man that is poor and contented; for such content is a certain proof of a base disposition, a disposition which is the enemy of all industry, all exertion, all love of independence.' If a man and woman chose to have a large family, instead of a small one, then they would have to work harder to pay for it. What he was fighting was a system of government in which a man could work to exhaustion and still be kept in poverty. His views on educating the poor would today seem hopelessly reactionary rather than revolutionary. Education for him has nothing to do with 'book learning' but should be a practical matter of passing on the skills needed to earn a living.

And is it not much more rational for parents to be employed in teaching their children how to cultivate a garden, to feed and rear animals, to make bread, beer, bacon, butter, and cheese, and to be able to do these things for themselves, or for others, than to leave them to prowl about the lanes and commons, or to mope at the heels of some crafty, sleek-headed pretend saint, who while he extracts the last penny from their pockets, bids them be contented with their misery, and promises them, in exchange for their pence, ever lasting glory in the world to come?

This might be thought a touch rich from the plough boy who had just shaken the hand of the Queen of England, thanks to book learning. It fits however with Cobbett's wider view, his dream of a return to an older, better way of life, where the land gave riches enough for everyone to be kept clear of poverty. It was part of the vision of old England, ruled by the seasons, where hardy sports brought pleasure not the tinkling of a drawing room piano. A good deal of the book is concerned with what he saw as modern fads, designed to take money from the poor. How ridiculous, he declared, to pay a baker to bake your bread when you could do it yourself, at a fraction of the cost, and proceeded to explain how it could be done. The book is wonderfully entertaining – far more so than its title suggests – largely because Cobbett felt completely free to follow his own prejudices. A pet hate is tea, and where others might mildly have suggested that this expensive commodity was not really worth its cost, he attacked it with as much ferocity as he spent on paper money and plural parsons.

It is notorious that tea has no useful strength in it: that it contains nothing nuturitious; that it, besides being good for nothing, has badness in it, because it is well known to produce want of sleep in many cases, and in all cases, to shake and weaken the nerves. It is, in fact, a weaker kind of laudanum, which enlivens for the moment and deadens afterwards.

Denunciation was not enough; he was prepared to back his claims with scientific statistics. He added up the cost of the tea and the price of the fires to heat the water on and the time wasted and triumphantly accounted an annual cost of £11-7-2 – somehow that twopence gives it a daunting credibility. The sensible alternative was to go back to the good old custom of brewing beer, and for £7-5-0 a year the family could get four pints a day in winter and ten in summer. Scientific experiment then joined statistics:

Put it to the test with a lean hog: give him the fifteen bushels of malt, and he will repay you in ten score of bacon or thereabouts. But give him the 730 tea messes, or rather begin to give them to him, and give him nothing else, and he is dead with hunger, and bequeaths you his skeleton at the end of about seven days.

The whole argument was then continued by pointing out that the home brew was infinitely more wholesome than the beverage provided by the professional brewers – a profession he compared to that of 'bug man' and 'rat-killer'. And in the end everything was brought right back to the government tax on malt and hops, the only thing that prevented the English labourer enjoying his birthright.

No matter how practical a piece might have been when it was set on its way, it would inevitably end up in politics. One such began with instructions on preserving a flitch of bacon, and went on to a request to the Bishop of Winchester to make land on the edge of the common available for the poor to keep pigs. It then proceeded via an argument on the merits of lard against butter to the view that a luxury product gives a taste for other luxuries, such as cotton prints instead of homespun, from which it was only a few more steps to a denunciation of Wilberforce and Castlereagh. Even he seemed to feel that he had strayed rather a long way and provided his own interjection.

'What', says the Cottager, 'has all this to do with hogs and bacon?'

What indeed! And all he could say in reply was 'it has a great deal to do, my good fellow'. It has, of course, a great deal to do with Cobbett's main aim of combining practical help with political education, and a good deal to do with Cobbett the man. He really did regard the practical advice he gave as being of great importance in helping raise the living standards of the cottagers. Among the ideas he promoted with enthusiasm was straw plaiting, an occupation that could be followed at home, just as spinning and weaving had been before the factory age. This was just the sort of thing that pleased him – an occupation that was useful and profitable while at the same time bringing back something of the older and better times before the Industrial Revolution.

As he wrote to the labourers, so he also wrote to the farmers, emphasizing that they were as much victims of the tax system as the labourers. As prices fell, with massive deflation, so more and more farms were abandoned. The land was paying for the excesses of the town: an argument farmers have always been delighted to hear. Now as well as writing he began touring southern England addressing meetings with gratifying success. 'Papa is going about the country, making fine speeches at great dinners and making such a stir as you never heard. To be sure if his head can be turned by the applauses and homage he meets with, it certainly will be.'[12] He travelled at first by coach, then changed to horseback. His account of those journeys became the famous Rural Rides.

19

RURAL RIDES

If William Cobbett sometimes seems a mass of contradictions, with his bold changes in political allegiances, his snakes and ladders progress up and down the social board, then it is in *Rural Rides* that everything comes together. Here we meet the plough boy and the political leader, the farmer and the reforming radical, not as sometimes seems the case in his other writings, as quite separate individuals, but melded into one complete, if complex, character. The form, to a large extent, determines the content: each new scene calls for a different approach, sets a new train of ideas in motion. The pace of the steadily jogging horse gives the rider time to look around, time to record impressions, while still ensuring a good, steady rate of progress through the land. Travel books were certainly not new when Cobbett set out on his rides. In fact, there were so many gentlemen and their ladies touring Britain and setting their impressions down on paper that they had become figures of fun for the satirists. One of the best was Combe, whose 'hero', Dr Syntax,[1] offered his tour to the publishers, only to meet a firm rebuffal.

> A tour, indeed! – I've had enough
> Of Tours, and such-like flimsy stuff,
> What a fool's errand you have made
> (I speak the language of the trade),
> To travel all the country o'er,
> And write what had been writ before.

But Cobbett was not writing what had been writ before. The earlier writers had mostly been hunting out picturesque scenes and wild scenery. If they chanced to meet the people who inhabited the more remote regions, then they treated them as if they were as exotic as their surroundings. A visitor to the mining region of North Wales thought it perfectly reasonable to go, uninvited, into the locals' homes, just as any explorer in a distant land would call on the natives in their straw huts or tepees.

In Byron's voyage, there is a print of what he calls a whig-wham or Indian hut, which will give you a perfect idea of these habitations; and the people, except that they are clothed, bear a strong resemblance to the natives of Terra del Fuego.[2]

Cobbett never adopted such a condescending tone, if only because he has always aware how close his own background was to those he met out ploughing fields or repairing hedges. They were not exotic species, but the sort of people he had known since boyhood. And he certainly had no interest in picturesque scenery: wild places were simply areas that had not enjoyed the benefits of cultivation. They were to be avoided, not sought out. His view was the antithesis of the picturesque writers and the Romantics who followed them yet when he inadvertently found himself faced with a beautiful scene, he responded with such obvious pleasure that the reader shares his delight in finding himself suddenly presented with a magnificent view. In November 1822 he was making his way across from Hambledon to Thursley, and in order to avoid the bogs and heavy clays of the valley was heading for what sounded to be a very dangerous, precipitous route down Hawkley Hanger.

On we trotted up this pretty green lane; and indeed, we had been coming gently and generally *up hill* for a good while. The lane was between highish banks and pretty high stuff growing on the banks, so that we could see no distance from us, and could receive not the smallest hint of what was so near at hand. The land had a little turn towards the end; so that, out we came, all in a moment, at the very *edge of the hanger!* And, never, in all my life, was I so surprised and so delighted! I pulled up my horse, and sat and looked; and it was like looking from the top of a castle down into the sea, except that the valley was land and not water. I looked at my servant to see what effect this unexpected sight had upon him. His surprise was as great as mine, though he had been bred amongst the North Hampshire hills. Those who had so stren-uously dwelt on the dirt and dangers of this route, had said not a word about the beauties, the matchless beauties of the scenery.

Here there is none of the extravagant language of so many travel books of the time. Thomas Hurtley, visiting Gordale Scar in the Yorkshire Dales issued a piercing typographical yell of capitals and exclamation marks – 'Good Heavens! What was my Astonishment!' and then a clap of thunder produced an even more extravagant effect.

Struck with indescribable Terror and Astonishment, the natural apprehensions of instant destruction being over, a man must have been dead to rationality and reflection, whose mind was not elated with immediate gratitude to the Supreme Architect and Preserver of the Universe.[3]

No modern reader can imagine experiencing Hurtley's almost hysterical reaction, but one can easily join Cobbett on his hilltop and share his delight in the surprise view. Honest description is not the least of the virtues of *Rural Rides*. Scenery, however, came as a bonus: it had nothing to do with his motives for travelling. In this he was closer to Daniel Defoe who had set out as a reporter to record the life of his times. Yet Cobbett was much more complex in the way he wrote of his journeys. The very first ride, recorded in the book, started at his home in Kensington on 25 September 1822, when he set out for Uphusband with his son James for company. Right at the start, he described how and why he was to travel.

It is very true that I could have gone to Uphusband by travelling only about 66 miles, and in the space of about *eight hours*. But my object was not to see inns and turnpike-roads, but to see the *country*; to see the farmers *at home* and to see the labourers *in the fields*; and to do this you must go either on foot or on horseback. With a *gig* you cannot get about amongst *bye-lanes* and *across fields*, through bridle-ways and hunting-gates; and to *tramp* it is too *slow*, leaving the *labour* out of the question, and that is not a trifle.

He did exactly what he wanted to do: he took time to observe, and the reader sees the countryside through his expert eye. There is not generalized exclamation at the beauty of nature, but a reasoned assessment, based rather more on a sense of utility than any aesthetic. Yet, paradoxically, one has a far clearer idea of the countryside and what it was actually like than one does from more rhapsodic travellers. Here is a typical description, which has to be quoted at length to make its effect. Cobbett is near Winchester.

The weather being dry again, the ground under you, as solid as iron, makes a great rattling with the horses' feet. The country where the soil is stiff loam upon chalk, is never bad for corn. Not rich, but never poor. There is at no time any thing deserving to be called dirt in the roads. The buildings last a long time, from the absence of fogs and also the absence of humidity in the ground. The absence of dirt makes the people habitually cleanly; and all along through this country the people appear in general to be very neat. It is a country for sheep, which are always sound and good upon this iron soil. The trees grow well, where there are trees. The woods and coppices are not numerous; but they are good, particularly the ash, which always grows well upon the chalk. The oaks, though they do not grow in the spiral form, as upon the clays, are by no means stunted; and some of them very fine trees; I take it, that they require a much greater number of years to bring them to perfection than in the *Wealds*. The wood, perhaps, may be harder; but I have heard, that the oak, which grows upon these hard bottoms, is very frequently what the carpenters call *shaky*. The underwoods here consist, almost entirely, of *hazle,* which is very fine, and much tougher and more durable than that which grows on soils with a moist bottom. This *hazle* is a thing of great utility here. It furnishes rods wherewith to make fences; but its principal use is, to make *wattles* for the folding of sheep in the fields. These things are made much more neatly here than in the south of Hampshire and in Sussex, or in any other part that I have seen. Chalk is the favourite soil of the *yew-tree*; and at *Preston-Candover* there is an avenue of yew-trees, probably a mile long, each tree containing, as nearly as I can guess, from twelve to twenty *feet of timber*, which, as the reader knows, implies a tree of considerable size. They have probably been a century or two in growing; but, in any way that timber can be used, the timber of the yew will last, perhaps, ten times as long as the timber of any other tree that we grow in England.

This could have been written by any agriculturalist, by Arthur Young perhaps, but the next description could only have come from Cobbett's pen. The theme is familiar enough from his other writings, but the way in which he responds first to what he *sees*, then goes on to what he has *heard*, to reach a conclusion that is purely political, is very different from his earlier writings. It flows so naturally, there is no sense of the absurd, of the straining to make a point that one finds in the story of the bacon in *Cottage Economy* (p.199). This is Cobbett in a habitat he knows and understands, writing in a way that carries the reader along. Beyond his avenue of yew, he came to the parks laid out, in the manner suggested by Capability Brown and his disciples, by Sir Thomas and Alexander Baring of the famous merchant bank. One might have expected an immediate harangue against this representative of the fund-holders, but the subject in sight is still land and trees, and he slides his criticism easily forward with a good deal of subtlety.

But Mr *Baring*, not reflecting that the woods are not like funds, to be made at a heat, has planted his trees *too large*; so that they are covered with moss, are dying at the top, and are literally growing downward instead of upward. In short, this enclosure and plantation have totally destroyed the beauty of this part of the estate. The down, which was before very beautiful, and formed a sort of *glacis* up to the park pales, is now a marred, ragged, ugly looking thing. The dying trees which have been planted long enough for you not to perceive that they have been planted, excite the idea of sterility in the soil. They do injustice to it; for, as a down, it was excellent. Every thing that has been done here is to the injury of the estate, and discovers a most shocking want of taste in the projector.

Now he had Barings written down, no longer great bankers but inept countrymen, who do not understand the world into which they have intruded. So he can move as easily to more important matters.

I do not like to be a sort of spy in a man's neighbourhood; but I will tell Sir Thomas Baring what I have heard; and if he be a man of sense I shall have his thanks, rather than his reproaches, for so doing. I may have been misinformed; but this is what I have heard, that he, and also Lady Baring are very *charitable*; that they are very kind and compassionate to their poor neighbours; but that they tack a sort of *condition* to this charity; that they insist upon the objects of it adopting their notions with regard to *religion*; or, at least, that, where the people are not what they deem *pious*, they are not objects of their benevolence. I do not say, that they are not perfectly sincere themselves, and that their wishes are not the best that can possibly be; but of this I am very certain, that, by pursuing this principle of action, where they make one good man or woman, they will make one hundred hypocrites.

And he ends this section with a conclusion that seems a long way from the problems of badly planted trees, but which has been arrived at by a smooth and logical progression.

I think Sir Thomas Baring would do better, that he would discover more real benevolence, by using the influence which he must naturally have in his neighbourhood, to *prevent a diminution in the wages of labour*.

This is far more effective than many of his more overly political writings in the *Register*. We feel, with him, the loss of the old common and share his distaste for the inept work of the new men who have taken over the old estates. And because we see them as intruders, we share his distaste at their strings-attached charity. Who are these people who would act Lord and Lady Bountiful, but show no interest in paying a living wage? And, of course, Cobbett has slipped in a sly little reference to the funds to make sure his readers know exactly who they are. The *Rural Rides* are full of such passages that move easily from descriptions of the countryside to moralizing.

He was not always this subtle, if only because there are times when anger seemed the only response. On 11 October 1822 he went to Weyhill-fair, where he found a sheep fair which a few years before had seen sales of £300,000 struggling to turn over £70,000, yet the rents of the sheep farmers remained the same. He moved on to the horse fair, and now he could tie his argument down to one specific event.

> A pretty numerous group of the *tax-eaters* from Andover and the neighbourhood were the only persons that had smiles on their faces. I was struck with a *young farmer* trotting a horse backward and forward to show him off to a couple of *gentlemen*, who were bargaining for the horse, and one of whom finally purchased him. These *gentlemen* were two of our '*dead-weight*', and the horse was that on which the farmer had pranced in the *Yeomanry Troop!* Here is a turn of things! Distress; pressing distress dread of the bailiffs alone could have made the farmer sell his horse. If he had the firmness to keep the tears out of his eyes, his heart must have paid the penalty. What, then, must have been his feelings, if he reflected, as I did, that the purchase-money for the horse had first gone from his own pocket into that of the *dead-weight*! And, further, that the horse had pranced about for years for the purpose of subduing all opposition to those very measures, which had finally dismounted the owner!

Again it is the sense of a logical development from the particular to the general that strengthens the argument, reinforced by the fact that Cobbett goes back in memory to a much happier visit when he came here as a boy with his father. Cobbett, the reader feels once again, knows what he is talking about, and knows it from personal experience.

Time and again, he drew on what he saw and found to give substance to his favourite views. Whenever he came across a large church in a small village he used it as evidence that Malthus must be wrong in claiming huge population increases. Here he is in Kent:

> At three miles from APPLEDORE I came through SNAR-GATE, a village with *five houses*, and with a church capable

of containing *two thousand people*! The *vagabonds* tell us, however, that we have a *wonderful increase of population!* These *vagabonds* will be *hanged* by-and-by, or else justice will have fled from the face of the earth.

One could go on quoting examples from almost any page. There was so much that infuriated him – not least the poverty of the workers in the richest lands. It was here, in the corn county of the Isle of Thanet, that he found some of the most miserable conditions.

The labourers' houses, all along through this island, beggarly in the extreme. The people dirty, poor-looking; ragged, but particularly *dirty*. The men and boys with dirty faces, and dirty smock-frocks, and dirty shirts; and, good God! what a difference between the wife of a labouring man here, and the wife of a labouring man in the forests and woodlands of Hampshire and Sussex!

And he has no doubt at all about the cause of such misery.

In this beautiful island every inch of land is appropriated by the rich. No hedges, no ditches, no commons, no grassy lanes: a country divided into great farms; a few trees surround the great farmhouse. All the rest is bare of trees; and the wretched labourer has not a stick of wood, and has no place for a pig or cow to graze, or even to lie down upon. The rabbit countries are the countries for labouring men. There the ground is not so valuable. There it is not so easily appropriated by the few.

Worse was soon to follow, for he came across a gang of seventeen men sent out by the parish to work on the roads, while four threshing machines stood in the fields. And then to make a day of seething anger complete, he found a notice stuck up in the garden of 'a neat little box of a house'.

The words were these. 'PARADISE PLACE. *Spring guns and steel traps are set here.*' A pretty idea it must give us of Paradise to know that spring guns and steel traps are set in it! This is doubtless some stock-jobber's place; for, in the first place, the name is likely to have been selected by one of that crew; and, in the next place, whenever any of them go to the country, they look upon it that they are to begin a sort of warfare against every thing around thcm. They invariably look upon every labourer as a thief.

It is easy to show Cobbett's anger at the conditions he found and described, but it is not quite so easy to imagine the effect of his words on his contemporaries. The labourers often seemed in the writings of others to be almost an alien species: to find a man such as Cobbett not treating them as the equals of the rich but rather suggesting that they might in many ways be a good deal better was still a novelty. He took the trouble to stop with the labourers, talk to them and find out at first hand just how they fared. The *Rural Rides* paint a depressing picture indeed of the state of the rural poor in the early 1820s.

If the work was no more than a social polemic, an airing of old political and economic arguments, then it is doubtful if it would still be in print a century and a half later. It is a great deal more. It provides a chance to see the countryside of the time through the eye of one who not only sees clearly, but understands what he sees. He speaks knowledgeably of the soil and the crops it supports, on the balance between woodland, arable and pasture and is a fine judge of a good turnip or cabbage. We do not see landscape as the picturesque writers saw it, as something to be judged on how it would look in a painting, but on how well it is adapted to feed and clothe the people. He was not, of course, alone in this view.

> I like a fine prospect, but not on picturesque principles. I do not like crooked, twisted, blasted trees. I admire them much more if they are tall, straight and flourishing. I do not like ruined, tattered cottages. I am not fond of nettles, or thistles, or heath blossoms. I have more pleasure in a snug farm-house than a watch-tower – and a troop of tidy, happy villagers please me better than the finest banditti in the world.[4]

It is doubtful, however, if Cobbett ever read those lines: somehow one cannot see him as an enthusiast for the novels of Jane Austen! Yet it is always worth remembering that the fund-holders, pensioned off admirals and absentee parsons who are the villains of Cobbett's world, were often the heroes of his great contemporary's work. It does require a real effort of the imagination to recognize that their two worlds overlapped. Yet it is an important part of understanding Cobbett, and *Rural Rides* in particular, to see them as sharing the same world. Jane Austen's fiction was set in Southern England; her characters lived in the grand houses which Cobbett trotted past: *Emma* predates the *Rides* by less than a decade, yet the two books might have been describing different planets, not the same area at around the same time.

There is one other aspect, perhaps more than any other, which has ensured the work's longevity: the very real presence of the author himself. He shared his emotions with his readers; his delight in a sunny day, the discomfort of a thorough soaking. He was always a man happy to give his prejudices a good airing – his notorious anti-Semitism crops up depressingly often – but then he surprises the reader by not being prejudiced just when one expects it. On a ride near Cheriton he met 'a grand camp of *Gipsys*' on the move, and warmed to them. Perhaps he recognized people who, like himself, refused to conform to the demands of contemporary society. He certainly saw their independence as something admirable. He also showed that he had lost neither the eye for a pretty girl, nor that taste for flirtation which had so aggravated his wife in America.

> The tall girl that I met at Tichbourne, who had a huckster basket on her arm, had most beautiful features. I pulled up my horse, and said, 'Can you tell me my fortune, my dear?' She answered in the negative, giving me a look at the same time, that seemed to say, it was *too late*; and that if I had been thirty years younger she might have seen a little what she could do with me.

Whatever it was she might have done, he would, it seems, not have objected very strongly. Women always seemed to bring out a rather roguish side of his character and certainly put him in a good humour. One of the few comic pieces that he tried out described a stay at an inn at Weston Grove in the New Forest, when he and his companion had to pass through another room to get to their own.

> I was, of course, awake by three or four; I had eaten little over night; so that here lay I, not liking (even after day-light began to glimmer) to go through a chamber, where, by possibility, there might be 'a *lady*' actually *in bed*; here lay I, my bones aching with lying in bed, my stomach growling for victuals, imprisoned by my *modesty*. But, at last, I grew impatient; for, modesty here or modesty there, I was not to be penned up and starved: so, after having shaved and dressed and got ready to go down, I thrusted GEORGE out a little before me into the other room; and, through we pushed, previously resolving, of course, not to look towards *the bed* that was there. But, as the devil would have it, just as I was about the middle of the room, I, like *Lot's wife*, turned my head! All that I shall say is, first, that the consequences that befel her did not befal me, and, second, that I advise those, who are likely to be hungry in the morning, not to sleep in *inner rooms*; or, if they do, to take some bread and cheese in their pockets.

The *Rural Rides* as published lasted right through to 1826, though he was to make a later addition, when he travelled to the north of England and Scotland in the 1830s. In these later encounters the tone is very different, for he was a stranger in unfamiliar territory (see pp. 239–42). It is in southern England that he can be seen to greatest advantage, where he can compare a little blue-smocked boy waiting on him at an inn with the little blue-smocked boy who had worked in the hop fields of Farnham so many years ago. It is the description of those journeys that make it a unique travel book, both in style and content, and a great one. His name would be remembered if he had done nothing else and never written another word. But he did do a good deal more and wrote a good deal more, even through the years when he was trotting around the countryside.

The campaigning for a whole variety of causes never ceased. His concern for the rural poor did not blind him to the fate of their industrial counterparts. In 1823 he wrote a blistering attack on the Combination Laws,[5] occasioned by a most curious case of a cotton spinner called Ryding who deliberately assaulted a manufacturer as the only way to get into a court to expose the iniquities of the Laws. This, in itself, might not have moved him, but as the trial came forward, Wilberforce chose that moment to pursue one of his favourite topics, emancipation – comparing the miseries of slaves across the Atlantic with the happy state of the free British labourers. Few subjects did more to arouse Cobbett's wrath, and this provided him with just what he needed, an opportunity to attack on two fronts. The very first words show how the whole would proceed: 'Wilberforce, I have you before me in a canting pamphlet.' Cobbett's view of slavery was, at best, simplistic: the American slave was generally well fed and well housed, so what was all the fuss about? He had, in any case, a strongly racist disposition, so that the status of 'the Blacks' simply did not interest him. But this piece is not about slavery as such, that is only a starting point for a more general claim of base hypocrisy and double standards. How dare he appeal to 'free British labourers' to help his cause when 'these poor, mocked, degraded wretches would be happy to lick the dishes and bowls out of which the Black slaves have breakfasted, dined or supped'? And who was the author of his misery? The government of which Wilberforce was a member. And so he moved onto the second main theme, the iniquity of the Combination Acts. He set out his own view of workers' unions, very simply.

> The cotton spinners had their labour to sell; or at least they thought so ... The purchasers were powerful and rich, and wanted them to sell it at what the spinners deemed too low a price. In order to be a match for the rich purchasers, the sellers of the labour agree to assist one another, and thus to

live as well as they can; till they can obtain what they deem a
proper price. Now, what was there wrong in this?

But such combinations were illegal, and men who combined in such
a way could be, and were, imprisoned by the magistrates. Cobbett
was now beginning to warm to his argument.

> This Combination Act does, however, say that the 'masters
> shall not combine against the workmen'. Oh! well then, how
> fair this Act is! ... Does not this law say that all contracts
> between masters and other persons for reducing the wages of
> men; does it not say, in short, that all such combinations of
> masters against workmen 'shall be, and the same are hereby
> declared to be, *illegal*, null and void, to all intents and
> purposes whatsoever'? Does not the law say this; and does it
> not empower the two justices to *send the masters to the
> common gaol and the House of Correction*? No, the devil a bit
> does it do such a thing! No such a thing does it do. However
> flagrant the combinations; however oppressive; however
> cruel; though it may bring starvation upon thousands of
> persons; though it may tend (as in numerous cases it has
> tended) to produce breaches of the peace, insurrections and all
> their consequences; though such may be the nature and
> tendency of these combinations of masters, the utmost punish-
> ment that the two justices can inflict is a *fine of twenty
> pounds*!

It was writing such as this that caused those early chronicleers of
labour history, the Hammonds, to dub Cobbett, 'the greatest living
master of controversial prose'.[6]
Cobbett's deep hatred of Wilberforce never abated with the
years, and he was a good, hearty hater. In 1822, Castlereagh
suffered a complete mental breakdown and killed himself. Whatever
one might think of Cobbett's response even his worst enemies could
not accuse him of cant and hypocrisy. It took the typical form of a
'private' letter made public.[7]

TO JOSEPH SWANN,
Who was sentenced by the Magistrates of Cheshire to FOUR
YEARS AND A HALF *imprisonment in Chester Gaol, for
selling Pamphlets and being present at a Meeting for
Parliamentary Reform; who was imprisoned many Weeks, for*
WANT OF BAIL, *before his Trial; who has now* TWO
YEARS OF HIS IMPRISONMENT UNEXPIRED; *and who,
when Imprisoned, had a Wife and four* helpless Children.
Kensington 15 August, 1822.

MR. SWANN,
CASTLEREAGH HAS CUT HIS OWN THROAT, AND IS
DEAD! Let that sound reach you in the depth of your
dungeon; ad let it carry consolation to your suffering soul! Of
all the victims, you have suffered most. We are told of the
poignant grief of *Lady Castlereagh*; and, while he must be a
brute indeed, who does not feel for her, what must he be, who
does not feel for *your wife* and your four helpless children,
actually torn from you when you were first thrown into the
dismal cells?

He also began to sound a new note in the early 1820s, and one that
caused some surprise. It began with recounting the poverty to be
found in Ireland, and he pepped it up with a spot of titillation.
Women there, he said, were so poor that they went naked – but the
gentry took no notice: 'A GENTRY (pretty gentry!) who are "*not
aware*" that *nakedness* is not "the *proper* way for females to
exist"?'

It might seem odd that the man who roundly declared that the
fate of African slaves was none of his business should trouble
himself over Irish peasants. But he had the answer to that: Irish
poverty was directly attributable to laws made in England. And even
worse than that, the Irish had very little say in the matter, since
most of the population, being Catholic, was denied the vote. He
went on from this point to argue for Catholic emancipation, and
indulged in increasingly severe attacks on the Church of England.

He had always been opposed to the non-conformist sects, and
over the years he had drifted further and further away from the
Church of England. All those religious issues were brought together
in an innocuous sounding *History of the Protestant Reformation*,
which he began writing during this period.[8] His argument begins
with the very obvious point that 'this same Catholic religion was,
for *nine hundred years*, the only Christian religion known to our
forefathers' and the Catholic Church represented 'nine-tenths of all
the Christians in the world.' His knowledge of history proved to be
distinctly shaky, as he explained how the priests being unmarried
and childless had no need to amass wealth, and at their deaths
everything, in any case, passed to charity. It is difficult to believe
that anyone, including the author, would regard this as a fair
summary of several centuries of Catholic history. It might do well
enough to tie the Reformation in England to Henry VIII's flouting
of church law to get rid of an unwanted wife – to his 'beastly lust'
as Cobbett put it – but it is rather more difficult to set up the likes
of Cardinal Wolsey as models of pious rectitude. But it suited the
argument. The Reformation could be presented as totally unnecessary and initiated out of pure greed. This is a very odd book for an

avowed Protestant to write, but it is soon pretty clear to the reader that history lessons, however dubious, are secondary to the main themes: it is no more than another way of attacking old enemies, and that he does with great panache. To get the full effect of the next passage, try reading it aloud, when the list of livings swells into a great percussive rhythm.

If the *late Bishop of Winchester* had lived in Catholic times, he could not have had a *wife*, and that he could not have had a *wife's sister*, to marry Mr. Edmund Poulter, in which case, I may be allowed to think it possible, that Mr Poulter would not have quitted the *bar* for the *pulpit*, and that he would not have had the *two livings* of Meon Stoke and Soberton and a *Prebend* besides; that his son Brownlow Poulter, would not have had the *two livings* of Buriton and Petersfield; that his son, Charles Poulter, would not have had the *three livings* of Alton, Binstead, and Kingsley; that his son-in-law Ogle would not have had the *living* of Bishop's Waltham; and that his son-in-law, Haygarth, would not have had the *two livings* of Upham and Durley. If the Bishop had lived in Catholic times, he could not have had a son, Charles Augustus North, to have the *two livings* of Alverstocke and Havant, and to be a *Prebend*; that he could not have had another son, Francis North, to have the *four livings* of Old Alfresford, Medstead, New Alresford, and St Mary's, Southampton, and to be, moreover, a *Prebend* and *Master of Saint Cross*; that he could not have had a daughter to marry Mr. William Garnier, to have the *two livings* of Droxford and Brightwell Baldwin, and to be a *Prebend* and a *Chancellor* besides; that he could not have had Mr. William Garnier's brother, Thomas Garnier, for a relation, and this latter might not, then, have had the *two livings* of Aldingbourn and Bishop's Stoke; that he could not have had another daughter to marry Mr. Thomas De Grey to have the *four livings* of Calbourne, Fawley, Merton, and Rounton, and to be a *Prebend* and also an *Archdeacon* besides.

He could have simply said that the Bishop's family shared out twenty-four livings, but where would the fun be in that? And who would want to miss that drumbeat of italics – *living, living, living?* No one could pretend that the *History* is one of Cobbett's better works, nor that it has anything like the power of *Rural Rides*, but it certainly has its moments. By the time the book appeared, he had already passed his sixtieth birthday, but the fighting spirit was very far from being extinguished.

POLITICS AND THE PEN

In January 1823, there was an immense county meeting for the people of Norfolk to request agricultural relief. It was the brainchild of the great Whig landowners, including Thomas Coke of Holkham, who was widely known as a pioneer user of Jethro Tull's seed drill. He was also the local member of Parliament. The aim was to bolster Whig popularity by showing they were on the side of the distressed farmer and the poor, even though in practice all they were proposing was a weakly worded petition which could do nothing other than gain a party political point. Nevertheless, some thousands of people turned up, and so too did William Cobbett, who proceeded to put a very different set of proposals to the crowd. He demanded the sale of church property to pay off the national debt, which in turn would allow a cut in taxes, together with a reduction in the standing army, abolition of sinecures and a temporary halt to the payment of tithes. To the horror of the organizers this was enthusiastically carried by the meeting.

Among those who went to hear Cobbett was the twenty-five-year-old Thomas Beevor, Bart, who was so enthused by what he heard that he proposed a meeting of like-minded gentlemen to try to get Cobbett into Parliament. The meeting was finally held in February 1826 in London, in a hired room which was calculated to hold 300, which the organizers thought quite adequate. In the event ten times as many turned up, so most had to be kept waiting outside. Then when Cobbett himself appeared, there was no room left for him either, so they all trooped off to Lincoln's Inn Fields instead. As a direct result, almost £2000 was raised to provide funds for him to fight an election – though when an election would come and where he would stand were still to be decided. Eventually, he settled on the Lancashire mill town of Preston, where he knew he could rely on strong support from the textile workers.

The election was called for June of that year, and Cobbett travelled up to the town with his son John and Sir Thomas Beevor. The reception he got, as John described it, was everything they could have wished.

We made our triumphal entry at 6 o'clock this evening, in an open barouche from Liverpool. Such an immense, such a dense mass of people you never beheld! The Gr. [governor] was, with difficulty, got into the Inn (the Castle Inn in the market place, a very fine open space.) He took a little wine and water to drive down the dust he had swallowed in the entry, and then stepped up to a window in a bow front of the House. There he was received by really the largest meeting that I ever beheld, and he made a noble, beautiful speech of $\frac{3}{4}$ of an hour long; pleased them all mightily, and then dismissed them till tomorrow night at the same time, when he and Sir T.B. are to make them grand speeches![1]

It all seemed to be going remarkably well, and they seemed assured of success, but they had not allowed for corruption and dishonesty on a scale that was astonishing even for that day and age. The manufacturers made it known that they would take a poor view of anyone voting for Cobbett while at the same time Whigs and Tories were bribing the electorate. The Radical cause could have survived such chicanery and the voters showed every sign of refusing to be donkeys, by ignoring both stick and carrot, but it was the arrangement made for polling that killed their chances. The voters were penned up and only allowed to the polling booths a few at a time, but what made the system worse was that each of the candidates had his own pen and his own queue of voters: two lines for the Tory and Whig, two for Cobbett and his Radical running mate, John Wood. Constables controlled the flow of voters, and it soon became clear that as a steady stream went unhindered down two of the lines, the Radical lines scarcely moved at all. Those who wanted to vote for Cobbett and Wood were subjected to intense questioning by lawyers over their voting qualifications. As the voting entered its ninth day of the fortnight allowed, Cobbett gave up the futile attempt of getting the votes of his supporters recorded. He came bottom of a poll in which even the pretence of fairness had been removed. It went down in the records as a defeat, but it felt like a victory. As he made his way through the cotton towns of Blackburn, Bolton and Manchester, the crowds turned out in their tens of thousands, to cheer him on his way and shake his hand until it was numb. Two things were clear to him now. He would never be elected under the old system; reform of that system would make him unbeatable in the manufacturing areas. The fight for Parliament was abandoned, and all his political energies were channelled into the cause of reform. High on the agenda of necessary changes was the emancipation of Catholics, and the freeing of Ireland of Protestant rule.

Molly Townsend has argued[2] that if by the late 1820s Cobbett had not actually converted to Catholicism, then, at the very least, he looked more favourably on the Church of Rome than he did on the Church of England. In his history of Protestantism he made great play of the fact that he came from a strong Church of England tradition: his family were all churchgoers, his father was buried in the churchyard. What he did not do was say that he himself was still a Protestant. Can this be read as a significant indicator that he had changed his allegiances? If he had, there was no hint that the rest of the family followed his lead. Many years after her father's death, Ellen wrote to a friend in some horror, after seeing a Catholic magazine in her house, with a very Cobbetty rash of underlinings and exclamations. 'I hope you are not *Going Over*!'[3] A more likely reading of Cobbett's position was that he was disillusioned with organized religion as a whole, but was no more inclined to think any worse of Catholics than he did of the rest. He could certainly see no reason why they should be treated any differently from other citizens, nor could he see why limited reform was acceptable. Justice demanded complete equality.

The fight for emancipation was led in Ireland by the founder of the Catholic Association, Daniel O'Connell. His ultimate aim was for a free Ireland, entirely removed from English rule, but he was prepared to move forward by cautious steps. A Bill to give Catholics the vote was brought forward in 1825 with two provisos; that instead of the forty shilling threshold for Protestant freeholders, Catholics would have to leap a £10 barrier, and Parliament would agree to pay Catholic clergy in Ireland. O'Connell accepted this meagre portion as better than nothing, a view vigorously opposed by Cobbett. He had objections to both additions: the first on the grounds of manifest unfairness; the second because he could not see why the English taxpayer should pay for the priests when tithes were being collected from Irish Catholics on behalf of the Protestant parsons. It did not help that the Bill was being introduced by an old friend and now enemy, Sir Francis Burdett. Cobbett wrote a play lampooning O'Connell and Burdett as Big O and Sir Glory which he published in the *Register*.[4] He was very proud of it, and in 1830 when the press was full of accounts of empty theatres and unemployed actors he had no hesitation in offering a solution: 'I *write* plays, and they act them! We might begin at once with my Comedy of 'Big O and Sir Glory' or *Leisure to Laugh* ... Let them act *this*; I'll warrant them crowded houses; nay, I should not be afraid to engage in the concern myself ... This is the stuff the people now want.'

In the event, the Bill was thrown out of the Lords and O'Connell publicly admitted that he was wrong to settle for less than a half measure. Cobbett happily welcomed the Prodigal, and sent his message to the Irish: 'I advise them by no means to give way to lamentation; and never again to think of redress by humility.'[5] He still wanted O'Connell to come out more firmly for wholesale reform, but accepted that the decision must lie with the man who commanded such huge support in his native Ireland. This was most clearly demonstrated when, at the next election, he was the successful candidate for County Clare, even though it was well known that the law would prevent him from taking his seat. Cobbett understood this as well as anyone, but was still dismayed that he seemed to do nothing when Parliament again in 1829 brought an emancipation bill.

> He stands quietly, even under the gallery of the House of Commons, and hears the proposition for disenfranchising the forty shilling freeholders; and does not step down from the bench to demand his seat that he may defend them.[6]

He was constantly irritated that the Irish were prepared to settle for so little, but when O'Connell was finally due to take his seat in the Commons, he received the full support of Cobbett and the *Register*. But, as Cobbett constantly argued, the real problems of Ireland remained untouched.

Other predictions also came dramatically true. He had said that it would never be possible to exchange all the paper money in circulation for gold as the government had promised and the result must be a financial crash. By the middle of 1825, the gold reserves of the Bank of England had fallen to a third of what they had been a year before. The small country banks were still using one-pound and two-pound notes and Cobbett sarcastically dubbed these banks as 'Rag Rooks'. Things began to fall apart when a Bristol man tried to get his bank to change his notes into gold coin. He was refused, and as a self-confessed 'disciple of Mr Cobbett' passed the news on. It was given all the publicity that the *Register* could provide, and there followed the absolutely inevitable rush on the banks. Many could not pay, many closed their doors – and many citizens were left with their useless rags. One cannot really blame Cobbett too much for crowing over their financial disaster. He had said it would happen, he had issued warning after warning, and now those who had not bothered to listen had to bear the cost. Even so, it was hardly the time to be joyous: at least not quite as joyous as he seemed to be.[7]

> READER, did you ever pass a winter near the sand-hills of Surrey; did you ever, after a long and dreary season, the ground half the time covered with snow, and the other half drenched with wet; did you ever, at the end of such a winter's last-frost, followed by a gentle thaw, find yourself just after sunrise, upon a hillock, scores of linnets singing in an oak tree on your left, the plough-boy's whistle keeping time to the

jingle of the traces to your right, the hounds at unequal intervals giving tongue in the thicket in the vale below, and, then,
all at once, bursting out in full cry, come rattling up towards
the spot where you stood: did you ever feel *this joy*?

Then he turned from this orgy of rejoicing to sound a more sombre
note. He was not feeling such emotions just because he had been
proved right, but on behalf of all those who had been wronged by
the system. At the end he addressed the poor to bring them into the
celebration.

Were you ever snatched, in dead of night, from your wife and
children, hoisted away, and crammed into a dungeon, in
consequence of the Bills brought in by Sidmouth and
Castlereagh?

The panic continued on into 1826 and Cobbett noted, with ill-
disguised, if grim pleasure, that the country banks were collapsing;
'There are three or four now stop every month; and those which *still
pay* are, in fact, *stricken for dead*.'[8]

In 1819 Cobbett had offered himself up to be roasted on a gridiron – to be placed there by Castlereagh, Sidmouth stirring the fire
and Canning making jokes – if the government achieved its stated
aim of making paper money wholly convertible into gold. On 6
April 1826, he held a somewhat grim Feast of the Gridiron to celebrate his being proved right. Few wanted to join this particular celebration, as the country teetered on the edge of a major financial
collapse. It is easy to understand why he wanted to boast, since the
government had used its considerable powers to try to silence him,
but he might have remembered that prophets of doom are seldom
welcomed, especially when their prophecies come true. In a more
general sense, however, he could reasonably feel himself to be at
the height of his power. He was supremely confident and preened in
public – sometimes, one hopes with his tongue in his cheek. He
could surely never have quite believed in this defence of his own
'amiability'.[9]

My Correspondent asks, 'Why not *be amiable*?' Now, I have
no reason to think that I am not, and that I have not been as
amiable as most other men. Very pretty girls in two different
countries used, when I was young, to be reasonably fond of
me. I have never had a servant that did not like his or her
master; and, as to my family and friends, I leave them to say,
whether there is the company of any person on earth, in which
they delight more than they do in mine. I do not believe, that
I have experienced the breaking off of friendship with ten

persons in the whole course of my life. Why should he therefore suppose, that I am unamiable. I am not over-bearing in
personal intercourse; I am not churlish or niggardly; I am not
a gabbler; I am never melancholy or sulky; all that know me,
know my readiness to forgive; I have never brought but one
action in my life, and that was in the execution of my duty
towards other parties. Why the devil then, am I to suppose
myself unamiable?

Never breaking off friendships, forgiving, not over-bearing? Well!
if the tongue was not in the cheek, it certainly should have been.
What he then went on to say was that he was certainly not amiable,
if the word meant 'being mild towards offenders of a heinous character ... to creep to those that Truth and Justice bid me set at defiance, and that ought to be trampled under my feet, if I had the
power to do it.' In other words, he was perfectly pleasant to everyone except those who disagreed with him. He took a similarly
robust attitude towards those who accused him of coarseness. He
quoted his favourite poem:[10]

> Tender-handed press a nettle,
> And it stings you for your pains;
> Press it like a man of mettle,
> And it soft as silk remains.
>
> 'Tis the same with vulgar natures;
> Treat them kindly, they rebel;
> But be rough as nutmeg-graters,
> And the rogues obey you well.

It is quite clear that he revelled in such criticism, which
confirmed his own opinion of himself as a plain-speaking man of the
people and scourge of the wicked. Throughout the latter part of the
1820s he kept at his role with immense energy, turning out a quantity of work that most writers can only marvel at. In putting down
an opponent, he gave a picture of his own working day.

At what hour of the day do you write, Mr. ATWOOD? We
authors should communicate things of this sort to one another.
I write at this season from five o'clock to eight, and then
breakfast upon Indian meal. I then return to it till twelve,
when I dine; and if I intend to write any more that day, I
seldom drink anything but small beer. I am afraid that you are
in the habit of writing *after dinner*; that is to say, about the
time when I go to bed; for no man in his sober senses ever
could have put a thought like this upon paper.[11]

Even with such a regime he must have been a very fast worker to turn out the volume of material that he did. The *Register* appeared on time, always with long essays by Cobbett; the *Rural Rides* continued and he still found time even to write his books. In 1824 as well as his major work on the Protestant Reformation he published a French Grammar and *The Woodlands*, a practical treatise on growing trees. In 1826 he produced a short book, in the form of a series of letters to the workers of Preston, explaining their condition and how it arose: 'The recollection of the misery, in which I found so many of you; those melancholy effects of poverty produced by taxation, that I had the sorrow to witness amongst a people so industrious and so virtuous; the remembrance of these will not suffer me to be silent on the subject of the means necessary to the restoration of your happiness, especially when I think of the boundless kindness which I received at your hands, and which shall live in my memory as long as memory shall live in me.'[12] He described it as 'the most learned' book he ever wrote, but it was little more than a reworking of old arguments. Another slight work was designed to promote 'Cobbett's Corn' or maize.[13] Having discovered maize in America and successfully grown it in Britain he then proceeded to use it in all kinds of unlikely ways. He made it into beer for himself and his labourers, and even foisted it onto his family as a coffee substitute–without them knowing. 'For God's sake say nothing about the coffee!' he wrote to a friend. 'My wife and my family can find no difference between it and coffee.'[14] Even the sons seem to have shared his enthusiasm, for William wrote from Paris to say that he had conquered the distrust of the Duc d'Orleans.

said he had been so much disgusted with the corn-bread in America, that he should be very sorry to be *obliged* to eat it any more; however, in practising his palate upon that which was the result of the science of the Parisian artist, he determined to eat nothing else.[15]

1829 was a bumper year for publications. He rewrote *The American Gardener* for the home market, adding a good deal of new material.[16] Although it is essentially a practical guide for gardeners, a function which it performs extremely well, being written in his best plain style, there is still space for personal comment. He revisited Waverley Abbey where he had worked as a boy, and found it in what was to his eyes a miserable condition.

SIR ROBERT RICH tore everything to atoms, except the remaining wall of the convent itself. He even removed the high hill at the back of the valley; actually carried it away in carts and wheelbarrows; built up a new-fashioned mansion-house with grey-bricks, made the place look as bare as possible; and, in defiance of nature, and of all the hoar of antiquity, made it very little better than the vulgar box of a cockney.

He was particularly hard on those who preferred to keep the kitchen garden out of sight, whereas to his mind it was a thing of great beauty. And to wall off an orchard struck him as quite incomprehensible. Why, he asks, when people 'decorate their chimney pieces with imitations of those beautiful fruits', do they 'seem to think nothing at all of the originals'? As with many of Cobbett's books, much of its charm lies in the idiosyncrasies of the author. Under 'Burnet' for example, he simply notes – 'Some persons use it in sallads, for what reason I know not.' He also had a curious test for the worthiness of vegetables: the pig. Given a choice, this discerning animal will apparently give up cabbage for lettuce, and move on eagerly from lettuce to spinach. He is prepared grudgingly to give space to that despised vegetable, the potato, contenting himself with acknowledging that 'there is nothing unwholesome about it.'

His next publication set a gloomier note, with advice to emigrants and would-be emigrants.[17] It begins with a familiar refrain.

The state of the country is now such, that no man, except by mere accident, can avoid ruin, unless he can get at a share of the taxes. As to the labouring classes, hunger, and rags, and filth, are now become their uniform and inevitable lot.

Much of the book consists of practical advice about how to get to America – he recommends American ships as being fast and efficient – and having got there, how to set out on the new life. There are lengthy quotes from settlers' letters, offering the benefit of their experience. Some of the advice seems bizarre. He recommends the better-off not to take servants, on the grounds that they are probably going to get seasick, and the employers will finish up looking after them. In any case they are likely to leave soon after landing. 'Good girls' are scarce in America, he writes, and they will soon be snapped up as wives.

In many ways, quite the most interesting publication of the period is his *Advice to Young Men*,[18] not least for what it reveals about the author. He begins with a typically outrageous, immodest list of his qualifications for offering advice. He specifically mentions his authorship of the *Protestant Reformation* – 'unquestionably the book of greatest circulation in the whole world, the Bible only excepted'. His main claims are, however, his combination of natural genius and unremitting hard work, which have roused public admiration.

> There must be something more than genius: there must be industry: there must be perseverance: there must be, before the eyes of the nation, proofs of extraordinary exertion: people must say to themselves, 'What wise conduct must have been in the employing of the time of this man! How sober, how sparing in diet, how early a riser, how little expensive he must have been.

He admits that his readers might be a little surprised to find the great Radical and political thinker offering advice to a sighing lover, but assures them that they have no need to doubt his eligibility on that score either.

> Some persons will smile, and others laugh outright, at the idea of 'Cobbett's giving advice for conducting the affairs of love.' Yes, but I was once young, and lively. I may say with the poet, I forget which of them,
>
> > Though old I am, for ladies' love unfit,
> > The power of beauty I remember yet.

The book is divided into sections addressed to a youth, a bachelor, a lover, a husband, a father and a citizen. Many of the arguments are very much as one would expect, things which Cobbett does not personally like are made to seem slightly immoral if not downright wicked. On large meals, for example, he writes that 'it is truly horrible to behold the people who ought to be at work, sitting at the three meals, not less, than three of the about fourteen hours that they are out of their bed.' Expensive meals are even worse – 'More fuel, culinary implements, kitchen-room; what! all these merely to tickle the palate of four or five people.' His recipe for the successful life is simple – early to bed, early to rise, hard work, plain food washed down with good English beer and no 'foreign' drinks, such as wine, tea and coffee, and no personal vanity: 'a looking-glass is a piece of furniture, a good deal worse than useless'.

On education, he predictably emphasizes the importance of grammar, but has some interesting thoughts on history. There are no surprises at first. 'Our "historians" as they are called, have written under the fear of the powerful, or have been bribed by them; and, generally speaking, both at the same time,' but when he comes to promote history as he would teach it, he strikes a surprisingly modern note.

You hear enough, and you read enough, about the glorious wars in the reign of King Edward the Third; and it is very proper that those glories should be recorded and remembered; but you never read, in the work of the historians, that, in that reign, a common labourer earned threepence-halfpenny a day; and that a fat sheep was sold, at the same time, for one shilling and twopence ... These are matters which historians have deemed to be beneath their notice; but they are matters of real importance.

The arts are at best suspect, and even his admired Swift is not above reproach: 'there are certain parts of his poems which are much too filthy for any decent person to read.' No one could accuse him of being over-romantic. He lists the qualities to look for in a wife in order of importance: chastity, sobriety, industry, frugality, cleanliness, knowledge of domestic affairs, good temper, beauty. It is a list that would serve equally well for hiring a housekeeper. He is even firmer on what he loathes in a wife.

One hour she is capering about, as if rehearsing a jig; and the next, sighing to the motion of a lazy needle, or weeping over a novel: and this is called sentiment! Music, indeed! Give me a mother singing to her clean and fat and rosy baby, and making the house ring with her extravagant and hyperbolical encomiums on it. That is the music which is 'the food of love', and not the formal, pedantic noises, an affectation of skill in which is now-a-days the ruin of half the young couples in the middle rank of life.

His view of the husband's role gives some notion of life in the Cobbett household. 'Nature has so ordered it', he wrote with complete confidence, 'that men should become less ardent in their passion after the wedding-day, and that women shall not.' Poor woman, denied in her passion by her husband, she should be kept at home and allowed as few visitors as possible, in case that passion should find other outlets. There are no such things, according to Cobbett as 'innocent freedoms'. So what is she to do: music is out, plays and shows will not do, novels are a frivolous waste of time. Her role is to obey her husband, run a frugal household and bring up the children. He is quite certain that this will be as welcome to the wife as it clearly is to the husband. Of his own marriage he speaks in the highest terms, as bringing him happiness and the spur to work hard for his family. As for Nancy, 'though deprived of all opportunity of acquiring what is called learning', she is perfectly happy looking after her husband and family.

He constantly paraded this view of the happy family home at

least in his public writings, but it was very far from a complete story. Nancy was often left alone while he went off on his rides and public-speaking tours. Her life had been one in which she had been buffeted by circumstances; rich one day, poor the next; flattered by the leaders of the nation as wife of a great man one year, vilified as the partner of a dangerous revolutionary the next. She would perhaps have borne anything and everything with a good heart, but she could not stand the thought of being involved with what she saw as the revolutionary rabble. She had a particularly poor view of Hunt, who had publicly criticized her as being incapable of keeping the servants she hired, because of her quarrelsome nature. At least her husband had taken her side, as a result of which there had been a distinct cooling off between these two leading Radicals. Nancy could not have been more pleased. That all changed in May 1827.

Burdett had steadily moved further and further away from the Radical cause, and was by now more inclined to vote with the government than oppose it. He had been joined as member for Westminster in 1820 by John Cam Hobhouse, another notably luke-warm reformer. Now it was proposed to have a dinner to celebrate the twentieth anniversary of the famous victory of Burdett and Cochrane. Cobbett and Hunt now joined forces again to denounce the pair, and declared that they would both attend the dinner and address the gathering to expose the hypocrisies. What resulted was not so much a fight as a scuffle, in which the stewards tried to evict Cobbett and Hunt while their supporters resisted the attempts. Cobbett had his say, a window was broken and the whole affair was really something of a fiasco. It seems, however, to have been too much for Nancy. It was widely rumoured that she and her husband were no longer on good terms, and the press reports of the brawl and the involvement with Hunt led to a near-tragic consequence. Nancy must have thought of the return of all the old miseries of what she saw as public disgrace, but which her husband saw as a kind of martyroom. She might have borne that from the ties of loyalty that had always been at their strongest when the family was threatened by disasters, but now she saw the loyalty itself under threat. Disgrace was bad enough, but disgrace coupled with the man she was known to despise, who had publicly criticized her, was insupportable. She attempted suicide by cutting her throat.

The affair was kept silent, but gradually bits of news and infor-mation trickled out, putting the whole Cobbett family in a different light. There had been an earlier quarrel, which involved the growing disagreement between Cobbett and his sons, about the handling of the finances. Less scrupulous men let out other stories. One of his opponents, David French, put out a rumour that Cobbett was having a homosexual relationship with his amanuensis, Charles Riley. This at least brought the family together: they might be

arguing between themselves, but this was going too far, and French
was given a beating by the sons – who were later fined £24, a
lenient sentence as the judge declared in court that they had been
seriously provoked. But taken together, it presents Cobbett's
published advice in a new light. When he writes that a woman who
does not submit to her husband's will must be 'a virago in her very
nature', it no longer seems a piece of prejudiced bombast, but the
heartfelt expression of a wound at the heart of the Cobbett family.
He was advising others to do what he could not do himself.

There is absolutely no doubt that Cobbett was a most difficult
man to live with, and much that he did must have seemed hopelessly
imprudent. As fast as he made money from his books, he spent it on
new farming ventures. In 1826, he began an ambitious scheme to
turn his grounds into a nursery for trees grown from seeds, mostly
imported from America. The sons were by now studying law, so a
good deal of the work had to be left to others, which included the
grandiose plan for eventually planting a million trees as seedlings.
Even this was not enough to satisfy his farming ambitions, and he
took a second farm across the Thames at Barn Elm, which he used
for experiments in growing turnips, mangel-wurzels and maize. He
left the running of this largely in the hands of his elder brother who
had control of a work-force of 'ten or a dozen men'. But while he
had the experience for such an enterprise, he lacked physical
strength. So Cobbett advertised in the *Register*[19] for a young man of
sixteen to eighteen 'to supply legs'. Exactly what the lad should do
and what sort of lad he should be was explained in a typically
Cobbett fashion. The piece is worth quoting at length because it
shows not only the writer's views on what constituted a good
farmer, but because it shows even more clearly what he had hoped
his own sons would be.

He is not wanted to *work much*; but, if he learn to do every
thing on a farm, it will do him no harm. He is wanted to see
the orders of myself, or of my brother, obeyed. I do not want
a *Bailiff*; for bailiffs do not think that they earn their wages,
unless they furnish you with *science*, or, at least, with *advice*,
as well as with care; and I want neither science nor advice. I
want *legs* that will move nimbly and willingly, and a young
head capable of *learning*. The lad ought to be *stout*, and not
stunted; he ought to be able to read and write a little; but, two
things are indispensable; namely, that his father be *a farmer*,
and that his son has lived on a farm in *England*, all his life,
and at a distance of not less than forty miles from London;
and not less than twenty miles from Portsmouth, Plymouth,
Bath, Bristol, Cheltenham, Liverpool, Manchester, Leeds, or
Norwich. He is to sit at table with my brother and my niece

(who is the housekeeper), and, when I am at the farm, with
me also; and is to be treated with every respect as *the young
farmer of the house*. He is never to quit the farm; except on
my business, and to go to the parish church on the Sunday,
and is to be under the control of my brother as completely as
if he were his son ... Now, if any farmer, who is of *my political principles, full up to the mark*, have such a son, nephew,
or grandson, to dispose of in this way, I shall be glad to hear
from him on the subject. If the lad stay a year out, I will make
him a *present* of not less than ten or twelve guineas. It is, I
hope, unnecessary to add, that this is a farm-house without a
tea-kettle or a *coffee-pot* and without any of the *sweets* that
come from the *sweats* of African slaves. Please to observe,
that I do not want a '*young gentleman*;' but a good, sturdy
lad, whose hands do not instinctively recoil from a frozen
chain, or from the dirty heels of an ox or a horse. I hope that
the lad, or young man, that I am to have, will; never have
been at an '*establishment*,' vulgarly called a *boarding-school*:
if he unfortunately have, and should suit in all other respects,
I must sweat the boarding-school nonsense out of him; that is
all. If he have a mind to improve himself in study, here are
books, and all the other means of well employing his leisure
hours.

There were farmhands to pay and no farming profits from which
to pay them. His successes in farming, such as proving that maize
could indeed be grown in Britain, gave him immense personal satisfaction but at a high financial cost that all the family had to bear.

William Cobbett painted a picture of himself as the eternal
yeoman farmer, presiding over a large, contented family. The truth
was that he was one of the greatest political writers of the age, a
leading figure in the thriving Radical movement that would soon
achieve its first really important success. He was at best a good
amateur farmer, and he was presiding over an increasingly fractious
and rebellious family. Cobbett was definitely not moving into a
calm and peaceful old age.

REVOLUTION AND REFORM

In Europe, 1830 was a year of revolutions. In France Charles X reigned over a very unpopular ultra-conservative government, and when elections in July of that year saw an increase in the number of liberal opposition members of the Chamber, he and his supporters promptly dissolved the Chamber. It was one of the most inept attempted *coups d'état* in history. Within a day, republicans had put up barricades in the streets of Paris in protest, and within three days had control of the capital. Charles X abdicated in favour of his grandson, the Duke of Bordeaux. There was a moment of confusion, with some wanting a return to the Republic and the moderate liberals arguing for a new constitution under a new king, the Duke of Orleans. The liberals won, so within a bewilderingly short period, Charles X was in exile, the Duke took the throne as Louis-Philippe and a number of liberal reform measures were pushed forward, including a wider franchise. Revolution in France was rapidly followed by a rising in Belgium against Dutch rule; and unrest spread through Central Europe, even touching such unlikely regions as Switzerland. The questions could not be avoided: would revolution spread to Britain, or was there now sufficient momentum in the drive for reform as to make peaceful change inevitable? Something had to give, and Cobbett was unequivocal in his enthusiasm for what had been achieved in France and Belgium.[1]

> The Revolution in France was accomplished – not by the aristocracy – not by military gentlemen – not by gentlemen with whiskers or long spurs – not by gentlemen of any description, in fact – not even by the middle classes, but by the working people alone; by men who quitted their shops, who laid down their needles and their awls, and their saws, and rushing out into the streets of Paris, said 'If there be no alternative but slavery, let us put an end to the tyrants'.

If this stops short of inciting the British to revolution to achieve just reform, then it stops only a little way from it. On the other hand, there were hopes for peaceful change in Britain, with the possibility of a new beginning following the death of George IV and the accession of William IV. Cobbett, as was his way, spoke of the dead exactly as he had when they were living. His comments on the late king were pithy and to the point.[2]

> I can find no one good thing to speak of, in either the conduct or character of this king; and as an Englishman, I would be ashamed to show my head, if I were not to declare that I deem his reign (including his regency), to have been the most unhappy, for the people, that England has ever known.

By the end of the year, there was a new government to go with the new king: out went the Tories under Wellington and in came the Whigs under Earl Grey. By this time it made no difference to Cobbett who was in power, since as far as he was concerned both parties followed the same disastrous policies. He set about lambasting them all in a new monthly begun in 1830. The cheap *Register* had been dubbed 'twopenny trash' by his opponents, and he now impishly used it for the new journal.

> AGREEABLY to the hint that I gave in the Register of last week, I shall on the FIRST OF JULY, publish the FIRST NUMBER OF A MONTHLY PAMPHLET, to be called
>
> TWO-PENNY TRASH:
> OR
> POLITICS FOR WORKING PEOPLE.
>
> It will be in the DUODECIMO form; each Number will consist of *one sheet*, well filled with matter; the main *object* will be, to show the working people *what are the causes* of their being poor; *what it is*, that in spite of their ingenuity, industry, and frugality, makes them unable to provide in a suitable manner, for their wives and children; and the *motto* will be,
>
> > 'Yes, while I live, no rich or noble knave
> > Shall walk the world in credit to his grave.'[3]

Cobbett's *Two-Penny Trash* gave him once again a chance to speak directly to the poor, for being monthly it avoided the swingeing tax on newspapers. He used his most robust language and images in attacking the different factions.[4]

The words Tory and Whig now excite ridicule and contempt

at the bare sound of them. The words '*opposition,*' and '*gentlemen opposite*', are become equally contemptible. The people have long looked upon the whole as one mass of fellows fighting and scrambling for public money; some fighting to keep it, and others scrambling to get at it; some dogs in possession of the carcase, and some growling and barking because they cannot get a share.

He was equally blunt in the *Register* in his views on the moderate reforms led by Brougham. He compared them to country shoy-hoys or scarecrows.[5]

The great body of the factions, knowing the reality of their views, have been highly diverted by their sham efforts, which have never interrupted them in the smallest degree in their enjoyment of the great plunder. Just as it happens with the birds and the shoy-hoys in the fields or gardens. At first, the birds take the shoy-hoys for a real man or woman; and, so long as they do this, they abstain from their work of plunder; but after having for some little while watched the shoy-hoy with their quick and piercing eyes, and perceived that it never moves hand or foot, they totally disregard it, and are no more obstructed by it than if it were a post. Just so it is with these political shoy-hoys.

In Cobbett's view then, as in the view of many others, there was little real hope of peaceful change, a view which seemed to be confirmed by the violence that began to sweep through the country in the autumn of 1830. It was, at first, concentrated in the rural areas of southern England, and just as the industrial workers had earlier had their mythical leader, General Ludd, now the agricultural labourers rallied behind the colours of Captain Swing. Like the Luddites, they set about destroying machinery, but most action was concentrated on breaking down fences and hedges round newly enclosed fields and burning hay ricks. Their complaints were varied and many: enclosure had taken away their rights to the common land, draconian game laws kept the wild animals of the countryside for the exclusive use of the rich, new machines were creating unemployment. In the end, however, all the complaints came down to just one issue, the poor were starving while surrounded by evidence of plenty.

In the past, Cobbett had always been circumspect, carefully separating out his sympathy for the poor and their demands from his condemnation of the use of violence as a means of achieving them. He still made the same distinction, but with a great deal less clarity.[6]

A sardonic comment on the swing riots, a judge's wig and a black cap sit on the gallows as the ricks burn (The British Museum)

I know that English labourers would not lie down and die in any number, with nothing but sour sorrel in their bellies (as two did at Acton on the beginning of the summer); and know that they would never receive the *extreme unction* and die of hunger, as the poor Irish did, and he praised for their *resignation* by Bingham-Baring or Baring-Bingham, or whatever else he is. I knew that all the palaver in the world, all the wheedling, coaxing, praying; I knew that all the blustering and threatening, I knew that all these would fail to persuade the honest, sensible and industrious English labourer, that they had not an indefeasible right to live.

He pounded away at the issue time and again in the pages of the *Register* and *Two-Penny Trash*, always asking the same questions. What has driven the docile labourer to commit 'truly abominable' crimes? Who is to blame? No regular reader of Cobbett would have had to hold his breath waiting for the answer. The response of the authorities was twofold – stick and carrot yet again – and Cobbett was loud in his condemnation of the one and just as vocal in his contempt for the other. The carrot was tried first.

Parliament set up special commissions to investigate the complaints of the poor. Cobbett saw them more as secret police than as a charitable body, and when they delivered their verdicts on matters such as the needs of the poor, his anger erupted in full fury[7]

There is now before me a Report of a Committee of the House of Commons, on the subject of the Corn Laws. This Committee report the evidence of certain persons examined by them; and, amongst the rest, of a great landholder, in Wiltshire, named BENETT, who, upon being asked how much a labourer and his family ought *to have to live upon*, answered, 'We calculate, that every person in a labourer's family should have, *per week*, the price of a gallon load, and three-pence over for *feeding* and *clothing*, exclusive of house-rent, sickness, and casual expenses.'

Mark! pray mark! a gallon loaf; that is to say, not quite *a pound and a quarter of dry bread* and a *half-penny a day* for FOOD AND CLOTHING! And a SPECIAL COMMISSION is gone into Wiltshire! There is a God of justice, to be sure! That God will do justice, in the end, to be sure! Talk of blasphemy, indeed! Talk of Atheism! Who is not to be an Atheist, if he believe that there is no God to show displeasure at human creatures (and those, too, who make all the food and all the raiment to come) being doomed to exist on a pound and a quarter of bread a day, and a half-penny for clothing, and nothing for *drink*, and nothing for *fuel*, and nothing for

bedding, washing, or light! And, what are we to think of the
Parliament that received this evidence, and that never
bestowed so much as one moment on the subject? What are
we to think of that Parliament! Why, just what the people *did*
think of it, to be sure.

Meanwhile, the ultra-conservative press was setting up equally
loud cries, demanding still harsher penalties, including the death
sentence for rick burning and poaching. Cobbett would have nothing
to do with such arguments: '*The means of terror or of punishment
are not calculated to put an end to the fires. It is an old saying that,
if you kill a fly, twenty flies come to his burying.*' There were
disquieting reminders of earlier troubles which had been put down
by the yeomanry; Peterloo had not been forgotten. Now the yeomen
cavalry were out again, chasing down the rick-burners, and Cobbett
told his readers just who they were:

> more than one half of you are loan-mongers, tax-gatherers,
> dead-weight people, stock-jobbers, shag-bag attorneys,
> bailiffs (most Scotch), toad-eating shopkeepers, who are
> ready to perform military duty towards the '*lower orders*', in
> order at once to give evidence of your gentility and to show
> your gratitude towards your rich customers for their paying
> your long bills without scruple.[8]

The stick was a rotten stick, and no good could come from its use.

He went further than he had ever gone in sympathizing with the
rick-burners and, whilst condemning the violence, showed that he
understood why it was happening.

> there is no man, not of a fiend-like nature, who can view the
> destruction of property that is now going on in the Southern
> counties without the greatest pain; but I stand to it, that it is
> the strict natural course of things, where the labourer, the
> producer, *will not starve*.

The authorities were infuriated by the writings, and turned to the
trick that had been tried before with considerable success. Once
more he was hauled into court, and charged with seditious libel, and
once again he undertook his own defence. It was generally accepted
in the establishment that any riot had to be the work of malicious
men inciting the ignorant poor to violence rather than a spontaneous
response to unbearable conditions. Cobbett looked as good a candidate as any. The process began with a story in *The Times* about a
man called Thomas Goodman,[9] who claimed that he had been led to

rick-burning as a result of hearing a speech given by Cobbett at
Battle in Sussex.

> I, Thomas Goodman, never should af thought of douing aney
> sutch thing if Mr. Cobbet Cobet had never given aney lactures
> i believe that their never would bean any fires or mob in
> Battle or maney other places if he never had given aney
> lactures at all.

What the report did not make clear was that his confession impli-
cating Cobbett had earned him a reprieve from the noose. Cobbett
rapidly turned to the attack. Who had obtained this confession? A
curate from Crowhurst, some twenty miles away, had come
specially to the jail to look Goodman out and quiz him about
Cobbett. This did not look very convincing, so three magistrates
went along to get a brand new, and more elaborate confession.

> I Thomas Goodman, once heard of one Mr. Cobbit going A
> Bout gaving out lactures at length he came to Battel and gave
> one their and their was a gret number of peopel came to hear
> him and I went he had verrey long conversation concerning
> the state of the country and tilling them that they was verrey
> mutch impose upon and he said he would show them the way
> to gain their rights and liberals (liberties) and he said it would
> be verrey Proper for every man to keep gun in his house espe-
> sely young men and that they might prepare themselves in
> readiness to go with him when he called on them and he
> would show them which way to go on and he said that peopel
> might expect firs their as well as others places.

As Cobbett duly noted, 'Liars, should have good memories.' He
came up with a declaration signed by 103 people who had been at
Battle and were ready to swear he had said no such thing, and, to
clinch the defence, one of them was the actual farmer whose barn
had been burnt down by Goodman.

With the Goodman case so hopelessly unconvincing, the charge
had to fall back on Cobbett's own writings. The Attorney-General
chose a piece from the *Register*, the article quoted above in which
he railed against the iniquities of the gallon loaf. But Cobbett had all
his answers ready. In front of a packed court, he called his
witnesses, not his supporters from Battle, but all the leading figures
of the Whig cabinet, from the Prime Minister to Brougham, the
Lord Chancellor. They had to sit listening to Cobbett's speeches and
it fell to the unfortunate Brougham to admit that he had indeed
written himself to Cobbett asking permission to republish his 1817
'Letter to the Luddites' as a way of bringing sense to the rioters. It

was, to say the least, farcical. Here was a government simultane-
ously putting a man on trial for incitement to violence and at the
same time requesting his permission to quote similar works in order
to keep the peace. After that, the verdict was scarcely in doubt.
Cobbett had not so far had many successes at law, but this one, with
all his enemies in attendance, was a triumph and a very, very sweet
one.

> I had forced the Whig ministers to come by subpoena; and I
> intended to question them every one, if the Judge permitted
> me, with regard to the grounds on which they had advised his
> Majesty in dealing with the rural disorders. For this purpose
> I brought together, to sit upon the bench in front of me, Lords
> Grey, Brougham, Melbourne, Durham, Goderich, and
> Palmerston. There they sat, ranged in a row, to hear my
> defence; and there sat between two and three thousand intelli-
> gent men to witness the scene. From every county in England,
> I believe, some one man or more was present. Well might I
> say it was a day of joy to me! It was a reward going ten thou-
> sand times beyond all that I had ever merited.[10]

He left the court as a free man.

Though the country was in turmoil, hopes for reform had never
been higher. It had been generally thought in the summer of 1830
that Wellington would save his government by offering at least some
form of sop to the reformers. In the event, his failure to do so
brought down his government and Grey was quick to announce that
he was setting up a committee to draft a bill. Cobbett was equally
quick to offer his advice on what needed to be done.[11]

He began by pointing out that, given the examples set in Paris
and Brussels and the growing discontent in England, something was
now sure to be done. His own proposals were admirably succinct:

1. That a new Parliament shall be chosen every year.
2. That every man, having attained the age of eighteen, shall
   have a vote, and that no man shall have more than one
   vote.
3. That no man shall be excluded, whether pauper, soldier,
   sailor, or anything else, if he be of sane mind, and is not
   branded by sentence of a court of justice for some indeli-
   ble crime which renders him incapable of giving evidence
   in a court of justice in civil matters.
4. That there be no pecuniary qualification for members, and
   that the only qualifications necessary shall be, that the
   member be a native of the county, that he had resided in it
   three years previous to being elected; and that each

member be twenty-one years of age.
5. That the mode of choosing the members be by ballot.

He can hardly have expected that any bill would meet all these
demands – or, indeed, any of them – but it set a standard against
which the government proposals could be judged. In the event, the
bill was a good deal more adventurous than anyone had expected,
and included a wholesale sweeping away of no fewer than 107 rotten
boroughs, and greatly widened the franchise. It scraped through the
Commons by a single vote, thanks to the support of the Irish. With
such a slim majority, there was little chance of it progressing
further. Parliament was dissolved, and in the election that began in
April 1831, the anti-reform candidates received a complete drubbing. There was no doubt which way public opinion was moving
and when the Reform Bill again reached Parliament in September it
passed the Commons with a resounding majority of 109. Then, in
an act of the most crass stupidity, given the tense conditions and the
violence throughout much of the country, the Lords decided to exercise the veto. Cobbett had said often enough that if reform was
denied, revolution would inevitably follow and had pointed to the
events in France in the 1790s to illustrate the point. Now it looked
very much as if that prophecy was about to be fulfilled. He was also
certain that the bishops were largely to blame, having voted 21 to 2
against it. Others certainly thought so, for in the surges of violence
that swept through many cities they and their palaces were among
the main targets. The worst of all the riots took place in Bristol.
There the bishop's palace went up in flames, followed by the
Mansion House, the customs house, toll houses, workhouses and
private houses. There was a real fear that if the fires spread to the
wooden ships that were tied up at the wharves, the whole city might
be destroyed. The ferocity of the mob was terrifying, but so too was
the response of the military when they arrived at Queen Square. One
of the commanders of the day, Major Mackworth, described the
events in his own words.[12]

I called out 'Colonel Brereton, we must instantly charge' and
without waiting for his answer – he could not but approve – I
called out 'Charge men and charge home'. The troops obeyed
with the utmost alacrity, Colonel Brereton charging with great
spirit at their head; and I trust in God every man there injured
was actually engaged in plunder or in burning and that not a
single innocent person there fell beneath our sabres. Numbers
were cut down and ridden over; some were driven into the
burning houses, out of which they were never seen to return,
and our dragoons, after sabreing all they could come at in the
Square, collected and formed and then charged down Princes

Street and again returned to the Square, riding at the miserable mob in all directions; about 120 or 130 of the incendaries were killed and wounded here.

The prophecies of revolution now looked nearer than ever to reaching fulfilment and, in the face of such a clamour, the government had little option other than to try again, and a third bill went successfully through the Commons. There was still the Lords to contend with. No one doubted that most of their Lordships detested the notion of reform, but no rational observer could believe that they would oppose it for ever. Change would come, one way or the other, and the only peaceful way forward would come if they could be convinced of the force of public opinion. The leading reformers used the period between the Commons reading and the debate in the Lords to pile on the pressure, and no one did more than Cobbett. He set off on a lecture tour round the Midlands, travelling nearly a thousand miles, and, on his own estimate, stood to talk for a total of a hundred and thirty hours. It became increasingly evident by the beginning of 1832 that pressure was vitally needed, as the government showed signs of caving in to the Lords by agreeing to a much watered-down Bill. Cobbett thundered in the *Register*, encouraging his readers to raise petitions, hold public meetings and make certain that Grey and his cabinet were in no doubt about the mood of the country. The Bill already fell short of the reformers' demands: further dilution was unthinkable.

In May, Grey told the king that he must at once create new peers to carry the Bill in the Lords or his government would resign. The King was quite happy to accept the resignation and called back Wellington to form a government. Cobbett described the effect of the decision and offered his own remedy – to create another financial crisis by demanding gold, so forcing the government to capitulate.[13]

To describe the agitation in London, and the anger of the people against the Lords, the Bishops, Wellington, and particularly against the King, is a task that no tongue or pen can perform. Every man you met seemed to be convulsed with rage: to refuse to pay taxes was amongst the mildest of the measures that were proposed ... A cry for a republic was pretty nearly general; and an emigration to Hanover formed the subject of a popular and widely-circulated caricature. Resistance in every shape and form was publicly proposed; and amongst the means intended to defeat the King and the new Minister, was that most effectual of all means, *a run upon the Bank for gold.*

The cry was taken up in London, where placards and posters started to appear, bearing the message 'To stop the duke, go for gold'. And so they did, withdrawing around half a million from the Bank of England in just one day. This, combined with the growing threat of yet more public disorder, turned the situation round. It was now quite clear that Wellington had no hope of forming a government, and the king was forced to recall Grey. Faced with a bleak choice between creating new pro-reform peers or persuading the anti-reformists to abstain, the king opted for the latter course. On 7 June 1832 the Reform Bill was passed by the Lords and became law. It was no triumph for Parliament, but rather one for public opinion, and Cobbett was quite certain where the true merit of the success lay: 'we owe the Reform Bill more to the Country Labourers than to all the rest of the nation put together'. It was not the Bill he had wanted; it offered a limited franchise, gave no secret ballot and kept Parliaments to seven years. But it was undeniably a start and if it did nothing else it swept away the rotten boroughs. It was an event to celebrate.

Cobbett's own celebration was absolutely typical of the man. It was a Chopstick Festival held in the little Hampshire village of Sutton Scotney. It was here that 155 farm labourers had met in 1830 to petition the king for reform. Two of them who had walked sixty miles to the meeting had been charged with begging and transported for life. A month later, the labourers had met again 'to remonstrate' with the farmers, the parsons, and the landowners, with regard to the wages that had reduced them to a state of half-starvation'. In a scuffle after the meeting, one labourer, Henry Cook, had knocked off the hat of Bingham-Baring the great banker and landowner, for which heinous crime he had been executed. His body now lay three miles away, in Micheldever churchyard. So, for Cobbett, this was a place which represented both the steadfastness of the chopsticks and the viciousness of old corruption. Thousands gathered on the day, and Cobbett himself contributed three vast rounds of beef, a 72lb ham cooked by Nancy and 141 loaves of bread. He was, not surprisingly, in the highest good humour, and when the celebrations were over he toured the region visiting old friends and receiving the congratulations of enthusiastic supporters.

William Cobbett was now sixty-nine years old and much of his effort over the past years had been devoted to the cause of reform. A reformed parliament would, he believed, transform the country, wipe away the burdens of debt, reduce taxes and see Britain return to prosperity based on a rich and fruitful countryside. Now it had come about, and he would have been forgiven if he had withdrawn from public life. He had already managed to arrange for his withdrawal from the Great Wen, the hated city of London, by purchasing Normandy Farm at Ash in Surrey, just a few miles from his birthplace. But he was unable – or unwilling – to resist the clamour of those who would make William Cobbett one of the first men to take a lead in the reformed parliament. He was offered two candidacies, Manchester and Oldham. He agreed to stand.

> As far as my concerns my own personal tastes and interests, I shall undertake this arduous task with reluctance. By Michaelmas next I shall have a *farm*; and somewhere in my own native county. A FARMER I WILL LIVE AND DIE, But God has been pleased to give me great health and strength yet: I am convinced that I am able to render the greatest service to my country; that country has a right to those services at my hands; and the more perilous her state, the more base it would be in me not to do my utmost to rescue her from peril.[14]

It is hard to imagine him refusing. He had stood for Parliament before and been defeated first by the mob, then by the gross injustices of the system. Now he had every chance of a triumphant success, and one made possible by the Bill which he had done so much to promote. At Oldham, one of the great cotton manufacturers and ardent reformers, John Fielden, agreed to stand if, and only if, Cobbett was his running mate, and they made a formidable pair. When the election began in December 1832, it was quite clear that Cobbett was going to win Oldham, though by the curious nature of the political process, he was still standing at Manchester. Before the voting ended, he withdrew from Manchester. When the votes were counted Fielden had 670, Cobbett 642 and their nearest rival 153. William Cobbett the ploughboy had become William Cobbett, Member of Parliament for Oldham.

THE LAST YEARS

Cobbett might have been thought to have had enough to do in 1832 in the drama of the fight for reform and the election, but there were still the bread-and-butter jobs to attend to. The *Two-Penny Trash* might have made a bright splash in the world, but it was the unglamorous works that provided a more solid financial basis. That year's solid work was *A Geographical Dictionary of England and Wales*, though it is doubtful if he did very much of the writing himself and a good deal was handed over to his son John and one of the daughters, presumably Anne. Just before the election, he set off on a tour of Scotland. In the past he had mercilessly ridiculed the great Scots thinkers of the day, such as Adam Smith and David Hume as 'feelosofers', and had not taken kindly to men such as the bailiffs who had come to England to manage some of the great estates. Never one for half-measures, he was happy to condemn the entire country on the basis of these few examples. Now, a little apprehensive about the reception he might receive, he travelled north and in his account of the journey he had the good grace to admit he had been mistaken – at least in some of what he had written.[1]

It was not just Scotland that was new to him, but also the north of England, particularly Northumberland. He may have set off with the best of intentions of keeping an open mind, but that did not mean that he was leaving all the old prejudices behind. He reached Alnwick on 14 October, 1832 and viewed its majestic castle 'with every feeling of contempt which haughtiness and emptiness can excite in the human mind, the endless *turrets* and *lions* of the descendent of SMITHSON, commonly called PERCY... . There was a flag flying on the battlements to indicate to the vassals around that the descendent of HOTSPUR was present in the castle.'

After this bit of playing to the reformist gallery, he came to a much more interesting phenomenon. The larger estates of Northumberland had been among the most ardent enthusiasts for modernization: even today, one can still see farms sprouting what appear to be factory chimneys, marking the engine-houses that powered the steam threshers. The workers were brought together and housed in what Cobbett described as barracks: 'that is to say they had neither gardens nor privies nor back-doors, and seem altogether to be kept in the same way as if they were under military discipline.' And as he travelled north, so the chimneys grew higher and the barracks larger until he exploded in rage. 'Gracious God! have these fellows the impudence; have they the insolent assurance, to hope to be able to bring the people of Kent, Sussex and Surrey, into this state? This is *rural life* with the devil to it!'

He crossed the Tweed and at last reached the land of 'antalluct' and 'feelosofers' and liked much of what he saw. He admired the sheep and the cattle, spoke well of the productive fields and the wooded valleys. All that was lacking was the people, forced out in the modernization programmes. Here was what he abhorred, rich landowners producing food not for the locals but to meet the demands of the indolent cities.

> We found the road (which is very fine and broad) actually covered with carts, generally drawn by one horse, all loaded with sacks of corn. For several miles it appeared to be a regular cavalcade of carts, each carrying about twelve English sacks of corn, and all going to DUNBAR, which is a little sea-port (though a large town) apparently made for the express purpose of robbing Scotland of all its produce, and of conveying it away to be squandered in scenes of dissipation, of gambling, and of every vice tending to vitiate man and enfeeble a nation.

He was to discover still worse in the treatment of the labourers, bound by annual hirings and unable to move on without a reference from the last master. Their living conditions were poor, in earthen-floored bothies, pay was wretched at £4 a year, made up with an allowance of oats, barley, peas and potatoes, with grazing for one cow. Here, at least, one prejudice was confirmed: 'There, chopsticks, of Sussex, you can now see what English scoundrels, calling themselves "gentlemen" get Scotch bailiffs for. These bailiffs are generally the sons of some of these farmers, recommended to the grinding ruffians of England by the grinding ruffians of Scotland.'

Edinburgh, however, delighted him and he declared it the finest city he had ever seen. The Edinburgh papers were less enthusiastic about the visitor, denouncing him as a revolutionary blackguard. To his huge delight, the people did not share the views of the leader writers. His lectures were packed and everywhere he was greeted with immense enthusiasm. He began to think Scotland not such a bad place after all.

From Edinburgh, he moved west to the manufacturing districts round Glasgow. He viewed them with distaste, and refused to look closely at any machines, 'lest I should be tempted to understand them'. There was, however, one factory village that could not be overlooked, New Lanark. This was arguably the most famous industrial site in the world, as a result of the social experiments of its manager, Robert Owen. He ranks with Cobbett as one of the great pioneers of the Radical movement in British politics and, like Cobbett, he was a man whose life was filled with contradictions, but there the similarities end. It was more than the difference of opinion between a manufacturer and a farmer, it was a much more fundamental difference towards the philosophy of the poor. Owen had a great vision of what he called 'Villages of Co-operation', where members of the community would work together and each be allotted his or her own task. To Cobbett this was at best regimentation, at worst something akin to the workhouse: he sarcastically dismissed Owen's Utopian villages as 'parallelograms of paupers'. Owen was ensconced in the ranks of Scots 'feelosofers' – even if he was a Welshman.

So, Cobbett arrived at New Lanark ready to be unimpressed. He refused to look at the mills, but went to the school and the New Institution. Owen set great store by teaching the children, and he encouraged his workers to take healthy exercise, including dancing, all of which was anathema to Cobbett. The school disgusted him:

> There was one boy pointing with a stick to something stuck up upon the wall, and then all the rest of the boys began bawling out what it was ... the fellow who leads the lazy life in the teaching of whom, ought to be sent to raking the kennel, or filling a dung-cart.

The dancing display was even worse.

> There were these eighteen couples, marching, arm in arm, in regular files, with a lock-step, slow march, to the sound of a fiddle, which a fellow, big enough to carry a quarter of wheat or to dig ten rods of ground in a day, was playing in the corner of the room with an immense music book lying open before him.

Even worse was the sight of 'half-naked lads of twelve or thirteen, putting their arms round the waists of the thinly-clad girls of the same age'. So he passed on his way to a land very much more to his liking. The valley of the Clyde, with its rich farmland, enchanted him and 'I cling to it', he wrote 'as Adam is said to have clung to Paradise'. But it was not in England, and he was not too sorry to be heading back south. At least he was able to tell his readers that

Scotland was not the barren wilderness they might have thought from the work of travellers such as Johnson.

If Cobbett was forced to change his mind about Scotland, so the Scots raised their opinion of him. He made a good impression by lecturing whenever asked and not once quibbling about fees. Those with whom he stayed found him straightforward and unpretentious, full of bonhomie and a great favourite with the children of the house. Given his schedule as reported by one of his hosts, and quoted in the *Fife Herald*,[2] it is difficult to see how families got to know him at all.

> His host ... though himself called on to get up at 5, to see if his guest wanted light or fire, but he was behind hand; his guest had been up at 4, and lighted the fire for himself, and was busy writing. He continued to do so until he joined the breakfast table, where he remained 4 minutes, leaving the savant to philosophise with Madame and her young folks. The amanuensis came at 9, and together they kept at it the whole day. He came another 4 *minutes* to the dinner table, and ate a very spare slice of mutton, without tasting anything else, or anything in the shape of drink. At tea he remained 6 minutes, from the incidental circumstances that news of the proroguing of Parliament ... was then brought in, and was treated at some length, as giving a more determinable shape of his future motions in Scotland. He resumed and continued his labours throughout the evening.

The paper's correspondent ended, with a surprised note. 'So you know we are beginning to think that the imputation of sordidness made against Cobbett is not warranted.' Cobbett and Scotland parted on better terms than they had met.

Returning home after the Scottish tour and the Oldham election, the Cobbetts rented a house in Westminster, conveniently close to the House. They moved in for the opening of the new Parliament on 29 January 1833. Cobbett arrived suitably dressed for the occasion, having exchanged his old unfashionable blue jacket for an equally unfashionable black one, and ready, in his own words, 'to fight the devil'. He did not regard himself, as many MPs are said to do, as the 'new boy' overwhelmed by the dignity and age-old ceremonial of the place. He was the 'new man' arriving to give the old place a thorough shaking, and to emphasize the point, he plonked himself down on the Treasury Bench in the place traditionally reserved for the Leader of the House. It was a defiant gesture, but in many ways an empty and slightly absurd one. He had seen Reform as the great turning-point in the country's political history, and in many ways it was, but it marked the start of a slow movement in a new direction, not a violent convulsion. Lord Grey still presided over a Whig government, just as he had before the election. Cobbett's voice inside the House could never have the influence that his pen had wielded outside it.

Cobbett's parliamentary career has generally been depicted as an anti-climax. It was, in the sense that Reform itself proved a terrible anti-climax. Cobbett had been prepared to accept these limited measures as a necessary step on the road to complete Reform, a movement that was later to be taken on by the Chartists. But there was no denying that the rural poor in whose name he had fought so many battles, were as unrepresented in the new Parliament as they had ever been in the old. Not all the Radicals accepted the half-measures. Hunt, in particular, had been a passionate advocate of all-or-nothing, and was inclined to view anyone who did not share his views as traitors to the cause. He represented a sizeable body of Radical opinion, which saw the Bill as adding a new class, a middle class, to Parliament, but one whose interests were little different from those of the old aristocrats who had ruled for so long. As one Radical paper put it, the whole thing was a fraud.[3]

> The only difference between the Whigs and the Tories is this
> – The Whigs would give the shadow to preserve the substance; the Tories would not give the shadow, because stupid as they are, the millions will not stop at shadows but proceed onwards to realities.

Cobbett and Hunt, who had argued so often in the past, were now irreconcilable, which was an outcome which at least pleased Nancy Cobbett. For the Radical movement as a whole, the split in the ranks could hardly have come at a worse time, just when they seemed poised to exert a real influence in the political world. As Cobbett was soon to discover, the pronouncements and deeds of the reformed Parliament would not be changed. No Radical measure would be accepted: no oppressive Bill defeated. The best he could now hope for was to be part of a group that would see itself as having a duty to question and criticize, without fear or favour.[4]

> What is wanted in the House, is this: ten men, who care not one single straw for all the noise that can possibly be raised against them; who would be just as insensible to the roarings and the scoffings as they would be to the noise of a parcel of dogs howling at the moon; who would preserve their good humour in spite of all the cheerings drawn forth by attacks upon them; and above all things, who would constantly, readily and boldly, persevere in looking scrupulously into every grant of the public money, however small.

It was by no means a despicable role, but it left Cobbett where he had always been, looking on events as a critical outsider, and not where he hoped Reform would have put him, as an insider helping to shape them. At least, as he proved by speeches inside the House and by his writings, he had not lost the zest for a battle. He had promised to fight and fight he did.

He fought, with no success in changing legislation, against the tax system that favoured the rich at the expense of the poor. He fought against the repressive legislation that tried to break the strength of the developing Trade Union movement. The Combination Acts had been repealed, but the authorities still found other ways to attack Unions. The most famous case of all was that of the Tolpuddle Martyrs, transported for seven years, ostensibly for administering illegal oaths, in practice for joining a Union. Cobbett's voice was loud among those who denounced the judgement. The champion of the rural poor proved also to be champion of the industrial workers.

He even found himself making common cause with an old enemy, Robert Owen. There was one thing on which the two did agree, that the employment of very young children for unlimited hours was evil. Lord Ashley's Factory Bill of 1833 sought to reduce the hours worked by children under eighteen to ten hours a day. The opponents prophesied doom and disaster, the ruin of the nation and all its industries if such a monstrous piece of legislation were passed. Cobbett spoke for the Bill, and his words still ring clear and loud, and one can only hope that those who heard them and voted against the Bill felt at least a twinge of discomfort at the scorn he poured upon them.[5]

Sir, I will make but one single observation upon this subject; and that is this: that this *'reformed'* House has, this night, made a *discovery* greater than all the discoveries that all former Houses of Commons have ever made, even if all their discoveries could have been put into one. Heretofore, we have sometimes been told that our ships, our mercantile traffic with foreign nations by the means of those ships, together with our body of rich merchants; we have sometimes been told that these form the source of our wealth, power, and security. At other times, the land has stepped forward, and bid us look to it, and its yeomanry, as the sure and solid foundation of our greatness and our safety. At other times, the Bank has pushed forward with her claims, and has told us, that great as the others were, they were nothing without 'PUBLIC CREDIT,' upon which, not only the prosperity and happiness, but the very independence of the country depended. But, Sir, we have this night discovered, that the shipping, the land, and the

Bank and its credit, are all nothing worth compared with the labour of three hundred thousand little girls in Lancashire! Aye, when compared with only an eighth part of the labour of those three hundred thousand little girls, from whose labour, if we only deduct two hours a day, away goes the wealth, away goes the capital, away go the resources, the power, and the glory of England!

Cobbett's greatest disappointment came with changes to the Poor Law. A Royal Commission under the Bishop of London had been set up to investigate the issue. He was confident that nothing would be done – 'the chopsticks will see to that' – and that a reformed Parliament would stand by the rural poor. He was wrong. A set of proposals was put forward, entirely based on the theories of Malthus, that the poor were growing in number and must be kept in check. Out went the old system of parish relief, overseen by magistrates, and in came the Poor Law Commissioners based in London. They were empowered to set up Union Workhouses, and they were specifically ordered to make them as unpleasant as possible. All able-bodied paupers were to be given work far worse than any they could possibly get outside, and husbands and wives were to be kept separate to prevent their breeding. The aim was clear: only the most desperate would ever again seek relief.

Cobbett attacked the Bill from many directions. He argued a case for a Rousseau-like social contract, in which the still disenfranchised poor consented to be governed only return for fair treatment.

There must be two parties to an obligation: without protection on the one side there can be no right to demand obedience on the other.[6]

It was part of a deplorable movement to take control of local affairs away from local people and hand it over to central government. 'This bill will totally abrogate all the local government of the kingdom: the gentlemen and the magistrates will be totally divested of all power tending to uphold their character, and to secure their property and their personal safety in the country.'[7] Above all else, it was immoral. Cobbett never ceased to campaign against the New Poor Law, and in his very last book he came closer than he had ever come before to arguing that if those who owned the land would not treat fairly with those who lived on the land, then the poor would rise and take the land.[8]

Well, then, what is the conclusion to which we come at last? Why, that the labourers have a right to subsistence out of the land, in all cases of inability to labour; that all those who are

AUTHOR OF "THE POLITICAL REGISTER".

Published by James Fraser, 215 Regent Street, London.

Cobbett sketched in the House of Commons, shortly after his election (Warden and Fellows of Nuffield College, Oxford)

able to labour have a right to subsistence out of the land, in exchange for their labour; and that, if the holders of the land will not give them subsistence, in exchange for their labour, they have a right to the land itself. Thus we come to the conclusion, that, if these new, inhuman and diabolical doctrines were acted upon, instead of giving that 'security to property,' which is their pretence, there would be an end of all respect for, and of all right to, property of every description!

Everywhere there seemed to be conspiracies against the poor, and even proposals which today seem eminently sensible were greeted with intense suspicion. Peel's new police force was regarded as something closer to the KGB than to the honest British 'Bobby' or 'peeler' which the Bill created. They were seen as *agents provocateurs* and spies and, worst of all, foreign. 'I have a rooted hatred of police establishment: I hate it because it is of foreign growth, and because it is *French.*'[9]

Cobbett fought many lonely battles, but he did have allies outside the sparse ranks of the Radicals and, in particular, he often found himself making common cause with O'Connell and the Irish Catholics. He was, by now, firmly set against the whole idea of an established church. The arguments begun in his history of the Reformation were carried further in *Legacy to Parsons.*[10] To the question, 'does the Establishment conduce to religious instruction?' he answered, 'No: flatly no; if "religious instruction" mean a teaching of the people the principles and practice of a pious worshipping of God.' Religious instruction should be paid for by those who wanted it, not by the state. He drew his examples of the iniquities of the present system mainly from the non-conformists. For example, a labourer called Jeremiah Dodsworth was required to pay 4s. 4d. out of an annual pay of £13 to the local rector, whose church he did not attend. When he refused to pay, he was given three months in gaol. And what applied to non-conformists applied in even greater measure in Ireland, where the majority of the population was Catholic.

Cobbett and O'Connell were not always in complete agreement. Who, indeed ever was in complete agreement with Cobbett? But they had enough in common to outweigh the differences, and the Irishman was particularly grateful for the support of such a very English Englishman. He urged Cobbett to go and see for himself just what the situation was in his own land.[11]

I want to thank you most heartily for all the good – the unmixed good you have done for Ireland, and the still greater good your visit and your knowledge of the state of the country must produce. Accept my warmest thanks in the name of and on behalf of Ireland.

So Cobbett went to Ireland and received a welcome scarcely matched among the chopsticks of England. Here, very near the end of his life, he showed that his literary powers were as strong as ever. He was always at his best when his heart was moved, and the plight of the poor Irish moved him deeply. He was at his best because it was at such times that he found the perfect means to express his feelings. He could simply have written essays for the readers of the *Register*, but instead he couched them as letters to John Marshall, back home at Cobbett's own farm. As a result, he told his story in a way that went straight to the heart, talked directly to the personal experience of his readers. If one were asked to explain Cobbett's appeal to the ordinary, often disregarded, country people of England, then one could scarcely do better than quote this passage. It is as good as anything in the better known *Rural Rides*.

> Marshall, you know how I scolded Tom Denman and little Barratt and your own son Dick, on the Saturday before I came away, for not sweeping the *sleeping-place* of the *yard-hogs* out clean, and what a strict charge I gave George to fling out the old bed, and to give them a bed of fresh straw every Saturday. Oh, how happy would thousands upon thousands in this city be, if they could be lodged in a place like that roughest hog bed! I this morning saw a *widow* woman and her four children, in the spot where they had slept; on *their bed*, in short. George remembers my looking over at the sows and their sucking pigs, and at the two youngest calves, just before I came away; and that I told him to keep them in that nice condition all the time that I should be away. Now Marshall, this poor widow and her little children were lying upon a quantity of straw not a twentieth part so great as that allotted to one of the sows and her pigs; and if I, on my return, were to see, as I am sure I shall not, the straw of the calves as dirty, and so broken, as that upon which this widow and her children were lying, I should drive George out of the house, as a slovenly and cruel fellow.[12]

The letters are moving testimonials to the horrors of Irish poverty, and also seem to suggest that the fires of anger at injustice still burned fiercely.

Reading Cobbett's work of the 1830s, one is scarcely conscious of any reduction of enthusiasm, any abatement of indignation or any falling off in the standards of the writing. This is astonishing, not because he was getting older, for many great writers have been at their best in later years, but because here was a man moving into his seventies and starting a new career as a Member of Parliament, and still producing a huge volume of written work while never stinting his duties to Parliament. When the Factory Bill was being debated in 1833, he stayed throughout the proceedings, went to vote at 1 a.m., eventually got to bed at 2.30 and by 6 a.m. was up and writing to make sure his account was available for the afternoon edition of the *Register*.

It was almost inevitable that such a regime would take its toll, and with so much effort concentrated on politics and writing it was his family life that suffered. If things had been bad before, they were now a good deal worse. He began to see all the family as ranged behind his wife and determined to oppose him. His public utterances were as rational as ever, but public life seemed to demand all his energy and common sense; his private correspondence shows a depressing decline into paranoia.

His relations with Nancy never really recovered from the miserable days of her attempted suicide. For years before that, he had spoken of her as his most stalwart supporter, now even the past was called into question. One night in July 1833, he came home after a Select Committee meeting on the police spy William Popay that ended in the small hours of the morning. He had expected to find a warm fire, and a bowl of hot milk as a comfort.

I found neither bowl nor fire, and nobody but the man to let me in, though there was wife, three daughters, two sons, and two maid servants in the house, all in good beds of my providing. Too happy should I have been, however, if this had been *all*. But, when I got into that bed which I so much needed for rest as well as for sleep, that *tongue*, which, for more than 20 years has been my great curse, and which would have worried any other man to death, suffered me not to have one moment's sleep, after my long fatigues and anxious labours; and, as I saw that this was a mere *beginning* of a month of it, she breakfasting in bed every day, and having the sofa to lounge on, and the park to take exercise in, to provide strength of lungs and the power of sustaining wakefulness at night, I also saw, that I must give up the affair of Popay, or get out of my house. Therefore as soon as it was light, I called up my man, and decamped to Bolt Court; and there I remained 'till the day when the king prorogued us.[13]

Bolt Court was the office and there he shut himself away and brooded. He began to see conspiracies everywhere. There were plots to deprive him of the *Register*, to have him booted out of Parliament, but he announced to his readers that he would fight them all. His biggest fights now, however, were with his own family.

It is difficult to unravel the tangled thread of the family quarrel, but somewhere near the heart of it was a growing exasperation on the part of the younger members with their father's financial mismanagement. They were no longer children, and could hardly be expected to bow to his every whim as they had once done. In 1832 he had sold Barn Elm Farm and bought Normandy Farm, very much against the family wishes. The new farm was big, expensive, and quite clearly set to lose money, not make it. William Cobbett Junior ran it as a reluctant manager. The seed business was already in deep trouble. In the past, Cobbett had always been able to rely on his pen to write himself into funds, but even this was failing. He took his Parliamentary duties seriously, and had little time left for the *Register*. He would make the effort when necessary, as he did at the time of the debate on the Factory Bill, but there was more news, more letters and less personal comment. The *Register* was Cobbett or it was nothing, and as he wrote less and less so the circulation fell. His books in the latter days were no more successful. His *History of the Reign of George IV* was dull, there was no great market for his new French–English Dictionary; and all the time his debts, especially those to Sir Thomas Beevor, were mounting. In the middle of this financial shambles, a new family row broke out in which he accused his own sons, John and James, of at best misman-agement and at worst embezzlement.

The cause of this quarrel was the will of an old family friend, Miss Boxall. Cobbett had been made an executor and now he was accusing the two sons of misusing the funds, a claim which they vigorously denied, with the backing of the rest of the family includ-ing their mother. This threw Cobbett into a complete rage and he poured his anger out in a letter full of pitiful resentments and accu-sations.[14]

They have discredited me to the utmost of their powers, and have stripped me of my means of paying. If they had not done this, there were copy-rights and stocks too for them. But, I am not thus to be plundered and my credit destroyed, and to be buried under printers' bills and arrears of rent and taxes, without insisting on their helping to pay this *Debt*. Their harbouring of the infamous Blundell, and their harbouring of Eagle under *my own roof*, after they had *heard* the latter abuse me, and after I had told them, that I had affidavits to produce of the foul calumnies of the former against me; these acts, in coccurence with the assertion of James Cobbett to Mr Nicholson, that *my character* might be *destroyed without affecting theirs*, and which he said in the name of '*all my family*'; these acts, coupled with this assertion, explain the motives that have been at work from the beginning. I showed you the *ferocious letter* of James Cobbett of 16 July, 1831, very soon after he had spent £60 of my money at Paris, and not long after he and his sister had spent £500 of it, in an European tour.

After the tirade, matters settled down a little, and Cobbett worked out a scheme to pay off his debts. A settlement was reached with John and James, his stock of books was sold and a down payment was made to Beevor, with arrangements to clear the whole debt. He also agreed on an annuity for Nancy. It was not done, it has to be said, with a good grace. 'Mind,' he wrote, 'all this may be done *in this very year*, if she let alone; and, if not, by God, I will not provide one single farthing for her.'[15] And when the annuity was agreed, the bitterness remained. 'As to the *wife*, there is the husband's *house* and *home*. I have my *legal rights* left at any rate. If the wife will not live in the husband's house, he is not bound to give her anything out of it.'[16]

It was a pitiful affair, and no one can pretend that Cobbett emerges from it with much credit. In his defence one can only say that he was by now a sick man. He had prided himself always on his physical prowess. Now he could hardly take a short walk without pausing for breath. He suffered from a bad cough and hoarseness, but still insisted on appearing regularly in the House and speaking in debates. He once remarked '*An old Quaker*, at Philadelphia, when I was writing away at a furious rate, used to send me a letter about once a week, containing those words, and no more: "Friend William, keep thyself cool".' He never did. He looked out on the countryside, and heard the spring call of the cuckoo and was at once reminded of all those he had fought against throughout his life.[17]

And now this cuckoo will, on Midsummer-Day, cease to call us up in the morning, and cease its work of sucking the hedge-sparrow's eggs, depositing its own in the next, making the poor hedge-sparrow bring it up until it is big and strong enough to eat the hedge-sparrow: in all which respects it so exactly resembles the at once lazy and greedy and ungrateful and cruel vagabonds, who devour the fruit of our labour.

In London, he saw the Marble Arch and the National Gallery and fulminated against them and the city.[18]

Hating the smoke of London as I do; my ears, violated as they are by the rattle of the infernal hackney coaches; my eyes, blasted as they are by the sight of the seventy-five-thousand-pounds gateway, and by the hundred-and-fifty-thousands picture gallery, the expenses of which are extracted from the sweat of the working people.

Here at least was evidence that the old Cobbett was alive and
kicking – kicking, indeed, as hard as ever. He had the satisfaction
of finding his last published book, *Legacy to Parsons*, become a
hugely popular success.

In January 1835 there was a general election, and Cobbett and
Fielden were again returned for Oldham. In February, when
Parliament reassembled he was back in place, still trying to speak
though by now his voice was scarcely audible. The very last debate
he attended was on 25 May, when, appropriately, the subject was
agricultural distress and though he was now too weak to speak at
all, he insisted on staying to cast his vote. The next day he went
down to Normandy Farm.

John and James Cobbett collaborated to write an account of this
last visit.[19]

> On Thursday night ... he felt unusually well, and impru-
> dently drank tea in the open air; but he went to bed apparently
> in better health. In the early part of the night he was taken
> violently ill, and on Friday and Saturday was considered in a
> dangerous state by the medical attendant. On Sunday he
> revived again, and on Monday gave us hope that he could yet
> be well. He talked feebly, but in the most collected and
> sprightly manner upon politics and farming; wished for four
> day's rain for the Cobbett corn and root crop; and on
> Wednesday he could no longer remain shut up from the fields,
> but desired to be carried round the farm; which being done,
> he criticized the work that had been going on in his absence,
> and detected some little deviation from his orders, with all the
> quickness that was so remarkable in him. As he was carried
> to see the fields a little boy in a blue smock-frock happened to
> come by us, to whom my father gave a laughing look, at
> which I thought I should have dropped, I knowing what was
> passing in his mind. He seemed refreshed at the sight of the
> little creature, which he had once precisely resembled, though
> now at such an immeasurable distance.

It is a charming account, and well meant, but it tells only a
part of the story. Although he had moments of lucidity, and was
even able to joke with the doctor, he also lapsed into delirium.
Reading this piece gives the impression that he was surrounded by
a loving family, but they were only summoned at the very last, on
18 June, when William sent a note, 'If you are to see my poor
father again it must be today.' They came straight down, but there
was no great death bed reconciliation, and although the children

were allowed in to see him, Nancy had to wait until he had lost consciousness. She sat by him, bathed his head and remained with him. 'In the last half-hour his eyes became dim, and at ten minutes after one pm. he leaned back, closed them as if to sleep, and died without a gasp.'

EPILOGUE

There are many ways in which a man's life can be assessed. One is to look at his position in life at the start and compare it with that at the finish. The little boy in the blue smock had ended owner of a farm and land, houses in London and offices from which he had published one of the most influential journals of the day. The child who had been born in a public house, son of a farm labourer, now had a seat in Parliament. If such things are measures of success, then Cobbett's life was a triumph. But there are other standards, the standards a man sets for himself. His great ambition was to change society. He wanted to see an end to corruption in public life. He wanted, above all, to see a country in which agriculture was seen as the only truly important way of life, and where those who worked the land could do so secure in the knowledge that they would always receive a fair return for their labour, and would never be allowed to sink into destitution. Set against these aims, he was a failure. The industrial world was steadily gaining in strength, and at Cobbett's death a new manifestation was to quicken the rate of change, as a network of iron rails spread first across Britain and then over the world. The agricultural labourer, far from looking to a better future, faced the new horror of the workhouse, deliberately designed not to make life better but to make it as grim as possible.

None of this, however, really measures Cobbett's true greatness. Anyone seeing a brief note on his life must be struck with the apparent inconsistencies, the violent swing from reactionary to radical; but it becomes comprehensible once one absolute fundamental is grasped. He never ceased caring about the poor, but not in the way that a charitable institution might care as it doled out funds as a favour, as a gift from the rich to those less fortunate than themselves. He believed that the poor were, in fact, those who did as much as anyone to create the wealth of a country and their share of that wealth was a right not a concession. He was no early Marxist, no believer in the rise of the proletariat. What he wanted for the poor was the fundamentals of a decent life: a good home, clothing and nourishing food. If they received more, that was all well and good, but they should never, under any circumstances, have to make do with less. All the other campaigns he fought, from paper money to rotten boroughs, were subsidiary to this one great theme.

In the age in which he was born and lived, few of those who had power and authority shared his views. So it fell to him to articulate the needs of the poor, to be their voice. He did so without any hint of condescension, and he did so with unique literary power. He found his own form of expression which was elegant and witty enough to appeal to a highly sophisticated readership whilst being direct enough to be recognised as an honest voice by the labourer in the cottage. There have been plenty of political writers and theorists who have taken it upon themselves to argue on behalf of the people, and from a position of conscious intellectual or moral superiority. Cobbett was a very much rarer creature. He argued as an equal, as a man who understood the poor because he came from the poor. There is absolutely no doubt that his regard for 'the chopsticks' was genuine, and his honesty comes through as an almost tangible thing. This is not to say that he did not use artifice. Far from it. One could argue that his greatest creation was a plain-speaking down-to-earth farmer called William Cobbett. He very deliberately took those aspects of his own character which suited the message he wanted to put across, and just as deliberately played down others. His whole approach was based on the idea that what he had to say was not based on some airy-fairy philosophy dreamed up in an academic's study, but came out of the direct experience of a man who had never lost his roots, who could spot a rotten apple in any barrel. At his best, he was brilliantly successful. In *Rural Rides,* one gets more notion of the realities of life in the countryside at that time than one could from a hundred other contemporary travel books. And it is because we believe he sees with a clear eye that we are prepared to listen to his views on what has gone wrong and attend to his notions on how they might be put right. When he tells his own farmhand in England about the conditions of the farmhands in Ireland, we share his anger and understand, without his having to spell it out, that he is also saying that if such inhumanity is possible in one place, then it is possible anywhere. Perhaps his greatest achievement was to make us all aware, ourselves reading him in a different world, in another century, as well as his contemporaries, that poverty is not an abstraction. He made the world look at real people enduring real suffering. And then he went one step further. He said that whatever Malthusians and others might argue, poverty was not the end result of a natural law. It was due to particular actions taken by specific men, and these actions could be changed. That they were not changed in his lifetime was his greatest sorrow, but the message has never lost its relevance and few have expressed it better.

As should be clear by now, his own life was very far from reaching the standards he set for others. No lover of Cobbett's writings can fail to be saddened by the miseries of the last years, and the sadness of the divided family. That the children must often have found their father impossible to live with is all too obvious, but they bore few grudges. Anne was, for many years, the closest to him and understood his moods better than most. On his death-bed in the grips of his dreadful paranoia, he rejected even her, but she did as much as anyone to preserve his memory. She became the publisher of his books and wrote books of her own, which were practical in a very Cobbetty way. Her *English Housekeeper* of 1835 was full of the sort of homely advice that was found in *Cottage Economy*. She lived on until 1877, like her other sisters unmarried. Whether the father frightened off would-be suitors, or whether the example of his life with Nancy made them think husbands a disposable commodity is not known. Nancy herself died in 1848 and was buried with her husband, so they finished up under the same roof after all. Susan became a teacher and in later life she set up house with Ellen at Wilmslow in Cheshire. A friend who knew them at that time described them as having 'beautiful old-world courtesy'.[1] Theirs seems to have been a quiet life, but they also retained an interest in their father's work. Susan was still writing around to friends for copies of his books in 1879, and when she died in 1889, her body was buried beside his. Ellen lived on until 1900.

The boys all opted for careers in law, with varying success. William (1798–1878) was tied the longest to his father's interests. He shared many of his views, but he, sadly, inherited his financial abilities as well. His life ended in farce, dying on his way to appear on behalf of the ludicrous Tichborne claimant. John (1800–77) eventually took over his father's Oldham seat in 1852, but was later to be returned in 1872 as a Conservative. He married John Fielden's daughter, Mary. James (1803–81) had a successful career, both as a lawyer and a writer, and worked with Anne to edit his father's political writings into six vast volumes, a task which, if it has done nothing else, has earned him the gratitude of at least one biographer.

Richard (1814–75) was the odd out among the children, very much the baby of the family and born at a time when his father was often away from home. He remained staunchly radical, editing and publishing *The Champion and Weekly Herald*, while establishing a successful firm of solicitors in Manchester. He was the only member of the family to produce an heir, and his descendants went on to have distinguished careers. How surprised Sergeant Cobbett would have been, had he known that his great-great-grandson would be an epaulette among epaulettes, General Sir Gerald Lathbury. More surprised, one suspects, than William Cobbett would have been to find that his name was remembered and cherished more than a century and a half after his death. He would be even more delighted to know that readers can still share his sense of outrage at the wrongs he encountered and join in his anger. And if he never quite found the Eden that he was sure England could become, we can still share his dreams and just occasionally catch a glimpse of those scenes that were dearest of all to him. He knew where his ideal would be located, in 'some vale in Wiltshire. Water meadows at the bottom, corn-land going up towards the hills, those hills being down land, and a farmhouse, in a clump of trees, in some little cross vale between the hills, sheltered on every side but the south.'[2]

This is the image of Cobbett's England, a true Arcadia, an ideal as appealing now as it was then. What makes Cobbett's so much greater was his conviction that this rural idyll could never make a man happy while a single farmworker and his family remained hungry. He dreamed of his perfect land: he fought all his life for justice for the poor.

BIBLIOGRAPHY

Cobbett's Published Works

The principal works, including important pamphlets and the journals he wrote and edited are listed below, in alphabetical order. Many books and pamphlets first appeared in the journals, but they are listed here under the title and date of their separate publication in final form. Many of the works have extremely long titles, but they are given here in their generally accepted abbreviated form. It does not include works by others, translated by Cobbett.

Advice to Young men and (incidentally) to Young Women, 1830
The American Gardener, 1821
Big O and Sir Glory, 1825
The Bloody Buoy, 1796
A Bone to Gnaw for the Democrats, 1795
Cobbett's American Political Register, 1817–18
Cobbett's Collective Commentaries, 1822
Cobbett's Complete Collection of State Trials, 1809–12 [continued afterwards as
    Howell's State Trials]
Cobbett's Evening Post, 1820
Cobbett's Legacy to Labourers, 1834
Cobbett's Legacy to Parsons, 1835
Cobbett's Manchester Lectures, 1832
Cobbett's Parliamentary Debates, 1804–12 [Continued afterwards as *Hansard*]
Cobbett's Parliamentary History of England, 1804–12
Cobbett's Poor Man's Friend, 1833
Cobbett's Sermons, 1821–2
Cobbett's Spirit of the Public Journals, 1804
Cobbett's Tour in Scotland, 1832
Cottage Economy, 1822
Country Porcupine, 1798–9
The Democratic Judge, 1798
Detection of a Conspiracy, 1798
The Emigrant's Guide, 1829
The English Gardener, 1828
French Arrogance, 1798
A French Grammar, 1824
A Full and Accurate Report of the Trial of William Cobbett, 1831
A Geographical Dictionary of England and Wales, 1832
Good Friday, 1830
A Grammar of the English Language, 1818

The Gros Mousqueton Diplomatique, or Diplomatic Blunderbuss, 1796
History of the Regency and Reign of King George IV, 1830–1
A History of the Protestant Reformation, 1824–6
Impeachment of Mr Lafayette, 1793
Important Considerations for the People of the Kingdom, 1803
A Kick for a Bite, 1795
*Letters to the Right Honourable Lord Hawkesbury and the Right Honourable Henry
    Addington*, 1802
The Life and Adventures of Peter Porcupine, 1796
Life of Andrew Jackson, 1834
A Little Plain English, 1795
A New French and English Dictionary, 1833
A New Year's Gift to the Democrats, 1796
Observations on the Emigration of Joseph Priestley, 1794
Paper against Gold and Glory against Prosperity, 1814
The Political Consort, 1796–7
The Political Register, 1802–35
The Porcupine, 1800–1801
Porcupine's Gazette, 1797–9
Porcupine's Works, 1801
A Prospect from the Congress-Gallery, 1796
The Republican Judge, 1798
Rural Rides, 1830
The Scare-Crow, 1796
The Soldier's Friend, 1792
A Spelling Book, 1831
Surplus Population, 1835
A Treatise on Cobbett's Corn, 1828
Two-Penny Trash, 1831–2
The Woodlands, 1825–8
A Year's Residence in the United States of America, 1818–19

Books on Cobbett

This selection mainly concentrates on biographies, or books with a substantial biographical content. It also includes bibliographies and major compilations.

Anon, *The Life of William Cobbett, Esq, Late MP for Oldham*, 1835
Anon, *The Life of William Cobbett*, Dedicated to his Sons, 1835
Anon, *Memoirs of William Cobbett, Esq. MP for Oldham*, 1835
W. Baring Pemberton, *Cobbett*, 1949
Marjorie Bowen, *Peter Porcupine, A Study of William Cobbett*, 1935
Asa Briggs, *William Cobbett*, 1967
E.I. Carlyle, *William Cobbett: A Study of his Life as Shown in his Writings*, 1904
G.K. Chesterton, *William Cobbett*, 1926
Mary E. Clark, *Peter Porcupine in America*, 1939
John Clarke, *The Price of Progress, Cobbett's England 1780–1835*, 1977
John N. Cobbett and James P. Cobbett, *Selections from Cobbett's Political
    Writings*, 1835–7
G.D.H. Cole, *The Life of William Cobbett*, 1924 (revised 1947)
G.D.H. Cole (ed.), *William Cobbett's Letters to Edward Thornton*, 1932
G.D.H. Cole and Margaret Cole (eds.), *The Opinions of William Cobbett*, 1944

G.D.H. Cole and Margaret Cole (eds.), *Rural Rides Including Irish Ride and Scottish Tour*, 1930

John Derry, (ed.), *Cobbett's England*, 1968

Gerald Duff (ed.), *Letters of William Cobbett*, 1974

Pierce W. Gaines, *William Cobbett and the United States*, 1792–1835, 1971

Daniel Green, *Great Cobbett*, 1983

Robert Huish, *Memoirs of the late William Cobbett*, 1836

Denis Knight, *Cobbett in Ireland*, 1984

Lewis Melville, *The Life and Letters of William Cobbett*, 1913

John W. Osborne, *William Cobbett*, 1966

M.L. Pearl, *William Cobbett, A Bibliographical Account*, 1953

William Reitzel (ed.), *The Autobiography of William Cobbett*, 1933

James Sambrook, *William Cobbett*, 1977

Edward Smith, *William Cobbett*, 1878

George Spater, *William Cobbett*, 1982

Molly Townsend, *Not by Bullets and Bayonets*, 1983

Raymond Williams, *Cobbett*, 1983

David A. Wilson, *Paine and Cobbett*, 1988

NOTES

In quoting Cobbett's own works, his name has not been used. The title is given in full at the first appearance and subsequently in abbreviated form e.g. *The Life and Adventures of Peter Porcupine*, 1796 becomes *Peter Porcupine*. The Political Register is PR throughout. The Cobbett Papers held at Nuffield College, University of Oxford are referred to as (Nuffield). The quotations from the Cobbett Papers have been used with the kind permission of the Fellow Librarian.

CHAPTER 1

1. Daniel Defoe, *A Tour Through The Whole Island of Great Britain* 1724–6.
2. *Cobbett's Tour in Scotland*, 1833 (1984 ed. Daniel Green)
3. Ibid.
4. Ibid.
5. *The Life and Adventures of Peter Porcupine*, 1796
6. Quoted in William Reitzel (ed) *The Autobiography of William Cobbett*, 1933
7. *Rural Rides*, 1830
8. *Peter Porcupine*
9. Quoted in Pamela Horn, *Labouring Life in the Victorian Countryside*, 1976
10. *Autobiography*
11. Ibid.
12. Ibid.
13. Ibid.
14. Anne Cobbett's notes for a life of her father, (Nuffield)
15. *Peter Porcupine*

CHAPTER 2

1. J. Howlett, *Annals of Agriculture*, 1792, quoted in Allan Armstrong, *Farmworkers*, 1820
2. *PR*. February 1820
3. Jonathan Swift, *A Tale of a Tub*, 1704
4. *PR*. February 1820
5. Ibid.
6. Anne Cobbett, Account of the Family, (Nuffield)
7. *Peter Porcupine*
8. Ibid
9. Ibid
10. *Autobiography*
11. *Peter Porcupine*
12. *Ibid.*
13. *Autobiography*
14. *Advice to Young Men*, 1829 [1980 edition]
15. Ibid.
16. *Peter Porcupine*
17. *Autobiography*
18. *The Emigrant's Guide*, 1829
19. *Advice to Young Men*
20. *Autobiography*
21. *Advice to Young Men*
22. Ibid.

23. *Autobiography*
24. *.Advice to Young Men*

20. *Observations on Priestley's Emigration*, 1794
21. P.R. 29 September 1804

CHAPTER 3

1. *PR*, 13 December 1817
2. *Advice to Young Men*
3. *The Soldier's Friend*, 1792
4. *Autobiography*
5. *PR*, October 1805
6. Tom Paine, *Rights of Man*, part 2, 1792
7. Quoted in Simon Schama, *Citizens*, 1989
8. *Peter Porcupine*
9. *Advice to Young Men*
10. Ibid.
11. Letter from Susan Cobbett to John Cobbett, 30 September 1835

CHAPTER 4

1. Tom Paine, *Common Sense*, 1776
2. Cobbett to Jefferson, 2 November 1792
3. *Autobiography*
4. *The Emigrant's Guide*, 1829
5. Ibid.
6. *Advice to Young Men*
7. Ibid.
8. *Autobiography*
9. *Advice to Young Men*
10. *Autobiography*
11. *Advice to Young Men*
12. *Le Tuteur Anglais*, 1795
13. *Autobiography*
14. Letter to James Mathieu, 19 July 1793
15. Letter to Rachel Smithers, 6 July 1794
16. *PR*, 12 October 1805
17. Undated letter quoted in Henry Collington Botton, *Scientific Correspondence of Joseph Priestley*, 1892
18. *PR*, 29 September 1804
19. Quoted in G.D.H. Cole, *The Life of William Cobbett*, 1947

CHAPTER 5

1. Quoted in James Thomas Flexner, *Washington – The Indispensable Man*, 1976
2. *The Bone to Gnaw for the Democrats*, 1795
3. *A Kick for a Bite*, 1795
4. *Porcupine's Works*, 1801
5. Remarks on the Pamphlets lately published against Peter Porcupine: *Porcupine's Works*, 1801
6. *A Little Plain English*, 1795
7. Ibid.
8. *Advice to Young Men*
9. *Autobiography*
10. Edmund Randolph, *A Vindication of Mr Randolph's Resignation*, 1795
11. *A New Year's Gift to the Democrats*, 1796
12. *The Bloody Buoy, thrown Out as a Warning to the Political Pilots of America*, 1796
13. Remarks on the Pamphlets lately published against *Peter Porcupine*, op cit.
14. *Autobiography*
15. *Porcupine's Works*

CHAPTER 6

1. *Autobiography*
2. Quoted in Flexner, op cit.
3. *Remarks on the Blunderbuss*, 1796
4. Quoted in Daniel J. Boorston, *The Americans: The National Experience*, 1965
5. *The Rushlight*, 15 February 1800
6. *Works*, Volume 4
7. Tom Paine, Letters to George Washington, 1796
8. George Chalmers, *The Life of Thomas Pain* [sic] 1791
9. *The Antidote for Tom Paine's*

Theological and Political Poison, 1786
10. Ibid.
11. John N. Cobbett and James P. Cobbett, *Selections from Cobbett's Political Writings*, 1835
12. *Porcupine's Works*, 1801
13. *Porcupine's Gazette*, June 1799
14. *The Cannibal's Progress*, 1798
15. *Porcupine's Works*
16. *Porcupine's Gazette*, 14 September 1797
17. *Political Works*
18. Letter to Edward Thornton, 29 August 1797
19. Letter to Edward Thornton, 27 August 1797
20. *Political Works*
21. G.D.H. Cole (ed.), *Letters from William Cobbett to Edward Thornton*, 1937
22. Letter to Thornton, 25 December 1799
23. *Autobiography*
24. *Porcupine's Works*
25. Letter to Thornton, 6 March 1800

CHAPTER 7

1. Letter dated 18 July 1800, Gerald Duff (ed.) *Letters of William Cobbett*, 1974
2. Anne Cobbett's notes
3. William Hazlitt, *Table Talk*, 1821
4. From Roy Palmer (ed.), *Poverty Knock*, 1974
5. *Commercial and Agricultural Magazine*, 1800, quoted in E.P. Thompson, *The Making of the English Working Class*, 1968 edition.
6. *PR*, April 1830
7. Letter dated 4 September 1800, Duff op. cit.
8. Letter to Edward Thornton, 20 January 1800
9. Quoted in Georges Duby and Robert Mandrou, *A History of French Civilisation*, 1964
10. John Locke, *Second Treatise on Government*, 1690
11. *Advice to Young Men*

12. *A Year's Residence in the United States of America*, 1813

CHAPTER 8

1. Quoted in Robert Reilly, *Pitt the Younger*, 1978
2. John Ferriar, pamphlet addressed to 'The Committee for the Regulation of the Police, in the Towns of Manchester and Salford', 1792
3. Andrew Ure, *The Philosophy of Manufacture*, 1835
4. Letter dated 1 October 1800
5. Quoted in Wendy Hinde, *Castlereagh*, 1981
6. Letter to N. Jekyll, 5 July 1800 in Duff, *Letters of William Cobbett*, 1974
7. *Autobiography*
8. Letter to Addington, 23 December 1801, *Political Works*
9. Letter to Addington, 24 December 1801, Ibid.
10. *Autobiography*
11. Ibid.
12. Cobbett to Lord Pelham, 11 October 1801.

CHAPTER 9

1. Letter to Thornton 19 February 1800
2. *PR*, 30 June 1802
3. *PR*, 2 October 1819
4. *Political Works*, July 1802
5. *PR*, 27 February 1802
6. *PR*, 27 October 1804
7. *PR*, 21 May 1803
8. Tom Paine, *The Decline and Fall of the English System of Finance*, 1793
9. *PR*, 10 December 1803
10. Letter to Thornton, 25 April 1800
11. *Important Considerations for the People of this Kingdom*, 1803

CHAPTER 10

1. *Autobiography*
2. Anne Cobbett's notes (Nuffield)
3. *PR*, 27 October 1804
4. Letter to William Windham 2 August 1805. Quoted in Gerald Duff (ed.) op. cit.
5. *PR*, August 1805
6. Anne Cobbett's notes (Nuffield)
7. Mary Russell Mitford, *Recollections of a Literary Life*, 1850
8. Letter to Lt Frederick Reid 13 December 1807 (Nuffield)
9. Letter dated 17 July 1808 (Nuffield)
10. Letter dated 21 February 1808 (Nuffield)
11. Letter dated 22 May 1810 (Nuffield)
12. Anne Cobbett's notes (Nuffield)
13. *Autobiography*
14. Ibid.
15. William Cobbett Jnr to his father 19 January 1808 (Nuffield)
16. *Autobiography*
17. *Advice to Young Men*
18. Ibid.
19. Quoted in *A Year's Residence in America*

CHAPTER 11

1. Cobbett to Windham 27 September 1803, quoted in Lewis Melville, *The Life and Letters of William Cobbett*, 1913
2. *PR*, July 1803
3. Laurence Sterne, *Tristram Shandy*, 1706–7
4. *PR*, April 1804
5. *PR*, April 1805
6. *Rural Rides*, 1830
7. *PR*, 8 February 1806
8. *PR*, 1 September 1804
9. *Political Works*
10. *PR*, March 1807
11. *PR*, 29 August 1807
12. *PR*, June 1805
13. *PR*, 1 February 1806

CHAPTER 12

1. *PR*, 6 December 1806
2. F.B. Cartwright (ed.) *The Life and Correspondence of Major Cartwright*, 1826
3. Quoted in E.P. Thompson, op. cit.
4. *PR*, 15 March 1806
5. Letter to John Wright dated 22 October 1807, quoted in Gerald Duff (ed.), op. cit., 1974
6. Letter to John Wright 29 May 1808. Quoted in Duff, op. cit.
7. Ibid.
8. *Political Works*
9. *PR*, 7 June 1806
10. *PR*, 28 June 1806
11. *PR*, 9 August 1806
12. *PR*, 20 August 1806
13. *Political Works*
14. *PR*, 20 December 1806
15. *PR*, 16 April 1808
16. *PR*, 9 December 1808
17. Cobbett to Wright, 12 February 1809, quoted in Melville op cit.
18. *Autobiography*
19. Ibid.
20. *PR*, 4 February 1809

CHAPTER 13

1. *PR*, 16 March 1811
2. *PR*, 1 July 1809
3. Cobbett to Wright, November 1809, Melville op. cit.
4. Letter to A. Tegart, 8 December 1809, quoted in Duff, op. cit.
5. Graham Wallas, *The Life of Francis Place*, 1918
6. *Autobiography*
7. Ibid.
8. Ibid.
9. Cobbett papers, (Nuffield)
10. Cobbett to Nancy 10 February 1802, quoted in Melville, op. cit
11. *Advice to Young Men*
12. Letter to Nancy, 3 February 1812, (Nuffield)
13. Letter to Nancy, 14 September 1811, (Nuffield)

14. Cobbett to Wright, 25 November 1808, Melville op. cit
15. Anne Cobbett's notes (Nuffield)
16. Ibid.
17. *PR*, 1 August 1812
18. Anne Cobbett's notes
19. *PR*, 25 July 1812
20. Anne Cobbett to Frederick Reid, 13 July 1812, quoted in Melville, op. cit.
21. Ibid.

CHAPTER 14

1. *Review of the Life of Thomas Paine*, 1796(?)
2. *Autobiography*
3. *Paper Against Gold*, 1815
4. *PR*, 1 June 1811
5. *PR*, 22 July 1815 and 30 September 1815
6. John Blackner, *History of Nottingham*, 1815
7. Broadsheet ballad, in Roy Palmer (ed.) *A Touch on the Times*, 1974
8. Quoted in G.D.H. Cole, *The Life of William Cobbett*, 1924
9. *PR*, 2 November 1816
10. *PR*, 4 May 1816
11. *Autobiography*
12. *PR*, 23 March 1816
13. *PR*, 1 July 1815
14. *PR*, 29 July 1815

CHAPTER 15

1. *PR*, 12 July 1815
2. Anne Cobbett's notes, (Nuffield)
3. *PR*, 10 April 1830
4. Samuel Bamford, *Passages in the Life of a Radical*, 1893
5. *PR*, 8 June 1816
6. Ibid.
7. *PR*, 8 March 1817
8. Quoted in E.P. Thompson, op. cit
9. *Autobiography*
10. *PR*, 22 November 1817
11. Ibid.
12. Anne Cobbett's notes (Nuffield)

13. *Autobiography*
14. Ibid.

CHAPTER 16

1. *Autobiography*
2. Letter from John to Anne Cobbett, 6 June 1817 (Nuffield)
3. *A Year's Residence in America*, 1818–9
4. Ibid.
5. Ibid.
6. PR, 3 October 1818
7. Ibid.
8. *PR*, 23 January 1819
9. *A Year's Residence in America*
10. Daniel Green, *Great Cobbett*, 1983
11. *PR*, 29 December 1819
12. Letter 6 February 1819, *Political Works*
13. *The American Gardener*, 1821
14. *A Grammar of the English Language*, 1818
15. Lines written in New York, 1819 (Nuffield)
16. Letter to William Cobbett, junior, 20 September 1819 (Nuffield)
17. Letter dated 30 November 1819 (Nuffield)

CHAPTER 17

1. *Black Dwarf*, 5 March 1817
2. *PR*, 25 October 1817
3. *PR*, 23 May 1818
4. *Rural Rides*, 30 August 1826
5. Quoted in John and Barbara Hammond, *The Town Labourer*, 1917
6. Percy Bysshe Shelley, *The Mask of Anarchy*, 1819
7. *PR*, 4 December 1819
8. Ibid.
9. Anne to James Cobbett, 24 December 1819 (Nuffield)
10. Untitled and undated press cutting, (Nuffield)
11. *PR*, 24 December 1819
12. *Autobiography*

13. Ibid.
14. Anne Cobbett's notes, (Nuffield)
15. *PR*, 25 March 1820
16. James to John Cobbett, 12 April 1820 (Nuffield)
17. Anne to James Cobbett, 20 April 1820 (Nuffield)
18. Ibid.

CHAPTER 18

1. Letter from Cobbett to the Queen, June 1820
2. Anne Cobbett's notes (Nuffield)
3. Anne Cobbett to James 25 August 1820 (Nuffield)
4. John Cobbett to James 26 November 1820 (Nuffield)
5. Anne Cobbett to James 6 December 1820 (Nuffield)
6. Ibid.
7. *PR*, 13 February 1821
8. E.J. Hobsbawm, *Labouring Men*, 1964
9. William Wilberforce, *A Practical View of the Prevailing Religious System of Professed Christians*, 1797
10. *Cobbett's Sermons*, 1822
11. *Cottage Economy*, 1822
12. Anne Cobbett to James, 23 January 1822 (Nuffield)

CHAPTER 19

1. Richard Combe, *The Tour of Dr Syntax*, 1812
2. Mary Morgan, *A Tour to Milford Haven in the Year 1781*, 1795
3. Thomas Hurtley, *Natural Curiosities of Malham*, 1786
4. Jane Austen, *Sense and Sensibility*, 1810
5. *PR*, 30 August 1823
6. J.L. and Barbara Hammond, *The Town Labourer*, 1917
7. *PR*, 17 August 1822
8. *A History of the Political Reformation*, 1827

CHAPTER 20

1. John Cobbett to William, 15 May 1825 (Nuffield)
2. Molly Townsend, *Not by Bullets and Bayonets*, 1983
3. Letter to Mrs Wilkes, 16 August 1894 (Southampton City Heritage Services)
4. *Big O and Sir Glory* or *'Leisure to laugh' A Comedy in Three Acts*, 1825
5. *PR*, 12 May 1825
6. *PR*, 21 February 1829
7. *PR*, 10 December 1825
8. Letter dated 5 January 1826 (Nuffield)
9. *PR*, 9 April 1828
10. *PR*, 24 May 1828
11. *PR*, 13 September 1828
12. *Poor Man's Friend*, 1826
13. *A Treatise on Cobbett's Corn*, 1828
14. Letter dated 25 November 1828, (Nuffield)
15. Letter from William Cobbett Jnr in Paris, 10 December 1830 (Nuffield)
16. *The English Gardener*, 1829
17. *The Emigrant's Guide*, 1829
18. *Advice to Young Men, and (incidentally) to Young Women, in the Middle and Higher Ranks of Life*, 1829. Quotes are from the 1980 edition
19. PR, 18 October 1828

CHAPTER 21

1. *Eleven Lectures on the French and Belgian Revolutions, and English Borough-Mongering*, 1830
2. *PR*, 3 July 1830
3. *PR*, 5 June 1830
4. *Two-Penny Trash* 1 September 1830
5. *PR*, 1 September 1830
6. *PR*, 13 November 1830
7. *PR*, 4 December 1830
8. *PR*, 7 January 1832
9. Cobbett told the whole story

himself in *A Full and Accurate Account of the Trial of William Cobbett, Esq*, 1831
10. *PR*, 16 July 1831
11. *PR*, 30 October 1830
12. *PR*, Quoted in Geoffrey Amey, *City Under Fire*, 1979
13. *PR*, 19 May 1832
14. *PR*, 30 June 1832

CHAPTER 22

1. *Cobbett's Tour in Scotland*, 1833 (1984 edition, ed. Daniel Green)
2. Ibid.
3. *Poor Man's Guardian*, 25 October 1832
4. *PR*, 16 March 1833
5. *PR*, 20 July 1833
6. *Hansard's Parliamentary Debates* Series 3 XXIV
7. Ibid.
8. *Cobbett's Legacy to Labourers*, 1834
9. *PR*, 17 August 1833
10. *Legacy to Parsons*, 1835 (Quotes from 1947 edition, ed. Ernest

Thurtle, MP)
11. O'Connell to Cobbett, November 1834, Letter quoted in Molly Townsend, *Not By Bullets and Bayonets*, 1983
12. Letter from Dublin, 22 September 1834, *Letters to Charles Marshall*, 1834
13. Letter dated 22 September 1833, (Nuffield)
14. Letter dated 9 January 1834, Sapsford Letters (Nuffield)
15. Letter dated 2 February 1834, Sapsford Letters (Nuffield)
16. Letter dated 18 March 1834, Sapsford Letters (Nuffield)
17. *PR*, 18 April 1835
18. *PR*, 2 May 1835
19. *Autobiography*

EPILOGUE

1. Letter from G.A. Fryer, 10 February 1900 (Southampton City Hertitage Services)
2. *Rural Rides*, 1830

INDEX